SHORT STORY THEORIES

SHORT
STORY
THEORIES

Edited by Charles E. May, 1941 -

OHIO UNIVERSITY PRESS

"Quotation beginning on page 94 of remarks by John Cheever, Shirley Hazzard, Harry Mark Petrakis, Elizabeth Janeway, reprinted from *The Writer's World* (published by McGraw-Hill Book Company) (Copyright © 1969 by The Authors Guild, Inc.,) by permission of the Guild and the authors."

Copyright © 1976 by Charles E. May
ISBN 0-8214-0189-0 cloth, 0-8214-0221-8 paper
Library of Congress Catalog Number: 75-36982
All rights reserved
Printed in the United States of America by
Watkins Printing Company

TO JOAN, HILLARY AND HAYDEN

Acknowledgments

I am particularly grateful to the California State University, Long Beach Foundation for a summer fellowship grant, 1973, which aided in the completion of this work. Thanks also to Ms. Victoria Nakagawa and Ms. Patricia Treadway for their assistance in preparation of the manuscript.

Sources

Bader, A. L. "The Structure of the Modern Short Story." *College English,* 7 (November 1945), 86–92. Reprinted by permission of the National Council of Teachers of English and A. L. Bader. Copyright © 1945 by the National Council of Teachers of English.

Baldeshwiler, Eileen. "The Lyric Short Story: The Sketch of a History." *Studies in Short Fiction,* 6 (Summer 1969), 443–53. Reprinted by permission of *Studies in Short Fiction* and Eileen Baldeshwiler.

Bates, H. E. "The Modern Short Story: Retrospect." from *The Modern Short Story: A Critical Survey.* Boston: The Writer, Inc., 1941, 1972. Reprinted by permission of the Estate of H. E. Bates.

Bowen, Elizabeth. "The Faber Book of Modern Short Stories." From *The Faber Book of Modern Short Stories.* London: Faber and Faber, Ltd., 1936, and *Collected Impressions.* New York: Alfred A Knopf, 1950. Reprinted by permission of Curtis Brown, Ltd. London and Curtis Brown, Ltd. New York on behalf of the Estate of Elizabeth Bowen.

Fitz Gerald, Gregory. "The Satiric Short Story: A Definition." *Studies in Short Fiction,* 5 (Summer 1968), 349–54. Reprinted by permission of Gregory Fitz Gerald.

Friedman, Norman. "What Makes a Short Story Short?" *Modern Fiction Studies,* 4 (Summer 1958), 103–17. Reprinted by permission of the Purdue Research Foundation and Norman Friedman. Copyright © 1958 by the Purdue Research Foundation, West Lafayette, Indiana.

Gordimer, Nadine. "The Flash of Fireflies." Originally appeared as "South Africa" in International Short Story Symposium in *Kenyon Review,* 30 (Issue 4, 1968), 457–61. Reprinted by permission of Russell & Volkening, Inc., as agents for Nadine Gordimer. Copyright © 1968 by Nadine Gordimer.

Gullason, Thomas A. "The Short Story: An Underrated Art." *Studies in Short Fiction,* 2 (Fall 1964), 13–31. Reprinted by permission of *Studies in Short Fiction* and Thomas A. Gullason.

"Is the Short Story Necessary?" from *The Writer's World.* Ed. Elizabeth Janeway. New York: McGraw-Hill Book Co., Inc., 1969. Reprinted by permission of The Author's Guild, Inc. and the panel participants.

Jarrell, Randall. "Stories." from *The Anchor Book of Stories.* New York: Doubleday & Co., Inc., 1958, and *Sad Heart at the Supermarket.* New York: Atheneum Publishers, 1962. Reprinted by permission of Atheneum Publishers. Copyright © 1958, 1962 by Randall Jarrell.

Kostelanetz, Richard. "Notes on the American Short Story Today." *Minnesota Review,* 5 (1966), 214–21. Reprinted by permission of Richard Kostelanetz. Copyright © 1966 by Richard Kostelanetz.

Lawrence, James Cooper. "A Theory of the Short Story." *North American Review,* 205 (February 1917), 274–86.

Marcus, Mordecai. "What is an Initiation Story?" *The Journal of Aesthetics and Art Criticism,* 14 (Winter 1960), 221–27. Reprinted by permission of *The Journal of Aesthetics and Art Criticism* and Mordecai Marcus, with minor revisions for this reprinting by the author.

Matthews, Brander. "The Philosophy of the Short-Story." From *The Philosophy of the Short-Story*. New York: Longmans, Green and Co., 1901.

Moravia, Alberto. "The Short Story and the Novel." From *Man as End: A Defense of Humanism*, trans. Bernard Wall. New York: Farrar, Straus & Giroux, Inc., 1969. Reprinted by permission of Farrar, Straus & Giroux, Inc. English translation copyright © 1965 by Martin Secker & Warburg, Ltd.

O'Connor, Frank. "The Lonely Voice." From *The Lonely Voice: A Study of the Short Story*. Cleveland: The World Publishing Co., 1963. Reprinted by arrangement with The New American Library, Inc., New York, New York. Copyright © 1962, 1963 by Frank O'Connor.

Poe, Edgar Allan. "Review of *Twice-Told Tales*." *Graham's Magazine*, May, 1842.

Rohrberger, Mary. "The Short Story: A Proposed Definition." From *Hawthorne and the Modern Short Story: A Study in Genre*. The Hague: Mouton and Co., 1966. Reprinted by permission of Edicom N.V. and Mary Rohrberger. Copyright © 1967 by Mouton, The Hague.

Stroud, Theodore A. "A Critical Approach to the Short Story." *The Journal of General Education*, 9 (January 1956), 91–100. Reprinted by permission of The Pennsylvania State University Press and Theodore A. Stroud.

Welty, Eudora. "The Reading and Writing of Short Stories." *The Atlantic Monthly*, 183 (February and March 1949), 54–58 & 46–49. Reprinted by permission of Random House, Inc. This essay will appear in a collection of essays by Eudora Welty to be published by Random House, Inc. Copyright © 1949 by Eudora Welty.

"A Survey of Short Story Criticism in America" originally appeared in A Symposium on the Contemporary Short Story in *Minnesota Review*, Spring, 1973, pp. 163–69.

Preface

The essays collected here approach the short story as a generic form of literature unique in its own right. Although it is obvious that these twenty short-story writers and critics believe the form deserves such generic consideration, such a view is not widely accepted. Compared with the vast amount of theoretical criticism on the novel, serious approaches to the short story have been embarrassingly few. My hope is that bringing the most provocative of these approaches together in a single book, new interest in the genre might be stimulated and more serious criticism forthcoming.

However, the book should also be a valuable tool for the student of short fiction. In the essays reprinted here he will surely find intuitions and analyses which he will accept and wish to pursue further. Just as surely he will find ideas and suggestions which he wishes to refute. This kind of serious dialogue is precisely what the short story needs. The annotated bibliography of approximately 130 items, representing most of the criticism of the form to appear in English, should help the student pursue the study further.

In addition to being a tool for the scholarly researcher and critic, the book also can serve as a practical aid for the teacher. One of the basic problems in teaching a genre class in the short story is that the course often is either structured around artificial divisions of stories which illustrate plot, character, theme, and symbol; or else it becomes a process of student-teacher explication of a different story each class meeting. It is not to disparage formalist criticism to suggest that in the latter procedure the semester's work is not so much a progression as it is a repetition. To those who object that this is the way it should be, I can only agree with Northrop Frye who says that such a repugnance toward a unified poetics "is the result of a failure to distinguish criticism as a body of knowledge from the direct experience of literature where every act is unique and classification has no place."

The essays included here do not attempt to establish an elaborate organon with which the reader can then test individual works to see if they are "short stories." But they do offer theoretical and practical perspectives on the form which might serve as materials toward a unified approach. They should be read as general rules of art, descriptive, not prescriptive, in nature. As Edith Wharton says, such rules are "useful chiefly as a lamp in a mine, or a hand-rail down a black stairway; they are necessary for the sake of the guidance they give, but it is a mistake, once they are formulated, to be too much in awe of them."

Charles E. May

California State University,
Long Beach

CONTENTS

SHORT STORY THEORIES

charles e. may

A SURVEY OF SHORT STORY CRITICISM
IN AMERICA

Although the short story is respected by its practitioners, it is largely ignored by both the popular and the serious reader. Moreover, the most valuable critical remarks made about the form have been made not by the critics but by the short story writers. The question for the short story seems to be: can the writer alone keep a genre alive once it has lost both its basic audiences?

In a four-part symposium in the now-defunct *Kenyon Review* between 1968 and 1970, nearly thirty writers from all over the world sent in their views on the artistic nature of the short story and its current economic status. Almost unanimously they praised the short story as the most natural, yet most artistically demanding, fictional form. However, nearly all lamented and admitted that they could not survive writing short stories. On November 20, 1970, Doubleday held a day-long symposium on the form in New York to celebrate and boost the publication of *Fifty Years of the American Short Story,* a compilation of the yearly O. Henry Award Stories. Although the writers there—John Barth, William Saroyan, Peter Taylor—praised the short story as an artistic form, the publishers, editors, and literary agents were not so rhapsodic.

If the short story is not popular with popular readers, it is not taken seriously by serious critics either. In a four-part annotated bibliography of periodical articles on the American Short Story published in the *Bulletin of Bibliography* in 1960 and 1961, Frank R. Smith found so few items giving serious critical attention to the form that he suggested his work might almost be considered a negative bibliography. And in the Fall, 1964, issue of *Studies in Short Fiction,* Thomas Gullason pointed out that not only is there only one scholarly journal devoted to the short story as compared to at least a half-dozen devoted to the novel, there is no full-length theoretical study of the short story, although several attempts have been made to establish a poetics for the novel. The standard bibliographies of critical work in literature include separate subject listings for drama, poetry, and the novel; there is not even a category for the short story.

During the Doubleday Symposium, Wallace Stegner, complaining that there has been little systematic criticism of the short story in America except in college textbooks, said that we badly need a good critical history of the form. Although I cannot agree that there has been valuable criticism of the form in the textbooks (See my survey of over a hundred texts in *College English,* January 1972), Stegner is surely right in saying that we do not have a good critical history. Fred Lewis Pattee's *The Development of the American Short Story* (1925) is certainly historical—filled with titles, dates, and names—but it is hardly critical. Ray B. West's 1952 book, *The Short Story in America: 1900–1950,* apparently takes up where Pattee leaves off, but lacks completeness and continuity. For example, only chapter one is a short survey of the form since Irving, Poe, and Hawthorne; the other chapters deal with more limited areas. Although Austin Wright's *The American Short Story in the Twenties* (1961) is quite detailed, it covers an even narrower period of time. Danforth Ross's *The American Short Story* (1961) measures the short story since Poe against Aristotelian criteria of action, unity, tension, and irony, but is still only a short pamphlet in the University of Minnesota series. Finally, William Peden's *The American Short Story* (1964), subtitled, unfortunately and erroneously, *Front Line in the National Defense of Literature,* does little more than illustrate some rather obvious thematic trends in the form since 1940.

The obvious question is: Why is the form so underrated by the critics? William Abrahams, editor of the O. Henry collection, suggested that the unhealthy state of the short story might be due to "something built into the form itself.'' And indeed the increasing movement away from plot in the short story in the last thirty years has perhaps made the popular reader prefer the novel. Finishing a novel, even the most pessimistic and fragmented one, the reader feels a sense of fulfillment and satisfaction. He has lived in a self-contained ''world'' for some time, has become intimately acquainted with its inhabitants, and has had time to accustom himself to the general consistency of the author's tone. The short story does not allow him to relax so much. Moreover, the novel usually proceeds through a spatial linearity and a temporal beginning, middle, and end. The short story, however, with its insistence that beginnings and ends are not so neat and that ''middles'' are always a mixed business impossible to judge, has become for the reader fragmentary, static, and irresolute. But this doesn't explain why the form is ignored by serious critics. If the contemporary short story is fragmentary and inconclusive, perhaps it is because the form is best able to convey the sense that reality itself is fragmentary and inconclusive. Such a view should be especially pertinent to the modern world.

I suggest that the lack of systematic criticism of the short story today is largely a reaction to too much systematic criticism in the first few decades of the twentieth century when the form became solidified by rules and tainted by commercialization. The problem began in 1901, when Brander Matthews, claiming himself to be the first to assert that the short story was in reality a genre essentially different from the novel, published *The Philosophy of the Short Story.* Attempting to create ''set rules'' out of Poe's cryptic suggestions in his review of *Twice-Told Tales,* Matthews borrowed his methodology from ''The Philosophy of Composition.'' Obviously taking Poe's description of his creation of ''The Raven'' quite seriously, Matthews made the short story seem merely a question of taxidermy after all. Even then, Matthews' formal rules for the genre might not have had such a disastrous effect if O. Henry had not had such great popular success with his formula at about the same time. The writers rushed to imitate O. Henry and the critics rushed to imitate Matthews, both with the same purpose in mind: popular financial success. Anyone could write short stories if he only knew the rules. J. Berg Esenwein's *Writing the Short Story* (1909), Carl H. Grabo's *The Art of the Short Story* (1913), and Blanche Colton Williams's *A Handbook of Story Writing* (1917), are only three of the many such books published in the first twenty years of the century. The serious readers and critics called for an end to it, filling the quality periodicals with articles on the "decline," the "decay," and the "senility" of the short story. Gilbert Seldes summed up the reaction at its most extreme in *The Dial* in 1922: "The American short story is by all odds the weakest, most trivial, most stupid, most insignificant art work produced in this country and perhaps in any country." Even Edward J. O'Brien, probably the greatest champion of the form America has ever had, wrote his book *The Dance of the Machines* in 1929, censuring the mechanized structure of American society and the machine-like story that both sprang from it and reflected it.

Reservations about the form continued on into the thirties with critics demanding that to save itself, the short story had to come more into line with the traditional purposes and foundations of the novel. In 1936, José Garcia Villa lamented that the short story was taking on the characteristics of the sketch, becoming a mere episode which was "functionless, directionless, and pointless." James T. Farrell urged in 1937 that the short story should address itself to social criticism, and in 1938, Howard Baker recommended that the form be made more intellectual, that it be built on a substructure of ideas. Although these same three complaints about the short story—lack of plot, lack of social concern, lack of ideology—have continued up through the sixties, in the last thirty years the critics have recognized that the short story is closer to the lyric than the novel and must be judged accordingly.

The first task for the critic in the forties was to make distinctions between the "old" story and the "new" one and between the "quality" story and the "commercial" one. Bonaro Overstreet (*Saturday Review of Literature*, Nov. 22, 1941) suggested that the usual critical complaint that the short story is not as good as it used to be is really the result of the critics' expecting still the same plotted story which was dominant in the nineteenth century. Noting that the two basic faiths of the nineteenth century—that it was possible to know the difference between right and wrong, and that people actually were what they seemed to be—have been lost, Overstreet claimed that the action or plotted story was no longer viable. Since the drama of the century has become the drama of what goes on in the mind, the short story has more and more become an expert medium for the expression of our "deep concern about human moods and motives—moods and motives that have shown themselves to be far less transparent than what we once thought they were."

Focusing on the division between the quality literary story and the formula commercial story, Warren Beck (*College English,* Nov. 1943) described the difference between the two as a difference in outlook. Calling the commercial story "fable founded on sentimental mottoes," Beck posed that the literary story was not so much a revolt against plot as it was a revolt against wooden formulas; it moves beyond mere eventfulness and has some kinship to the reflective essay, occasionally sounding a lyric tone. Gorham Munson (*The University Review,* Autumn 1943) was probably saying much the same thing when he claimed that the short story was escaping from formula and recapturing the "storyable incident." Whereas Poe aimed at a "patterned dramatization of life," for which he needed an anecdote, O. Henry and those that followed him made this dramatic pattern mechanical. Writers have revolted against this formula and have stopped trying to concoct plots; they have directed their attention to unveiling the latent value in an incident or episode.

This effort to reveal "latent value" in an episode tends to push the short story closer to the lyric with its emphasis on the artist's subjectivity and technique. Critical response to this predominantly modern trend in the form has been quite divided. Herschel Brickell (*The University of Kansas City Review,* Summer 1949) claimed that the short story has experimented with a greater variety of forms than the novel in that it has become more subjective. He cites approvingly Walter Havighurst's suggestion that it is the tone of the short story, more than the plot, that carries the reader further into the story. Irving Howe (*Sewanee Review,* Winter 1949) also noted the increasing dependence on tone in the short story and added that such a dependence poses a danger as well; for tone can be easily wrenched from its content and become a stereotype. "In the novel," Howe suggested, "the second-rater tends to parrot a vision of life; in the story, he tends to echo a tone of voice."

Herschel Brickell claimed in 1951 that the psychological story moving toward the lyric was at a very high plateau (*Atlantic Monthly,* Sept.) He attributed this increase in good short stories to the new surge of short-story writing courses at colleges and universities, not teaching the O. Henry formula as they did thirty years earlier, but rather teaching the new psychological, poetic story. Two years later Falcon O. Baker chose this fact as the most important reason for the short story's decline (*Saturday Review,* Dec. 19, 1953). He charged that the college-associated writers, influenced by the New Criticism, have made the short story even more concerned with technique and psychological case studies. Thus a new formula had been created to replace the old one, and the short story belonged only to the professors, the critics, and the literary quarterlies.

Other commentators have noted that the movement away from plot in the modern short story has been accompanied by a movement away from character as well. Granville Hicks (*Saturday Review,* Dec. 20, 1958) suggested that character in the form no longer seems to be used for itself as it is used as a means to an end, the end being an emotional experience for the reader. A few years later, George P. Elliott (*Harpers,* April 1965) noted the movement away from basic human character to the extremes of character and warned that such a concern leads to a deper-sonalizing of character: "At the brink, people are apt to behave much alike, less according to their personal natures than according to human nature generally." Maxwell Geismar (*Studies on the Left,* Spring 1964) mounted the most severe attack on the new focus in the short story. He charged that our modern short story writers, primarily those of the *New Yorker* school—Salinger, Roth, Updike, Malamud, Powers—are not interested in the deeper realms of human character but rather in the intricate craftsmanship of the well-made story. Furthermore, the con-temporary short story, Geismar claimed, is characterized by a lack of social, ideological, and metaphysical horizons; it has shrunk more and more into the "labyrinthian recesses of the tormented and isolated psyche of the individual soul."

The most balanced assessment of the short story in the sixties is, in my opinion, Richard Kostelanetz's discussion (*Twentieth Century,* Autumn 1965). Actually expanding on and illustrating what various critics had merely hinted at before, Kostelanetz shows that contemporary short story writers have indeed focused on experiences which are not typical but extreme and that they have also tended to be concerned more and more with the medium of language itself. In a shift that pulls the genre farther away from narrative and pushes it closer to nonlinear forms of poetry, the contemporary short story writer attempts through language and technique to depict the workings of the mad mind, attempts, as in poetry, to simulate the feel of madness itself.

As the seventies begin, the extreme result of this focus as well as the extreme reaction to it seems to be exemplified by a new collection of stories edited by Philip Stevick (*Anti-Story,* Free Press, 1971) and Malcolm Cowley's impatient, even angry, response to it (*Saturday Review,* Sept. 25, 1971). In his introduction, Stevick says that the works collected illustrate reactions against the classic attributes of story:

against mimesis, against reality, against event, against subject, and against meaning. All this is obviously too much for Cowley who is still very much for story. He says that most of the pieces in the book really deal with the theme of the extreme difficulty the writer has "when he knows a hell of a lot about technique and has nothing but that knowledge to offer us."

Discussion of the short story by the academic critics has not been as spirited as this on-going controversy among the cultural commentators. In fact, the scholars did not really begin to consider the short story until *Understanding Fiction* made analysis of the form respectable in 1943. A. L. Bader's article, "The Structure of the Modern Short Story," (*College English,* November 1945), confronts the common complaint that the modern short story has no structure by showing that although a narrative structure is still present in the form, its presentation and resolution are so indirect that the reader must work harder to find the perceived relationships of the parts of the story. Walter Sullivan begins to develop this rather simple and general assessment into a more rigid methodology in 1951 (*Vanderbilt Studies in Humanities,* vol. 1). Using Mark Schorer's comment that the short story is an art of "moral revelation," Sullivan asserts that the fundamental methodological concept of the short story is a change from innocence to knowledge—a change that can be either "inter-concatinate" (occurring within the main character) or "extra-concatinate" (occurring within a peripheral character). Theodore Stroud, extending Bader and Sullivan's Epiphanic and New Critical approaches, focuses more on aesthetic than on narrative pattern. He shows that the best way to discern the pattern in the short story is to examine how the completeness of a story results from the units or episodes in a work combining to make credible a change in one of the characters or to create a sense of realization in the reader (*The Journal of General Education,* Jan. 1956).

At least two critics have focused on rhetorical modes of presentation in the short story. Norman Friedman, in his essay "What Makes the Short Story Short?" (*Modern Fiction Studies,* Summer 1958), uses Elder Olson's terms for different actions to try to account for the basic problem of the short story—its shortness. To deal with the problem, Friedman says, we must ask the following questions: What is the size of the action? Is it composed of a speech, a scene, an episode, or a plot? Does the action involve a change? If so, is the change a major one or a minor one? Peripherally, Friedman also discusses several authorial techniques which may affect the length of the story such as omission, contraction, expansion, and point of view. James Moffett (*ETC.*, December 1964) focuses entirely on point of view, or what he calls methods of abstraction, in fiction. Presenting eleven such methods, with short definitions and examples of each, Moffett charts a sequence which he says covers the "entire range in which stories can be told," from the most subjective and personal (interior monologue) to the most objective and impersonal (anonymous narration).

A few critics recently have attempted to approach the problem of the short story by isolating and defining certain sub-genres. Mordecai Marcus (*Journal of Aesthetics and Art Criticism,* Winter 1960) notes two basic elements of initiation which might account for the predominance of the theme in the short story: initiation's focus on an activity that causes a significant change and its focus on an activity that is formally patterned. Gregory Fitz Gerald (*Studies in Short Fiction,* Summer 1968) discusses the satiric short story, which he defines as a sub-genre that sustains throughout a reductive attack upon its objects and conveys to its intended reader an "import different from its apparent surface meaning." Although Fitz Gerald does not explore the possibility, his definition may really be pointing toward a general characteristic of the short story: its ability to convey a meaning that often lies beneath the surface of the narrative. Eileen Baldeshwiler's sketchy history of the lyric short story (*Studies in Short Fiction,* Summer 1969) does not add a meaningful distinction since many critics have noted the lyric nature of the twentieth-century short story; however, she does pose an explicit definition: the lyric short story concentrates on "internal changes, moods, and feelings, utilizing a variety of structural patterns depending on the shape of the emotion itself."

This brief survey of academic attempts to grapple with the nature of the short story must convince us that critics have not really performed the necessary task: they have not formulated a unified theory of the genre which would help us understand the unique kind of experience the short story deals with and the unique way it imitates and creates that experience. The short story writers, those who, as Eudora Welty says, have a much less sure but a much more passionate point of view of the form, have given us more helpful suggestions, especially about how the short story differs from the novel. Elizabeth Bowen, in her introduction to the *Faber Book of Modern Short Stories,* 1939, made two interesting suggestions about the typical experience the short story deals with and its typical structural difference from the novel which Frank O'Connor and Nadine Gordimer have since stated more explicitly. Bowen says that the short story, more than the novel, is able to place man alone on that "stage which, inwardly, every man is conscious of occupying alone," and that, exempt as it is from the novel's often forced conclusiveness, the short story may more nearly "approach aesthetic and moral truth." Frank O'Connor develops his well-known thesis about the short story (*The Lonely Voice,* 1963) around Bowen's first suggestion. O'Connor says, although he can only guess at the reason why, that in the short story at its most characteristic we find something we do not find often in the novel—"an intense awareness of human loneliness." Perhaps Nadine Gordimer's expansion of Bowen's second suggestion gives us a clue as to why loneliness is so pervasive in the form. In the second installment of the *Kenyon Review* Symposium, Gordimer suggests that the strongest convention of the novel, its prolonged coherence of tone, is false to the nature of what can be grasped as reality in the modern world. The novel cannot convey that quality of human life "where contact is more like the flash of fireflies, in and out, now here, now there, in darkness." Short story writers, Gordimer says, deal with the only thing one can be sure of—the present moment: "A discrete moment of truth is aimed at—not *the* moment of truth, because the short story doesn't deal in cumulatives." Perhaps it is not too much to suggest that the relation between O'Connor's theories about the typical short story vision and Gordimer's theories about its typical form is an integral one: modern man's realization that he can depend only on the present moment is precisely what makes him lonely, and his sense of loneliness is best manifested in a form that focuses only on the present moment.

Eudora Welty, Randall Jarrell, and Joyce Carol Oates have also made suggestive comments on the nature of the short story which are related to the Bowen, O'Connor, and Gordimer ideas. Welty says the most characteristic aspect of the short story is that we cannot see the solid outlines of it: "it seems bathed in something of its own. It is wrapped in an atmosphere." The first thing we really see about a story is its mystery (*Atlantic Monthly,* Feb. & March 1949). Randall Jarrell, in his introduction to *The Anchor Book of Stories* (1958), says that in reading stories we must recall Freud's belief that the "root of all stories is in Grimm, not in La Rochefoucauld; in dreams, not in cameras and tape recorders." And finally, Joyce Carol Oates, in a short note published recently (*Southern Humanities Review,* Summer 1971), agrees with

Welty that the most interesting thing about the short story is its mystery, and goes beyond Jarrell to assert that story is the "dream verbalized." Although in their present form these suggestions about mystery and dream, loneliness and fireflies are much too impressionistic to be of any real help in understanding the short story, they seem to me to be the best place to begin if one wishes to develop a theory of the genre. For what is needed is a theory in the modern sense, starting not from external elements of form or even various classes of subject matter, but rather from the underlying vision of the short story, its characteristic mode of understanding and confronting reality. Such a vision is not to be deduced from a nugget of absolute knowledge thematically embedded in the story, nor from the glue of technique that holds the parts together, but rather from that atmosphere which Welty says stories are wrapped in.

The problem of the short story writer often seems to be the same problem that Conrad's master story-teller, Marlowe, faced as he tried to verbalize the mystery of his journey into the Heart of Darkness: "Do you see the story? Do you see anything? It seems to me I am trying to tell you a dream, making a vain attempt, because no relation of a dream can convey the dream sensation, that commingling of absurdity, surprise, and bewilderment in a tremor of struggling revolt, that notion of being captured by the incredible which is the very essence of dreams. . . ."

The problem of the short story critic is that he has seldom made any attempt at all.

THOMAS A. GULLASON

The Short Story: An Underrated Art

I

Today in the 1960's the short story still has an audience, and there are many practitioners in the field, but both short story and short-story writer are clearly underrated, even ignored, by professional and academic critics, publishers, some literary artists, and by general readers. When a genre such as the short story has been a part of our world heritage from the beginning of oral and written literature, one would expect that it would have "its day," its period of kingship. This has not been the case. The Bible stories, Aesop's *Fables, The Arabian Nights, The Decameron* are a few of many early examples of the international interest in this form which at various stages of its history has been known by other names: anecdote, fable, narrative, tale, story, sketch, yarn, short fiction. As Aristotle and many later critics remind us, both poetry and drama have had periods of kingship. Since the 19th century, however, the novel, given great impetus by Flaubert's *Madame Bovary,* has become the king of imaginative literature. And the novel does not have a long tradition behind it as poetry, drama, and the short story do, though some have traced it to the epic.

The short story has kept pace with the modernity of the novel by becoming modern itself at about the same time in the 19th century, as seen in the work of Anton Chekhov and Guy de Maupassant in Europe, and Edgar Allan Poe in America. Many readers still have, however, an old-fashioned picture of the short story: a rambling, simple, balladlike narrative, a public, oral art, the property of the storyteller and his community. The present-day short story is mainly a private art, between writer and reader, and it is as sophisticated as the novel, with as great a concern for craft, for technique and style, and for complexity of emotions and ideas—all presented, of course, on a miniature scale. Yet the short story is still running a poor fourth to the novel, poetry, and drama.

Some great novelists, like William Faulkner, readily accept the importance of the short story. Once, Faulkner explained his position, and as he did so, he gave insight into the pattern of his own literary career. "I'm a failed poet," he said. "Maybe every novelist wants to write poetry first, finds he can't, and then tries the short story, which is the most demanding form after poetry. And failing at that, only then does he take up novel writing."[2] Frequently, short-story writers and their sympathizers have had to protest against their deriders, and their low status. They feel that their medium is unfairly treated as a "kind of literary pimp," as a "finger exercise," as the "blood kinsman of the quick-lunch," as a "modern toy," and as "a poor relation of the novel."

Some great short-story writers, like D. H. Lawrence, never have seemed too concerned about the fate of the medium. In fact, Lawrence continually showed his allegiance to the novel, and he is read by the general public and studied by the critics mainly as a novelist. But Lawrence really worked best in the short medium (a few critics concede this), which demanded discipline; and he needed this badly. For his gift was essentially poetic, immediate, spontaneous. And it is in his more than sixty short stories—like "The Horse Dealer's Daughter," "Odor of Chrysanthemums," "The Man Who Loved Islands" and others—that Lawrence displayed a control and sustained lyric beauty not always present in his ten novels. While his novels are never dull, there are frequent and serious lapses in style and structure. Still the countless books on Lawrence, since his death in 1930, deal with his psycho-biography, his Utopian ideas, and his novels. Only in 1962, with Kingsley Widmer's *Art of Perversity*, have we had the first full-scale study of his short fiction. The undisputed leadership of the novel form has made any substantial comment on the short story seem irrelevant.

Besides, if critics do refer to short stories, like Lawrence's, they often see them as miniature pieces echoing the novels to come, or pieces left over from novels already published.

Ernest Hemingway illustrates a problem similar to Lawrence's. As a novelist in *The Sun Also Rises, A Farewell To Arms,* and *For Whom The Bell Tolls,* he so well illuminated the temper of an age that he may well be forever linked with the expatriate, the lost generation, the twenties, and war. It is harder to link Hemingway with his age in his short stories, because they do not present a unified and full-blown canvas of his times. Not long after Hemingway's death, a few critics hazarded a guess that his future reputation would rest on his short stories—not on his novels. Generally, there is far too much treatment for the subjects chosen in his novels; and his style and themes seem too studied and too shrill. It is in his short stories that Hemingway maintains a skillful balance between subject and treatment, that his compact style and themes gain in power and in meaningfulness: in stories like "The Short Happy Life of Francis Macomber," "The Snows of Kiliman-jaro," "In Another Country," "A Clean, Well-Lighted Place," and others. Of the many recent books on Hemingway, not one deals fully with his craft as a short-story writer, the craft with which Hemingway began his literary career, and a craft which he has deeply influenced. If critics refer to the short stories, like *In Our Time,* they study them mainly in terms of Nick Adams, who in the later novels becomes the great Hemingway hero. Hemingway's short stories function chiefly as stepping stones to an appreciation and understanding of his novels. The most rounded treatment of Hemingway's short fiction occurs in one chapter of Carlos Baker's book *Hemingway: The Writer As Artist* (1956). Just recently, Joseph DeFalco used "modern psychoanalytical procedures" to present *The Hero in Hemingway's Short Stories* (1963).

Hemingway's partner in themes and in the art of fiction, and who earlier fought the first major battle for modernism in American litera-ture, is Stephen Crane. He is continually associated with one book, the great novel, *The Red Badge of Courage.* Then, periodically, the talk falls on *Maggie,* labeled the first naturalistic novel in America, which has many unnaturalistic qualities, especially in style. Crane, then, is discussed mainly as a novelist, though some critics have mentioned his short stories. In his own literary development Crane continually warred against the novel form. He was critical of the long novels of Tolstoy, Zola, Twain, and Henry James. Even his own *Red Badge* Crane considered too long; and *Maggie* and *George's Mother* were in reality short novels. Crane's lengthy novels, such as *Active Service* and *The O'Ruddy,* showed him at his worst, for his effects were sprawling and melodramatic. He was consciously or unconsciously moving toward his best medium, the short story, and he wrote over one hundred of them. In the novel form, Crane was too repetitious, too artificial, and too brittle. In the short story form he was triumphantly Greek—especially in "The Open Boat," "The Blue Hotel," "The Monster," and "Death and the Child." For here he had the tautness and the epic richness of classic tragedy. Like Lawrence, Hemingway, Sherwood Anderson and others, Crane had a poetic gift, darting and intense. His works inspired Anderson and Hemingway further to revolutionize the short story in the 1920's. Still, there is not a single book-length treatment of his fiction. Critics are lost in his bizarre life and in *The Red Badge.* At present there are two biographies of Crane, and at least two new ones are in the making.

Even Edgar Allan Poe, called by many the father of the American short story, is not represented by anything that resembles a full-length study of his short fiction. Scholars can afford to rewrite his biography over and over, though we have very little or no new information. But we can't afford to study his stories, which have made his artistic reputation secure, and which have stimulated the fast growth of the short story in America.

The most shocking European examples of this same dilemma are the two giants, Chekhov and Maupassant. Both had a profound influence on the modern British and American short story; both were known mainly through translations. Chekhov's influence on the short story even extends to China, where he inspired Lu Hsün (Lusin), China's greatest storyteller. The major share of the English criticism on Chekhov deals with his great impact on world drama. Probably next to the novel, the drama receives the widest attention, and so, though Chekhov is generally regarded as the world's greatest short-story writer, no one has dared to evaluate his short stories. Again, the short story functioned as a stepping stone, for Chekhov adapted some of his stories for the stage. Chekhov has influenced many of our present-day fiction writers, but there is not a single thorough study of his short-story craft available in English. There are some reasons for this neglect: many of his stories have not been translated; and we have no idea of the chronology of his work. Even without the ideal complete and chronological works, how-ever, it would still seem urgent to appraise his existing short fiction.

The same problem exists with Maupassant, characterized by Henry James as a "lion in the path." Besides Francis Steegmuller's biography, there are appreciations of Maupassant by such famous students of his as Henry James and W. Somerset Maugham. We even have a book-length study of Maupassant as a novelist available in English, but not one on his short-story craft, though his name is synonymous with the short story.[3]

Not only this, many of the greatest short-story writers are not even represented by their complete works in volume form, and they should be. If their complete stories were available at one time, they are now out of print. Chekhov's short fiction is a case in point. The very popular Hemingway still is not represented by his complete short stories. Some of the short-story collections of Sherwood Anderson and F. Scott Fitzgerald are now out of print. And just recently, the first complete and chronological edition of Stephen Crane's stories was published.[4]

In another area—the literary journal and the scholarly magazine—one finds an almost total absence of comment on the short story. Only last year the first journal devoted largely to the short story was begun—*Studies in Short Fiction*. The many journals generally pay the most attention to the novel, poetry, and drama. A review of the annual *Publications of the Modern Language Association* bibliographical guide for 1962 demonstrates this. Under the section Twentieth Century (English), there are three categories, one each devoted to drama, poetry, and the novel—none to the short story. Under the section Twentieth Century (American), the term "fiction" replaces "novel," though the majority of the entries relates specifically to the novel. Then a glance at an individual author, like Lawrence, shows that one article was pub-lished on his short stories—out of almost thirty entries. The case with Hemingway is somewhat better: of over forty entries, nine deal with his short stories.[5] Ironically, the most talked about short stories in recent years are those which are grouped like novels, and connected into a oneness by hero, theme, or mood: things like Sherwood Anderson's *Winesburg, Ohio;* James Joyce's *Dubliners;* and Hemingway's *In Our Time*.

There are other factors which clearly indicate that the short story is not highly regarded. Besides the lack of discussion on individual practition-ers, whether in books or in magazines, there are few critical essays and books on the theory and history of short fiction. Three serious critical studies on the short story stand out: H. E. Bates's *The Modern Short Story* (1941); Sean O'Faolain's *The Short Story* (1951), though a good portion of this volume is an anthology of stories; and Frank O'Connor's *The Lonely Voice* (1963). And even these books are too selective in their choice of authors and in their analyses.

The older histories of the short story are now outmoded curiosity pieces: Henry Seidel Canby's *The Short Story in English* (1909); Fred Pattee's *The Development of the American Short Story* (1923); and Edward J. O'Brien's *The Advance of the American Short Story* (1923). Ray West's recent *Short Story in America* (1952) and Danforth Ross's pamphlet, *The American Short Story* (1961), are too brief, especially the latter, and they become mere catalogues of writers and stories. There is a real need for an up-to-date general history—and not restricted to America as most of the previous ones are. There is as great a need for discriminating studies of the aesthetics of the short story. By contrast, there is an impressive number of serious and elaborate books on the novel and novelists, on poetry, and on drama. Take a highly specialized area in the novel—rhythm. This was first discussed at some length in E. M. Forster's *Aspects of the Novel.* Then an entire book, by E. K. Brown, was devoted to rhythm in the novel.

Commercial publishers themselves neglect the short story. A cliché current that publishers tell promising short-story writers is "Give us first a novel and then we will publish your short stories." If the writer succeeds in his novel, he will obviously be encouraged to write more novels—and not short stories. After non-fiction, the novel has a good chance to reach and surpass the break-even point for publishers. Short-story collections rarely reach the break-even point. One can only guess how many skillful short-story writers move to the novel medium because the financial returns are better. There have been—already—some tragic cases which have developed out of this publishing dilemma. Eudora Welty, for one, who gained her first fame as a short-story writer, changed to the novel medium and failed in *The Robber Bridegroom* and *Delta Wedding;* presently she is at work on a long comic story. Irwin Shaw is another case in point.

The general reader may be as much to blame as the publisher, if not more, for ignoring the short story. To the general reader, the novel's bulk is equated with big events and big ideas, all told in one continuous story, a kind of extended serial which makes the reader eager to come back for more. The novel has become a status symbol of intellectual curiosity. The short story—even in collections—is treated as though it were trivia, small talk, a potpourri of abrupt, scattered episodes, which leaves the reader impatient with something that ends before it really begins. The many short stories in literary quarterlies, sponsored usually by universities, and the annual prize collections—like the O. Henry and Martha Foley's—do not have a large following. They do not seem to have stimulated the general reader, or the critic and others to appreciate the worth of stories, whether individually or collectively.

One final point clearly indicates that the short story is underrated. If recent trends continue, the short story of the future may even be without a name. More and more the professional and academic critics are relying on the word *fiction*—any prose fiction—to cover the short story, the short novel, and the novel. This is probably a reaction against the craze for divisions and subdivisions of art. The trend toward the word *fiction* was popularized by René Wellek and Austin Warren in their *Theory of Literature,* specifically in a chapter entitled ''The Nature and Modes of Narrative Fiction.'' They spend much of their time with the novel, and make only incidental reference to the short story. Many other critics have adopted this approach in their literary evaluations. Quite often anthologists have three categories for literature: fiction, drama, and poetry. Rarely are the short-story writers asked what they think of this, for if they were, critics, anthologists, and others would be shocked to learn that most modern short-story writers are agreed that their medium is closer to poetry than to the novel. And the many artists writing short stories have proven the validity of their art form by the very nature of its long life. They have explained their form and its special qualities lucidly enough in a famous series of interviews in *The Paris Review.* Still, present signs indicate that the short story may be only a piece of ''fiction.''

II

Why is the short story underrated? For many, the word *short* is responsible. Frank O'Connor uses another word—*time*. The short story presumably lacks the time which in the novel creates a ''sense of continuing life''—of the birth, growth, and fulfillment of people and ideas. The short story—because of its brevity—is accused of seeing life through a knothole, a kind of ''peep show.'' One of our leading critics, Mark Schorer, further suggests the limitations of the short story by terming it the "art of moral revelation," while he sees the novel as the "art of moral evolution."[6] To put it another way: the modern short story begins as near as possible to the end of an action, something like the final act of a play. Therefore, the reasoning goes, it has too many missing parts, and can show us something only abruptly. Due to all these factors and others, the short story has been denounced as episodic, one-dimensional, static, fragmentary, superficial. Especially "episodic," which supposedly proves the structural failing of a short story, and yet some of the most revered novels of the world—*Don Quixote* and *Huckleberry Finn* are good examples—are episodic. Then there is the word *static*. Because the action of a story is so small, nothing really happens in it. The classic example usually chosen is Chekhov, who has frustrated many readers, past and present.

Another single word—*formula*—has been so often attached to the short story that it suggests a robotlike, unimaginative craft—the kind of thing represented by the new IBM machine that can take one plot and create endless variations. The short story has been treated like the neglected sonnet, as though it were something rigid and inflexible, lost in a numbers game, somewhere between 500 words and 15,000 words. Charges of a more serious nature, relating to formula, can be traced to Edgar Allan Poe's review of Hawthorne's *Twice-Told Tales* in 1842. Here follows a key passage from what is now literary history:

> A skilful literary artist has constructed a tale. If wise, he has not fashioned his thoughts to accommodate his incidents; but having conceived, with deliberate care, a certain unique or single *effect* to be wrought out, he then invents such incidents—he then combines such events as may best aid him in establishing this preconceived effect. If his very initial sentence tend not to the outbringing of this effect, then he has failed in his first step. In the whole composition there should be no word written, of which the tendency, direct or indirect, is not to the one pre-established design.

Too often Poe's "deliberate care," "single effect," "preconceived effect," and his "one pre-established design" have been taken so seriously that today in the 1960's critics and readers expect nothing more than this thin, automated oneness from the short story. In his essay "The Philosophy of Composition," Poe added: "It is my design to render it manifest that no one point in its composition is referable either to accident or intuition—that the work proceeded, step by step, to its completion with the precision and rigid consequence of a mathematical problem." Carl Grabo's entire book *The Art of the Short Story* (1913) is based on Poe's theories as expounded in ''The Philosophy of Composition.'' The O. Henry plots have added to the mechanical formula charge. And Maupassant did not escape this charge either. Many critics and anthologists, influenced by Poe's mathematical approach, have made the short story seem a mechanical and standardized affair—with graphs and curves to show the exact movement of plots; and with certain ingredients—presently the magic number is seven—to show what makes a story. Whenever critics talk about fresh approaches, new experiments, a creative craft, they invariably go to the novel to study things like stream of consciousness, symbolism, or myth. Rarely do they bother with the short story, for they see it as extremely limited by hard-and-fast rules.

If Poe's formulas were not destructive enough, then we have Aristotle's theory of the beginning, middle, and end, something whole and complete, which he related to tragedy, and which has been applied by others to all imaginative literature. The fact that the short story is short enough to begin with makes it seem even flimsier when the reader expects it to have a wholeness made up of three parts. Many stories, before and after Chekhov, followed this pattern. Then when Chekhov struck out the beginning and the end, and left us with a so-called middle action, this created another monster in the eyes of the critical reader— the plotless story, beginning nowhere and going nowhere. So whether plotted or plotless, the short story seemed unable to justify itself either in form or in substance.

Another kind of formula has been created by the magazines, and this has further damaged the short story and made it seem a standardized and mechanized product. *The New Yorker, The Saturday Evening Post, Mademoiselle,* the old *Collier's* and others—all have set up, whether consciously or unconsciously, certain taboos and formulas to impose further controls on the short story. As if this were not enough, the magazines further created controls by the simple expedient of word count. This has helped to create another unhealthy image for the short story: art as a filler. And the filler suggests the newspaper world, something of short duration, a thing of the moment. Moreover, the fact that the short story is continually linked with popular magazines makes it seem a cheap potboiler.

The short story is underrated for still other reasons. Most of the masters of the short story have worked in other mediums, especially in the novel. This is supposed to prove that any talented writer escapes from the short story as soon as he can, for it is inferior, second-rate, a form for apprentices only. In 1887, the editor of *The Critic* went so far as to say: "As a rule, the short story is produced in youth, while the novel is a product of experience." It is very rare indeed that critics would acknowledge that a short-story writer could learn by his mistakes in other forms, and return with clearer perspective to his earlier and best medium. There are many examples of great writers who attempted to escape from the short story. Chekhov is one. In a letter he mentioned a novel in the planning stages: "It is a good theme," he said, "and it is pleasant to work on it, but unfortunately, owing to lack of practice in writing long things, and from fear of crowding in too many details, I go to the opposite extreme: each page comes out compact, like a short story. . . ." In another letter Chekhov added: "To me it appears bulky, dull, too crowded with details. I am in a hurry to start on something short, but I long for some large work." As Sean O'Faolain reminds us, "Set any short-story writer to work on a novel and he will inevitably break it up into episodes."[7] Chekhov could not escape from the short story; his were essentially miniaturist skills.

An American example of the escapist short-story writer is Sherwood Anderson, who tried his hand at novels, among them *Poor White, Dark Laughter,* and *Windy McPherson's Son.* He failed miserably in the form, for he was windy and repetitious, and his fine perceptions and delicate sensibility so appropriate to the short story were strained and dulled by the novel's length. Anderson deserved every satiric thrust made by Hemingway in his novel *The Torrents of Spring,* which was aimed specifically at *Dark Laughter.* Frank O'Connor moved to the novel twice in *The Saint and Mary Kate* and *Dutch Interior,* and failed. On the one hand, then, as short-story writers try other art forms they are supposedly escaping; on the other, when they fail in the novel form and move back to the short story, they move to something less demanding and really inferior.

The short story has been belittled in other ways, especially when compared to the novel. It is simply looked upon as a "subsidiary form of expression."[8] In other words, when novelists want holidays or relief from the strenuous work of novel-writing, they dabble in the lesser prose medium. Further, usually any novelist has something left over, a chapter or a scene that would not fit the novel, or the novelist wants to make a trial run into a new novel with a short piece of fiction. Thomas Mann's "Tristan" is often studied as a preparation for the novel *The Magic*

Mountain, rather than an impressive performance in the long short story. Perverse criticism often views Franz Kafka's short stories as trial flights into the metaphysics of his famous novels, *The Trial* and *The Castle;* or they are treated as side effects from these novels.

A lost art—the fine art of reading, Lord David Cecil calls it—has not helped the short story's plight. Too often the prose of short fiction is treated like the prose of the novel, but there is the poetry of "much in little" in the short story. Usually the novel takes some time warming up; there are further opportunities in the novel for the reader to rehearse characters and ideas. But the short story may end before the reader really warms up to it. And the writer—not the reader—is charged with a lack of empathy. Even in relatively easy modern short stories, the reader must be thoroughly awake from the opening word. For illustrative purposes, one can view the opening lines of Hemingway's "Short Happy Life of Francis Macomber":

> It was now lunch time and they were all sitting under the double green fly of the dining tent pretending that nothing had happened.
> "Will you have lime juice or lemon squash?" Macomber asked.
> "I'll have a gimlet," Robert Wilson told him.
> "I'll have a gimlet, too. I need something," Macomber's wife said.
> "I suppose it's the thing to do," Macomber agreed. "Tell him to make three gimlets."

Hemingway seems to be giving us very little information; in reality he is giving us a great deal. There is a flash of insight into the individual characters, their individual tones, the author's tone, the atmosphere, the theme, and expository information that points to the past, the present, and the future. Even the language used—the short, stunted, sparse, clipped rhythms—suggests the world of this short story: on the one hand, it is seemingly offhanded; on the other, nervously taut, potentially explosive. There is "calamity in this cablegram" of an opening. But the possibility that prose is *that* compressed and *that* flexible is never really accepted by the reader.

Another lost art suggests the older, more traditional short story; even some contemporary stories gain by it. This is the short story as public art, where an oral reading to an audience by an artist shows how important the manner, the way of telling, is to an appreciation of some stories.[9] Mark Twain recalled this art in his essay "How to Tell a Story." In part, Twain said: "The humorous story depends for its effect upon the *manner* of the telling; the comic story and the witty story upon the *matter.*" This does not always hold true, for there are a good many comic and witty stories that do not have matter, and do depend on manner: some of James Thurber's fables, some of the entertainments of Somerset Maugham. There is little matter in Thurber's "Unicorn in the Garden." Though it was published originally for the private reader in *The New Yorker,* the pleasure of the fable is enhanced by an artist who can capture the casual and matter-of-fact movements that gradually release the witty and humorous vapors. The one-sentence close to the tale—"*Moral: Don't count your boobies until they are hatched*"— shows us that the fable has been bubbling gently along and can be enriched by the artist.

A final art which some feel has always been lost—honest, careful criticism—has further shoved the short story into the background. This is suggested by another literary war that started a short time ago. The angry, middle-aged Maxwell Geismar has annoyed some angrier and younger critics in his new book, *Henry James and the Jacobites.* One of the things Mr. Geismar assaults in his book is the New Critics; secondly, one of their gods, James himself. So many of the younger critics, teachers, and students have gone to James's house of fiction that they are not too receptive to other points of view. As almost everyone agrees, the New Criticism, that is, the intensive analysis of the work of art itself, has done a great deal of good. But those who emphasize the Jamesian approach to fiction have passed over the brief, the loose, simple narratives, the horizontal stories with few technical devices in favor of the highly complicated style and theme and subtle technical devices. The Jamesian critics have found many of their treasures in the novel form— rarely in the short story—and in special novelists like James himself, Joseph Conrad, and Herman Melville, who are involved, abstruse, and symbolical, who have plenty of "stretch." The short story is too restricted and gives the imagination of the critic too little room in which to develop further the art of overreading—a favorite occupation of some of the New Critics. For example, there have been too many "turns" on James's worn out *The Turn of the Screw.*

III

What must we do so that the short story can receive the kind of consideration it deserves? We can try to rid the genre of the prejudices that have conspired against it. We can come to it as though it were a fresh discovery. We can settle on one term for the medium, like "short fiction'' or ''short story.'' References to names like ''anecdote,'' ''tale,'' ''narrative,'' ''sketch,'' though convenient, merely add to the confusion and suggest indecisions and a possible inferiority complex. Too many names attached to the short story have made it seem almost nameless. Even the provincial attitude of teachers and anthologists has not helped. Most often students are fed on a strict diet of British and American short-story writers. But the short story is not solely a British and American product; it is an international art form, and Continental as well as Oriental, and other authors should be more fully represented in any educational program. As Maurice Beebe reminds us, ''Once translated, Zola, Mann, Proust, Kafka become authors in English and American literature. . . .''[10] Once this philosoph is accepted, the short story will automatically increase in vitality and stature.

One way the reader can contribute to a fuller appreciation of an old art is by simply applying the negative criticisms already mentioned— oneness of effect, formulas, and so on—to examples of the modern short story. For an illustration of the older modern story of average length (5000 words), one can go to Chekhov's popular ''Gooseberries,'' written in 1898. Too many readers would probably be so frustrated and so bored by all the talk and the lack of action in this story that they would stop before they really started. A more patient reader would go on trying to understand and appreciate Chekhov's tone before attempting any kind of critical evaluation. For Chekhov tells a story so casually, almost so indifferently, that he himself seems bored. Now on the surface level a Hemingway story, like ''The Killers,'' moves very rapidly; and we in America are used to quickness. Chekhov insists on putting us into a rocking chair.

On a first study, ''Gooseberries'' seems to be about Nikolay and the realization of his dreams: of a man once lost as a clerk, who has now found his meaning and validity as a human being, and consequently his freedom. But as Ivan tells the story about his brother Nikolay to Burkin and Alyokhin, the story becomes a study in Nikolay's self-deception and hypocrisy. For as Nikolay achieves what Tolstoy said was all that man needed—six feet of earth—Ivan sees the blindness of both Nikolay and Tolstoy. He says:

> . . . six feet is what a corpse needs, not a man. . . . To retire from the city, from the struggle, from the hubbub, to go off and hide on one's own farm—that's not life, it is selfishness, sloth, it is a kind of monasticism, but monasticism without works. Man needs not six feet of earth, not a farm, but

the whole globe, all of Nature, where unhindered he can display all the capacities and peculiarities of his free spirit.

But then the story is also a study of Nikolay as a dead soul, the superfluous man. This is corroborated in many ways. The imagery of fatness clearly reveals Nikolay's dead life; Ivan says:

> I made my way to the house and was met by a fat dog with reddish hair that looked like a pig. It wanted to bark, but was too lazy. The cook, a fat, barelegged woman, who also looked like a pig, came out of the kitchen and said that the master was resting after dinner. I went in to see my brother, and found him sitting up in bed, with a quilt over his knees. He had grown older, stouter, flabby; his cheeks, his nose, his lips jutted out: it looked as though he might grunt into the quilt at any moment.

And yet, though Nikolay is living a life of self-deception and hypocrisy, and though he is a dead soul, he is enjoying every moment of it: to him, his gooseberries are delicious; to his brother Ivan, the realist, they are hard and sour. To Nikolay his illusions are not illusions—they are happy realities. This is only one layer of the several paradoxes relating to illusions and realities in the story.

The story, then, is far too elaborate to be limited merely to Nikolay and his gooseberries. The gooseberries become a focal and radiating symbol, for they also touch the lives of Burkin, Ivan, and Alyokhin specifically, and Russia generally. This story ever expands in meaning and meanings.

For before Ivan tells his story in Alyokhin's house we are told: "It was a large structure of two stories. . . ." Structurally this is a frame story, a story within a story, and gradually the life of Nikolay becomes a first stage in studying a general condition in Russian life. As Ivan tells his brother's story he also tells his own, and reveals, through his constant rationalization, that he too is a dead soul, the superfluous man. He shows the pathos of his whole life, for now an old man, he cries out: "If I were young!" And he has his own deceptions and his own illusions. As he sees Nikolay's failures and his own, he looks to Alyokhin—as a "young" man of forty—to carry the banner of freedom and his idealizations of life. But he can't see—neither can Alyokhin—that Alyokhin is paralleled to Nikolay: both are landowners, one is lost in the work of his farm, the other in his gooseberries. Alyokhin can never realize the ideals mouthed by Ivan; the omniscient author, Chekhov, reflects ironically: "The guests were not talking about groats, or hay, or tar, but about something that had no direct bearing on his [Alyokhin's] life, and he was glad of it and wanted them to go on."

Earlier, Ivan has generalized on Russian life, and, without knowing it, the life of the story. He says:

> Look at life: the insolence and idleness of the strong, the ignorance and brutishness of the weak, horrible poverty everywhere, overcrowding, degeneration, drunkenness, hypocrisy, lying—Yet in all the houses and on all the streets there is peace and quiet; of the fifty thousand people who live in our town there is not one who would cry out, who would vent his indignation aloud. . . . It is a general hypnosis.

The paralysis of the individual lives and this general hypnosis are sounded in the opening of the story. The atmosphere—the "still" day, "tedious," "gray" and "dull," and later "it was tedious to listen to the story of the poor devil of a clerk who ate gooseberries"—infects everything. By the skillful use of contrast—the "refreshing" rain, the brief entrances and exits of the beautiful and pleasant maid Pelageya, and the ladies and generals in the golden picture frames—Chekhov further ironically studies what becomes the "general hypnosis theme" in Russia. From the choric Burkin at the story's end, we hear that he "could not sleep for a long time, [and he] kept wondering where the unpleasant odor came from." The unpleasant odor refers to the burnt tobacco from Ivan's pipe; this unpleasantness becomes, in a sense, the man with the hammer, mentioned earlier in the story, who is knocking at the reader's mind about happy and unhappy man. The monotony of the day—the rain at the beginning and at the end—and the tediousness of the tale transfers to the reader the paralysis of lives and the hypnosis theme.[11]

The story does not end. Nothing is solved. But the story is like a delayed fuse; it depends on after-effects on the reader via the poetic technique of suggestion and implication. We have enough of the parts to complete a significant pattern. This particular, isolated action moves to a more general plane of significance.

We can use "Gooseberries" to counteract the usual charges leveled against the short story. First, let us counteract Poe's legacy of oneness of effect. This story has layer and layer of meanings and plenty of contradictions in these meanings. If there were Poe's oneness here, the reader would not be forced to reread the story. Then we counteract the issue of mechanical formulas. This story seems as artless, as unplanned, as unmechanical as any story can be; it seems to be going nowhere but it is going everywhere. There is no beginning, middle, and end; it is just an episode that dangles. Here Chekhov demonstrates how flexible the form of the short story can be. Further, Mark Schorer's claim that a story means "revelation" and the novel "evolution" does not fit. This story does study change (even on the reader's part), and it also suggests a sense of continuing life, of whole lives; the past, the present, and the future have coalesced to evolve the idea of general hypnosis. Here is the remarkable art of telescoping. The complaint that the story is only a fragment does not fit either; the part comes to represent the whole in "Gooseberries." Even the much criticized episodic structure fits Chekhov's intended rhythm, his manner of viewing life. Chekhov saw that life did not happen in neat beginnings, middles, and ends. Human problems are not solved so neatly; they go on and on. Chekhov conceived his plotless, episodic stories to capture this rhythm of life. And the characters—characters in short stories are usually criticized as "flat" and uncomplicated—work together to create a combination of moods and anxieties that humanize the ambivalences and ambiguities in the Russian soul.

A more modern illustration than Chekhov is South Africa's Nadine Gordimer in her 2400-word story "The Train from Rhodesia" (1949). What one discovers with this example is that even extreme brevity cannot stifle the short story. "The Train from Rhodesia" is a puzzling story, for Miss Gordimer is trying to say far more than she reveals on the surface. One sees that she is in a world of censorship, the possible loss of a passport, and possible imprisonment and therefore sends cryptic notes from underground. Miss Gordimer's art is the poetic art of ellipsis— much has been omitted; the reader must fill in.

What Miss Gordimer has done is to take a brief space of time and lives and make it suggest a large panorama of feelings and attitudes. For in the story we see the separateness of black and white, and white and white, the world of primitivism (suggested by the hunk of sheep's carcass dangling in a current of air) and civilization (suggested by the train and its inhabitants), and hunger (suggested by the piccanins and the animals) versus sloth (suggested by occupants of the train, who throw out chocolates). The train expands these various threads. For one, the train is from Rhodesia and is to be burdened with white and native problems. In the opening of the story we hear: the "train came out of the red horizon and bore down toward them. . . ." Before the train stops in the station, it "called out, along the sky; but there was no answer; and the cry hung on: I'm coming . . . I'm coming. . . ." The last paragraph of the story returns to the train and extends its meaning: "The train had cast the station like a skin. It called out to the sky, I'm coming, I'm coming, I'm coming; and again, there was no answer."

The specific actions lead us to the generalizations made above. The pitiful natives smile not "from the heart, but at the customer." Their primitive art, like the carved lion, is "majestic," but they as vendors are bent "like performing animals." The old vendor who sells his art work to the young husband for one-and-six has his opened palm "held in the attitude of receiving." The crisis of husband and wife at the story's end is not resolved; it merges with the tempo—gnarled, fierce, disconnected—of the humanized train which expands and heightens the various estrangements. In one place, the wife reflects: "How will they [the native goods] look at home? Where will you put them? What will they mean away from the places you found them? Away from the unreality of the last few weeks? The man outside. But he is not part of the unreality; he is for good now. Odd . . . somewhere there was an idea that he, that living with him, was part of the holiday, the strange places." This private reflection becomes a public estrangement with her husband: "If you wanted the thing [the carved lion] . . . why didn't you buy it in the first place? If you wanted it, why didn't you pay for it? Why didn't you take it decently, when he offered it? Why did you have to wait for him to run after the train with it, and give him one-and-six? One-and-six!" The wife returns to her private world: "She had thought it was something to do with singleness, with being alone and belonging too much to oneself." The train's choric chant at the end—"I'm coming, I'm coming; and again, there was no answer"—helps to magnify a world of loneliness, separation, and discord.[12]

Like Chekhov's, this story defies the rules: Its action is small; its meanings are large. It is a poetic story—even more important, an impressionistic painting, for Miss Gordimer wants us to *see* and to *feel* the world of Africa through this one incident. The incident is not closed; there are the after-effects, nothing is finished off, the problem still exists.

Besides merely disproving the charges made against the short story, it is highly appropriate to show the story's virtues, some of which have already been suggested. First, concerning the relationship of these stories to the private reader: if one takes into account the aesthetic speculations of Edgar Allan Poe and Percy Lubbock, one must say that while the novel is one and continuous, it is forced into separateness, into pieces of short readings by the very nature of its length. The reader of the novel must rehearse mood, tone, characters, themes before he picks up the novel again; many do not do this. One wonders how many novels are really *read* and *understood*. And usually, after reading a novel once, the reader does not reread it.

Because the short story can be read in one sitting—and if one gives it the attention that one has to give to poetry—it gains by its compact impact and nothing is lost. In his *Poetics,* Aristotle felt that "the more compact is more pleasing than that which is spread over a great length of time." The short-story writer usually gains in control, in power, and in meaningfulness by his arts of distillation, telescoping, and understatement. And the short story can be easily reread; often it must be reread. Like the diamond, the short story throws off glints of meanings.

Because the novel falls into the category of pieces by the reading problem, one wonders if the short-story writers could be more appreciated if their complete stories were available in volume form. Here would be a novel of short stories, each distinct and separate, but yet gathered as a whole by the vision and style of one unique artist. Then some of the claims made for the novel could also be made for the short story. Critics say: here is Dickens' England, Flaubert's France. With the complete short stories of Crane and Anderson we can say: here is America of the 1890's and of the 1920's. Collected short stories could invite these and other large considerations usually reserved for the novel. Critics also say that the novel—specifically, *Madame Bovary*—is the proper place to study the art of fiction; a single story, like "The Open Boat," can serve just as well.

A surprising thing is this: the novel often has a number of errors, but we forgive these errors because the novel is ambitious. How many novels are loose and straggling? E. M. Forster once said that "nearly all novels are feeble at the end. This is because the plot requires to be wound up." There are other problems in the novel. Luckily because it is read in parts, a novel's possible lack of logic and proportion and loss of momentum are not noticed for the piecemeal reading of the novel. Now because the short story is read in one sitting it is always on trial. Every second counts. Like poetry, if a word, a sentence, is misplaced, if there is a loss of proportion, or if the momentum is not right, if there are platitudes, anything superfluous, any faking—the jig is up.

The novelist has been called the "long-distance runner," and he is not lonely. The short-story writer has been called a "sprinter," and he is lonely. Carlos Baker's reading of Hemingway's short stories is penetrating, as he uses Hemingway's own statement to explain the depths of the form. "The dignity of movement of an iceberg," Hemingway once said, "is due to only one-eighth of it being above water." Many of our great modern short-story writers write in short-hand; and one word, a phrase, can raise the short story to a new level of meaning. There is dignity and hidden depth in the short story. It has been in a deep freeze too long. One looks forward to a thawing out period.

1. This essay is a shortened version of my University Honors Lecture delivered at the University of Rhode Island on November 19, 1963.

2. *Writers at Work: The Paris Review Interviews,* edited by Malcolm Cowley (New York, 1958), p. 123.

3. An interesting yet very brief recent study of Maupassant's short fiction is Edward D. Sullivan, *Maupassant: The Short Stories* (New York, 1962).

4. *The Complete Short Stories and Sketches of Stephen Crane,* edited with an introduction by Thomas A. Gullason (New York, 1963).

5. In the *PMLA* bibliography for 1963, the editors retain the categories for Twentieth Century (American) but add a fourth section, Prose Fiction, under Twentieth Century (English). Lawrence and Hemingway still receive far more attention as novelists than as short-story writers.

6. *The Story: A Critical Anthology* (New York, 1950), p. 433.

7. *The Short Story* (New York, 1951), p. 52.

8. Dorothy Brewster and Angus Burrell, *Modern Fiction* (New York, 1934), p. 348.

9. Frank O'Connor tried to put back the "narrative impulse" in his stories during his readings on radio programs. He saw how the written word had robbed stories of "a man's voice, speaking." To be fully enjoyed, some of O'Connor's best stories should be read aloud. See *Stories By Frank O'Connor* (New York, 1958), p. vii.

10. *Approaches to the Study of Twentieth-Century Literature* (East Lansing, 1961), p. 161.

11. Though "Gooseberries" is most often studied singly, it forms part of a trilogy which also includes "The Man in a Shell" and "About Love." All three episodes present examples of the paralysis of souls and the hypnosis theme. Depending on a biographical approach, Ernest Simmons reads these stories differently. See his *Chekhov* (Boston, 1962), pp. 425–427.

This analysis of "Gooseberries" is not intended as a full explication; the story is being used mainly to illustrate the depths of the modern short story.

12. Though highly praised, Miss Gordimer is represented in very few anthologies. "The Train from Rhodesia" is reprinted only in *The World of Short Fiction: An International Collection,* edited by Thomas A. Gullason and Leonard Casper (New York, 1962), pp. 465–471.

This analysis of "The Train from Rhodesia" is not intended as a full explication; I use the story mainly to illustrate the depths of the modern short story.

Stories

Story, the dictionary tells one, is a short form of the word *history,* and stands for *a narrative, recital, or description of what has occurred;* just as it stands for a *fictitious narrative, imaginative tale; Colloq. a lie, a falsehood.*

A story, then, tells the truth or a lie—is a wish, or a truth, or a wish modified by a truth. Children ask first of all: "Is it a *true* story?" They ask this of the storyteller, but they ask of the story what they ask of a dream: that it satisfy their wishes. The Muses are the daughters of hope and the stepdaughters of memory. The wish is the first truth about us, since it represents not that learned principle of reality which half-governs our workaday hours, but the primary principle of pleasure which governs infancy, sleep, daydreams—and certainly, many stories. Reading stories, we cannot help remembering Groddeck's "We have to reckon with what exists, and dreams, daydreams too, are also facts; if anyone really wants to investigate realities, he cannot do better than to start with such as these. If he neglects them, he will learn little or nothing of the world of life." If wishes were stories, beggars would read; if stories were true, our saviors would speak to us in parables. Much of our knowledge of, our compensation for, "the world of life" comes from stories; and the stories themselves are part of "the world of life." Shakespeare wrote:

This is an art
Which does mend nature, change it rather, but
The art itself is nature . . .

and Goethe, agreeing, said: "A work of art is just as much a work of nature as a mountain."

In showing that dreams sometimes both satisfy our wishes and punish us for them, Freud compares the dreamer to the husband and wife in the fairy tale of The Three Wishes: the wife wishes for a pudding, the husband wishes it on the end of her nose, and the wife wishes it away again. A contradictory family! But it is this family—wife, husband, and pudding—which the story must satisfy: the writer is, and is writing for, a doubly- or triply-natured creature, whose needs, understandings, and ideals—whether they are called id, ego, and super-ego, or body, mind, and soul—contradict one another. Most of the stories that we are willing to call works of art are compounds almost as complicated as their creators; but occasionally we can see isolated, in naked innocence, one of the elements of which our stories are composed. Thomas Leaf's story (in Hardy's *Under the Greenwood Tree*) is an example:

> "Once," said the delighted Leaf, in an uncertain voice, "there was a man who lived in a house! Well, this man went thinking and thinking night and day. At last, he said to himself, as I might, 'If I had only ten pound, I'd make a fortune.' At last by hook or by crook, behold he got the ten pounds!"
>
> "Only think of that!" said Nat Callcome satirically.
>
> "Silence!" said the tranter.
>
> "Well, now comes the interesting part of the story! in a little time he made that ten pounds twenty. Then a little after that he doubled it, and made it forty. Well, he went on, and a good while after that he made it eighty, and on to a hundred. Well, by-and-by he made it two hundred! Well, you'd never believe it, but—he went on and made it four hundred! He went on, and what did he do? Why, he made it eight hundred! Yes, he did," continued Leaf, in the highest pitch of excitement, bringing down his fist upon his knee, with such force that he quivered with the pain; "yes, and he went on and made it A THOUSAND!"
>
> "Hear, hear!" said the tranter. "Better than the history of England, my sonnies!"
>
> "Thank you for your story, Thomas Leaf," said grandfather William; and then Leaf gradually sank into nothingness again.

Every day, in books, magazines, and newspapers, over radio and television, in motion-picture theaters, we listen to Leaf's story one more time, and then sink into nothingness again. His story is, in one sense, better than the history of England—or would be if the history of England were not composed, among other things, of Leaf's story and a million like it. His story, stood on its head, is the old woman's story in *Wozzeck*. "Grandmother, tell us a story," beg the children. "All right, you little crabs," she answers.

> Once upon a time there was a poor little girl who had no father and mother because everyone was dead and there was no one left in the whole world. Everyone was dead, and she kept looking for someone night and day. And since there was no one on earth, she thought she'd go to heaven. The moon looked at her so friendly, but when she finally got to it, it was just a piece of rotted wood. So she went on to the sun, and when she got there, it was just a dried-up sunflower. And when she got to the stars, they were just little gold flies stuck up there as if they'd been caught in a spider web. And when she thought she'd go back to earth, it was just an upside-down pot. And she was all alone. And so she sat down and cried. And she's still sitting there, all alone.

The grandmother's story is told less often—but often enough: when we wake into the reality our dream has contradicted, we are bitter at returning against our wishes to so bad a world, and take a fierce pleasure in what remains to us, the demonstration that it is the worst of all possible worlds. And we take pleasure also—as our stories show—in repeating over and over, until we can bear it, all that we found unbearable: the child whose mother left her so often that she invented a game of throwing her doll out of her crib, exclaiming as it vanished: "Gone! gone!" was a true poet. "Does I 'member much about slavery times?" the old man says, in *Lay My Burden Down;* "well, there is no way for me to disremember unless I die." But the worst memories are joyful ones: "Every time Old Mistress thought we little black children was hungry 'tween meals she would give us johnnycake and plenty of buttermilk to drink with it. There was a long trough for us they would scrub so clean. They would fill this trough with buttermilk and all us children would sit round the trough and drink with our mouths and hold our johnnycake with our hands. I can just see myself drinking now. It was so good. . . ." It is so good, our stories believe, simply to remember: their elementary delight in recognition, familiarity, mimesis, is another aspect of their obsession with all the likenesses of the universe, those metaphors that Proust called essential to style. Stories want to *know:* everything from the first blaze and breathlessness and fragrance to the last law and structure; but, too, stories don't want to know, don't want to care, just want to *do as they please.* (Some great books are a consequence of the writer's losing himself in his subject, others are a consequence of his losing himself in himself. Rabelais' "do what you please" is the motto of how many masterpieces, from Cervantes and Sterne on up to the present.) For stories vary from a more-than-Kantian disinterestedness, in which the self is a representative, indistinguishable integer among millions—the mere *one* or *you* or *man* that is the subject of all the verbs—to an insensate, protoplasmic egotism to which the self is the final fact, a galaxy that it is impracticable to get out of to other galaxies. Polarities like these are almost the first thing one notices about fiction. It is as much haunted by the chaos which precedes and succeeds order as by order; by the incongruities of the universe (wit, humor, the arbitrary, accidental, and absurd—all irruptions from, releases of, the unconscious) as by its likenesses. A story may present fantasy as fact, as the sin or *hubris* that the fact of things punishes, or as a reality superior to fact. And, often, it presents it as a mixture of the three: all opposites meet in fiction.

The truths that he systematized, Freud said, had already been discovered by the poets; the tears of things, the truth of things, are there in their fictions. And yet, as he knew, the root of all stories is in Grimm, not in La Rochefoucauld; in dreams, not in cameras and tape recorders. Turgenev was right when he said, "Truth alone, however powerful, is not art"—oxygen alone, however concentrated, is not water; and Freud was right, profoundly right, when he showed "that the dream is a compromise between the expression of and the defence against the unconscious emotions; that in it the unconscious wish is represented as being fulfilled; that there are very definite mechanisms that control this expression; that the primary process controls the dream world just as it controls the entire unconscious life of the soul, and that myth and poetical productions come into being in the same way and have the same meaning. There is only one important difference: in the myths and in the works of poets the secondary elaboration is much further developed, so that a logical and coherent entity is created." It is hard to exaggerate the importance of this difference, of course; yet usually we do exaggerate it—do write as if that one great difference had hidden from us the greater similarities which underlie it.

II

A baby asleep but about to be waked by hunger sometimes makes little sucking motions: he is dreaming that he is being fed, and manages by virtue of the dream to stay asleep. He may even smile a little in satisfaction. But the smile cannot last for long—the dream fails, and he wakes. This is, in a sense, the first story; the child in his "impotent omnipotence" is like us readers, us writers, in ours.

A story is a chain of events. Since the stories that we know are told by men, the events of the story happen to human or anthropomorphic beings—gods, beasts, and devils, and are related in such a way that the story seems to begin at one place and to end at a very different place, without any essential interruption to its progress. The poet or story-teller, so to speak, writes numbers on a blackboard, draws a line under them, and adds them into their true but unsuspected sum. Stories, because of their nature or—it is to say the same thing—of ours, are always capable of generalization: a story about a dog Kashtanka is true for all values of dogs and men.

Stories can be as short as a sentence. Bion's saying, *The boys throw stones at the frogs in sport, but the frogs die not in sport but in earnest,* is a story; and when one finds it in Aesop, blown up into a fable five or six sentences long, it has become a poorer story. Blake's *Prudence is a rich, ugly old maid courted by Incapacity* has a story inside it, waiting to flower in a glass of water. And there is a story four sentences long that not even Rilke was able to improve: *Now King David was old and stricken in years; and they covered him with clothes, but he got no heat. Wherefore his servants said unto him, Let there be sought for my lord the king a young virgin: and let her stand before the king, and let her cherish him, and let her lie in thy bosom, that my lord the king may get heat. So they sought for a fair damsel throughout all the coasts of Israel, and found Abishag a Shunamite, and brought her to the king. And the damsel was very fair, and cherished the King, and ministered to him: but the king knew her not. . . .* The enlisted men at Fort Benning buried their dog Calculus under a marker that read: *He made better dogs of us all,* and a few days ago I read in the paper: *A Sunday-school teacher, mother of four children, shot to death her eight-year-old daughter as she slept today, state police reported. Hilda Kristle, 43, of Stony Run, told police that her youngest daughter, Suzanne, "had a heavy heart and often went about the house sighing."*

When we try to make, out of these stories life gives us, works of art of comparable concision, we almost always put them into verse. Blake writes about a chimney sweep:

A little black thing among the snow
Crying "'weep! 'weep!" in notes of woe!
"Where are thy father & mother, say?"
"They are both gone up to the church to pray.

"Because I was happy upon the heath,
And smil'd among the winter's snow
They clothed me in the clothes of death,
And taught me to sing the notes of woe.

"And because I am happy & dance & sing,
They think they have done me no injury,
And are gone to praise God & his Priest & King,
Who make up a Heaven of our misery—"

and he has written enough. Stephen Crane says in fifty words:

In the desert
I saw a creature naked, bestial,
Who, squatting upon the ground,
Held his heart in his hands
And ate of it.
I said, "Is it good, friend?"
"It is bitter—bitter," he answered;
"But I like it
Because it is bitter
And because it is my heart."

These are the bones of stories, and we shiver at them. The poems one selects for a book of stories have more of the flesh of ordinary fiction. A truly representative book of stories would include a great many poems: during much of the past people put into verse the stories that they intended to be literature.

But it is hard to put together any representative collection of stories. It is like starting a zoo in a closet: the giraffe alone takes up more space than one has for the collection. *Remembrance of Things Past* is a story, just as Saint-Simon's memoirs are a great many stories. One can represent the memoirs with the death of Monseigneur, but not even the death of Bergotte, the death of the narrator's grandmother, can do that for *Remembrance of Things Past*. Almost everything in the world, one realizes after a while, is too long to go into a short book of stories—a book of short stories. So, even, are all those indeterminate masterpieces that the nineteenth century called short stories and that we call short novels or novelettes: Tolstoy's *The Death of Ivan Ilyich, Hadji Murad, Master and Man;* Flaubert's *A Simple Heart;* Mann's *Death in Venice;* Leskov's *The Lady Macbeth of the Mzinsk District;* Keller's *The Three Righteous Comb-Makers;* James's *The Aspern Papers;* Colette's *Julie de Carneilhan;* Kleist's *Michael Kohlhaas;* Joyce's *The Dead;* Turgenev's *A Lear of the Steppes;* Hoffmannsthal's *Andreas;* Kafka's *Metamorphosis;* Faulkner's *Spotted Horses;* Porter's *Old Mortality;* Dostoievsky's *The Eternal Husband;* Melville's *Bartleby the Scrivener, Benito Cereno;* Chekhov's *Ward No. 6, A Dreary Story, Peasants, In the Ravine.*

And there are many more sorts of stories than there are sizes. Epics; ballads; historical or biographical or autobiographical narratives, letters, diaries; myths, fairy tales, fables; dreams, daydreams; humorous or indecent or religious anecdotes; all those stories which might be called specialized or special case—science fiction, ghost stories, detective stories, Westerns, True Confessions, children's stories, and the rest; and, finally, "serious fiction"—Proust and Chekhov and Kafka, *Moby-Dick, Great Expectations, A Sportsman's Notebook.* What I myself selected for a book of stories was most of it "serious fiction," some of it serious fiction in verse; but there was a letter of Tolstoy's, a piece of history and autobiography from Saint-Simon; and there were gipsy and German fairy tales, Hebrew and Chinese parables, and two episodes from the journal of an imaginary Danish poet, the other self of the poet Rainer Maria Rilke. There are so many good short narratives of every kind that a book of three or four hundred pages leaves almost all of their writers unrepresented. By saying that I was saving these writers for a second and third book I tried to make myself feel better at having left them out of the first. For I left out all sagas, all ballads, all myths; a dozen great narrators in verse, from Homer to Rilke; Herodotus, Plutarch, Pushkin, Hawthorne, Flaubert, Dostoievsky, Melville, James, Leskov, Keller, Kipling, Mann, Faulkner—I cannot bear to go on. Several of these had written long narratives so much better than any of their short ones that it seemed unfair to use the short, and it was impossible to use the long. Hemingway I could not get permission to reprint. Any anthology is, as the dictionary says, a bouquet—a bouquet that leaves out most of the world's flowers.

My own bunch is named *The Anchor Book of Stories,* and consists of Franz Kafka's *A Country Doctor*; Anton Chekhov's *Gusev*; Rainer Maria Rilke's *The Wrecked Houses* and *The Big Thing* (from *The Notebooks of Malte Laurids Brigge*); Robert Frost's *The Witch of Coös*; Giovanni Verga's *La Lupa*; Nicolai Gogol's *The Nose*; Elizabeth Bowen's *Her Table Spread*; Ludwig Tieck's *Fair Eckbert*; Bertolt Brecht's *Concerning the Infanticide Marie Farrar;* Lev Tolstoy's *The Three Hermits*; Peter Taylor's *What You Hear from 'Em?*; Hans Christian Anderson's *The Fir Tree*; Katharine Anne Porter's *He*; a Gipsy's *The Red King and the Witch*; Anton Chekhov's *Rothschild's Fiddle*; the Brothers Grimm's *Cat and Mouse in Partnership*; E. M. Forster's *The Story of the Siren*; *The Book of Jonah*; Franz Kafka's *The Bucket-Rider*; Saint-Simon's *The Death of Monseigneur*; Isaac Babel's *Awakening*; five anecdotes by Chuang T'zu; Hugo von Hofmannsthal's *A Tale of the Cavalry*; William Blake's *The Mental Traveller*; D. H. Lawrence's *Samson and Delilah;* Lev Tolstoy's *The Porcelain Doll;* Ivan Turgenev's *Byezhin Prairie*; William Wordsworth's *The Ruined Cottage*; Frank O'Connor's *Peasants*; and Isak Dinesen's *Sorrow-Acre.*

I disliked leaving out writers, but I disliked almost as much having to leave out some additional stories by some of the writers I included. I used so many of the writers who "came out of Gogol's *Overcoat*" that *The Overcoat* was in a sense already there, but I wished that it and *Old-World Land-owners* had been there in every sense; that I could have included Chekhov's *The Bishop, The Lady with the Dog, Gooseberries, The Darling, The Man in a Shell, The Kiss, The Witch, On Official Business,* and how many more; that I could have included Kafka's *The Penal Colony* and *The Hunter Gracchus;* and that I could have included at least a story more from Lawrence, Tolstoy, Verga, Grimm, and Andersen. With Turgenev's masterpiece all selection fails: *A Sportsman's Notebook* is a whole greater and more endearing than even the best of its parts.

III

There are all kind of beings, and all kinds of things happen to them; and when you add to these what are as essential to the writer, the things that don't actually happen, the beings that don't actually exist, it is no wonder that stories are as varied as they are. But it seems to me that there are two extremes: stories in which nothing happens, and stories in which everything is a happening. The Muse of fiction believes that people "don't go to the North Pole" but go to work, go home, get married, die; but she believes at the same time that absolutely anything can occur— concludes, with Gogol: "Say what you like, but such things do happen—not often, but they do happen." Our lives, even our stories, approach at one extreme the lives of Prior's Jack and Joan:

> *If human things went Ill or Well;*
> *If changing Empires rose or fell;*
> *The Morning past, the Evening came,*
> *And found this couple still the same.*
> *They Walked and Eat, good folks: What then?*
> *Why then they Walk'd and Eat again:*
> *They soundly slept the Night away:*
> *They did just Nothing all the day . . .*
> *Nor Good, nor Bad, nor Fools, nor Wise;*
> *They wou'd not learn, nor cou'd advise:*
> *Without Love, Hatred, Joy, or Fear,*
> *They led—a kind of—as it were;*
> *Nor Wish'd, nor Car'd, nor Laugh'd, nor Cry'd:*
> *And so They liv'd; and so They dy'd.*

Billions have lived, and left not even a name behind, and while they were alive nobody knew their names either. These live out their lives "among the rocks and winding scars/ Where deep and low the hamlets lie/ Each with its little patch of sky/ And little lot of stars"; soundly sleep the Night away in the old houses of Oblomov's native village, where everybody did just Nothing all the day; rise—in Gogol's Akaky Akakyevich Bashmachkin, in the *Old-World Landowners,* to a quite biblical pathos and grandeur; are relatives of that Darling, that *dushechka,* who for so many solitary years "had no opinions of any sort. She saw the objects about her and understood what she saw, but could not form any opinion about them"; sit and, "musing with close lips and lifted eyes/ Have smiled with self-contempt to live so wise/ And run so smoothly such a length of lies"; walk slowly, staring about them—or else just walk—through the pages of Turgenev, Sterne, Keller, Rabelais, Twain, Cervantes, and how many others; and in Chuang T'zu disappear into the mists of time, looming before us in primordial grandeur: "In the days of Ho Hsu the people did nothing in particular when at rest, and went nowhere in particular when they moved. Having food, they rejoiced; having full bellies, they strolled about. Such were the capacities of the people."

How different from the later times, the other pages, in which people "wear the hairs off their legs" "counting the grains of rice for a rice-pudding"! How different from the other extreme: the world of Svidrigaylov, Raskolnikov, Stavrogin, where everything that occurs is either a dream told as if it were reality, or reality told as if it were a dream, and where the story is charged up to the point at which the lightning blazes out in some nightmare, revelation, atrocity, and the drained narrative can begin to charge itself again. In this world, and in the world of *The Devil, The Kreutzer Sonata, The Death of Ivan Ilyich,* everything is the preparation for, or consummation of, an Event; everyone is an echo of "the prehistoric, unforgettable Other One, who is never equalled by anyone later." This is the world of Hofmannsthal's *A Tale of the Cavalry,* where even the cow being dragged to the shambles, "shrinking from the smell of blood and the fresh hide of a calf nailed to the doorpost, planted its hooves firm on the ground, drew the reddish haze of the sunset in through dilated nostrils, and, before the lad could drag her across the road with stick and rope, tore away with piteous eyes a mouthful of the hay which the sergeant had tied on the front of his saddle." It is the world of Nijinsky's diary: "One evening I went for a walk up the hill, and stopped on the mountain . . . 'the mountain of Sinai.' I was cold. I had walked far. Feeling that I should kneel, I quickly knelt and then felt that I should put my hand in the snow. After doing this, I suddenly felt a pain and cried with it, pulling my hand away. I looked at a star, which did not say good evening to me. It did not twinkle at me. I got frightened and wanted to run, but could not because my knees were rooted to the snow. I started to cry, but no one heard my weeping. No one came to my rescue. After several minutes I turned and saw a house. It was closed and the windows shuttered . . . I felt frightened and shouted at the top of my voice: 'Death!' I did not know why, but felt that one must shout 'Death!' After that I felt warmer . . . I walked on the snow which crunched beneath my feet. I liked the snow and listened to its crunching. I loved listening to my footsteps; they were full of life. Looking at the sky, I saw the stars which were twinkling at me and felt merriment in them. I was happy and no longer felt cold . . .

I started to go down a dark road, walking quickly, but was stopped by a tree which saved me. I was on the edge of a precipice. I thanked the tree. It felt me because I caught hold of it; it received my warmth and I received the warmth of the tree. I do not know who most needed the warmth. I walked on and suddenly stopped, seeing a precipice without a tree. I understood that God had stopped me because He loves me, and therefore said: 'If it is thy will, I will fall down the precipice. If it is thy will, I will be saved.'''

This is what I would call pure narrative; one must go to writers like Tolstoy and Rilke and Kafka to equal it. In the unfinished stories of Kafka's notebook, some fragment a page long can carry us over a whole abyss of events: ''I was sitting in the box, and beside me was my wife. The play being performed was an exciting one, it was about jealousy; at that moment in the midst of a brilliantly lit hall surrounded by pillars, a man was just raising his dagger against his wife, who was slowly retreating to the exit. Tense, we leaned forward together over the balustrade; I felt my wife's curls against my temples. Then we started back, for something moved on the balustrade; what we had taken for the plush upholstery of the balustrade was the back of a tall thin man, not an inch broader than the balustrade, who had been lying flat on his face there and was now slowly turning over as though trying to find a more comfortable position. Trembling, my wife clung to me. His face was quite close to me, narrower than my hand, meticulously clean as that of a waxwork figure, and with a pointed black beard. 'Why do you come and frighten us?' I exclaimed. 'What are you up to here?' 'Excuse me!' the man said, 'I am an admirer of your wife's. To feel her elbows on my body makes me happy.' 'Emil, I implore you, protect me!' my wife exclaimed. 'I too am called Emil,' the man said, supporting his head on one hand and lying there as though on a sofa. 'Come to me, dear sweet little woman.' 'You cad,' I said, 'another word and you'll find yourself lying down there in the pit,' and as though certain that this word was bound to come, I tried to push him over, but it was not so easy, he seemed to be a solid part of the balustrade, it was as though he were built into it, I tried to roll him off, but I couldn't do it, he only laughed and said: 'Stop that, you silly little man, don't wear out your strength prematurely, the struggle is only beginning and it will end, as may well be said, with your wife's granting my desire.' 'Never!' my wife exclaimed, and then, turning to me: 'Oh, please, do push him down now.' 'I can't,' I exclaimed, 'you can see for yourself how I'm straining, but there's some trickery in it, it can't be done.' 'Oh dear, oh dear,' my wife lamented, 'what is to become of me?' 'Keep calm,' I said, 'I beg of you. By getting so worked up you're only making it worse, I have another plan now, I shall cut the plush open here with my knife and then drop the whole thing down and the fellow with it.' But now I could not find my knife. 'Don't you know where I have my knife?' I asked. 'Can I have left it in my overcoat?' I was almost going to dash along to the cloakroom when my wife brought me to my senses. 'Surely you're not going to leave me alone now, Emil,' she cried. 'But if I have no knife,' I shouted back. 'Take mine,' she said and began fumbling in her little bag, with trembling fingers, but then of course all she produced was a tiny little mother-of-pearl knife.''

One of the things that make Kafka so marvellous a writer is his discovery of—or, rather, discovery by—a kind of narrative in which logical analysis and humor, the greatest enemies of narrative movement, have themselves become part of the movement. In narrative at its purest or most eventful we do not understand but are the narrative. When we understand completely (or laugh completely, or feel completely a lyric empathy with the beings of the world), the carrying force of the narrative is dissipated: in fiction, to understand everything is to get nowhere. Yet, walking through Combray with Proust, lying under the leaves with Turgenev and the dwarf Kasyan, who has ever wanted to get anywhere but where he already is, in the best of all possible places?

In stories-in-which-everything-is-a-happening each event is charged and about to be further charged, so that the narrative may at any moment reach a point of unbearable significance, and disintegrate into energy. In stories-in-which-nothing-happens even the climax or denouement is liable to lose what charge it has, and to become simply one more portion of the lyric, humorous, or contemplative continuum of the story: in Gogol's *The Nose* the policeman seizes the barber, the barber turns pale, "but here the incident is completely shrouded in a fog and absolutely nothing is known of what happened next"; and in *Nevsky Avenue,* after Schiller, Hoffman, and Kuntz the carpenter have stripped Lieutenant Pirogov and "treated him with such an utter lack of ceremony that I cannot find words to describe this highly regrettable incident," Pirogov goes raging away, and "nothing could compare with Pirogov's anger and indignation. Siberia and the lash seemed to him the least punishment Schiller deserved . . . But the whole thing somehow petered out most strangely: on the way to the general, he went into a pastry-cook's, ate two pastries, read something out of the *Northern Bee,* and left with his anger somewhat abated''; took a stroll along Nevsky Avenue; and ended at a party given by one of the directors of the Auditing Board, where he ''so distinguished himself in the mazurka that not only the ladies but also the gentlemen were in raptures over it. What a wonderful world we live in!''

One of these extremes of narrative will remind us of the state of minimum excitation which the organism tries to re-establish—of the baby asleep, a lyric smile on his lips; the other extreme resembles the processes of continually increased excitation found in sex and play.

EDGAR ALLAN POE

Review of *Twice-Told Tales*

WE said a few hurried words about Mr. Hawthorne in our last number, with the design of speaking more fully in the present. We are still, however, pressed for room, and must necessarily discuss his volumes more briefly and more at random than their high merits deserve.

The book professes to be a collection of *tales,* yet is, in two respects, misnamed. These pieces are now in their third republication, and, of course, are thrice-told. Moreover, they are by no means *all* tales, either in the ordinary or in the legitimate understanding of the term. Many of them are pure essays; for example, "Sights from a Steeple," "Sunday at Home," "Little Annie's Ramble," "A Rill from the Town Pump," "The Toll-Gatherer's Day," "The Haunted Mind," "The Sister Years," "Snow-Flakes," "Night Sketches," and "Foot-Prints on the Sea-Shore." We mention these matters chiefly on account of their discrepancy with that marked precision and finish by which the body of the work is distinguished.

Of the essays just named, we must be content to speak in brief. They are each and all beautiful, without being characterised by the polish and adaptation so visible in the tales proper. A painter would at once note their leading or predominant feature, and style it *repose*. There is no attempt at effect. All is quiet, thoughtful, subdued. Yet this repose may exist simultaneously with high originality of thought; and Mr. Hawthorne has demonstrated the fact. At every turn we meet with novel combinations; yet these combinations never surpass the limits of the quiet. We are soothed as we read; and withal is a calm astonishment that ideas so apparently obvious have never occurred or been presented to us before. Herein our author differs materially from Lamb or Hunt or Hazlitt—who, with vivid originality of manner and expression, have less of the true novelty of thought than is generally supposed, and whose originality, at best, has an uneasy and meretricious quaintness, replete with startling effects unfounded in nature, and inducing trains of reflection which lead to no satisfactory result. The Essays of Hawthorne have much of the character of Irving, with more of originality, and less of finish; while, compared with the Spectator, they have a vast superiority at all points. The Spectator, Mr. Irving, and Mr. Hawthorne have in common that tranquil and subdued manner which we have chosen to denominate *repose;* but, in the case of the two former, this repose is attained rather by the absence of novel combination, or of originality, than otherwise, and consists chiefly in the calm, quiet, unostentatious expression of common-place thoughts, in an unambitious, unadulterated Saxon. In them, by strong effort, we are made to conceive the absence of all. In the essays before us the absence of effort is too obvious to be mistaken, and a strong under current of *suggestion* runs continuously beneath the upper stream of the tranquil thesis. In short, these effusions of Mr. Hawthorne are the product of a truly imaginative intellect, restrained, and in some measure repressed, by fastidiousness of taste, by constitutional melancholy and by indolence.

But it is of his tales that we desire principally to speak. The tale proper, in our opinion, affords unquestionably the fairest field for the exercise of the loftiest talent, which can be afforded by the wide domains of mere prose. Were we bidden to say how the highest genius could be most advantageously employed for the best display of its own powers, we should answer, without hesitation—in the composition of a rhymed poem, not to exceed in length what might be perused in an hour. Within this limit alone can the highest order of true poetry exist. We need only here say, upon this topic, that, in almost all classes of composition, the unity of effect or impression is a point of the greatest importance. It is clear, moreover, that this unity cannot be thoroughly preserved in productions whose perusal cannot be completed at one sitting. We may continue the reading of a prose composition, from the very nature of prose itself, much longer than we can persevere, to any good purpose, in the perusal of a poem. This latter, if truly fulfilling the demands of the poetic sentiment, induces an exaltation of the soul which cannot be long sustained. All high excitements are necessarily transient. Thus a long poem is a paradox. And, without unity of impression, the deepest effects cannot be brought about. Epics were the offspring of an imperfect sense of Art, and their reign is no more. A poem *too* brief may produce a vivid, but never an intense or enduring impression. Without a certain continuity of effort—without a certain duration or repetition of purpose—the soul is never deeply moved. There must be the dropping of the water upon the rock. De Beranger has wrought brilliant things—pungent and spirit-stirring—but, like all immassive bodies, they lack *momentum,* and thus fail to satisfy the Poetic Sentiment. They sparkle and excite, but, from want of continuity, fail deeply to impress. Extreme brevity will degenerate into epigrammatism; but the sin of extreme length is even more unpardonable. *In medio tutissimus ibis.*

Were we called upon, however, to designate that class of composition which, next to such a poem as we have suggested, should best fulfil the demands of high genius—should offer it the most advantageous field of exertion—we should unhesitatingly speak of the prose tale, as Mr. Hawthorne has here exemplified it. We allude to the short prose narrative, requiring from a half-hour to one or two hours in its perusal. The ordinary novel is objectionable, from its length, for reasons already stated in substance. As it cannot be read at one sitting, it deprives itself, of course, of the immense force derivable from *totality.* Worldly interests intervening during the pauses of perusal, modify, annul, or counteract, in a greater or less degree, the impressions of the book. But simple cessation in reading, would, of itself, be sufficient to destroy the true unity. In the brief tale, however, the author is enabled to carry out the fullness of his intention, be it what it may. During the hour of perusal the soul of the reader is at the writer's control. There are no external or extrinsic influences—resulting from weariness or interruption.

A skilful literary artist has constructed a tale. If wise, he has not fashioned his thoughts to accommodate his incidents; but having conceived, with deliberate care, a certain unique or single *effect* to be wrought out, he then invents such incidents—he then combines such events as may best aid him in establishing this preconceived effect. If his very initial sentence tend not to the outbringing of this effect, then he has failed in his first step. In the whole composition there should be no word written, of which the tendency, direct or indirect, is not to the one preestablished design. And by such means, with such care and skill, a picture is at length painted which leaves in the mind of him who contemplates it with a kindred art, a sense of the fullest satisfaction. The idea of the tale has been presented unblemished, because undisturbed; and this is an end unattainable by the novel. Undue brevity is just as exceptionable here as in the poem; but undue length is yet more to be avoided.

We have said that the tale has a point of superiority even over the poem. In fact, while the *rhythm* of this latter is an essential aid in the development of the poet's highest idea—the idea of the Beautiful—the artificialities of this rhythm are an inseparable bar to the development of all points of thought or expression which have their basis in *Truth*. But Truth is often, and in very great degree, the aim of the tale. Some of the finest tales are tales of ratiocination. Thus the field of this species of composition, if not in so elevated a region on the mountain of Mind, is a table-land of far vaster extent than the domain of the mere poem. Its products are never so rich, but infinitely more numerous, and more appreciable by the mass of mankind. The writer of the prose tale, in short, may bring to his theme a vast variety of modes or inflections of thought and expression—(the ratiocinative, for example, the sarcastic, or the humorous) which are not only antagonistical to the nature of the poem, but absolutely forbidden by one of its most peculiar and indispensable adjuncts; we allude, of course, to rhythm. It may be added here, *par parenthèse,* that the author who aims at the purely beautiful in a prose tale is laboring at great disadvantage. For Beauty can be better treated in a poem. Not so with terror, or passion, or horror, or a multitude of such other points. And here it will be seen how full of prejudice are the usual animadversions against those *tales of effect,* many fine examples of which were found in the earlier numbers of Blackwood. The impressions produced were wrought in a legitimate sphere of action, and constituted a legitimate although sometimes an exaggerated interest. They were relished by every man of genius; although there were found many men of genius who condemned them without just ground. The true critic will but demand that the design intended be accomplished, to the fullest extent, by the means most advantageously applicable.

We have very few American tales of real merit—we may say, indeed, none, with the exception of "The Tales of a Traveller" of Washington Irving, and these "Twice-Told Tales" of Mr. Hawthorne. Some of the pieces of Mr. John Neal abound in vigor and originality; but in general, his compositions of this class are excessively diffuse, extravagant, and indicative of an imperfect sentiment of Art. Articles at random are, now and then, met with in our periodicals which might be advantageously compared with the best effusions of the British Magazines; but, upon the whole, we are far behind our progenitors in this department of literature.

Of Mr. Hawthorne's Tales we would say, emphatically, that they belong to the highest region of Art—an Art subservient to genius of a very lofty order. We had supposed, with good reason for so supposing, that he had been thrust into his present position by one of the impudent *cliques* which beset our literature, and whose pretensions it is our full purpose to expose at the earliest opportunity; but we have been most agreeably mistaken. We know of few compositions which the critic can more honestly commend than these "Twice-Told Tales." As Americans, we feel proud of the book.

Mr. Hawthorne's distinctive trait is invention, creation, imagination, originality—a trait which, in the literature of fiction, is positively worth all the rest. But the nature of originality, so far as regards its manifestation in letters, is but imperfectly understood. The inventive or original mind as frequently displays itself in novelty of *tone* as in novelty of matter. Mr. Hawthorne is original at *all* points.

It would be a matter of some difficulty to designate the best of these tales; we repeat that, without exception, they are beautiful. "Wakefield" is remarkable for the skill with which an old idea—a well-known incident—is worked up or discussed. A man of whims conceives the purpose of quitting his wife and residing *incognito,* for twenty years, in her immediate neighborhood. Something of this kind actually happened in London. The force of Mr. Hawthorne's tale lies in the analysis of the motives which must or might have impelled the husband to such folly, in the first instance, with the possible causes of his perseverance. Upon this thesis a sketch of singular power has been constructed.

"The Wedding Knell" is full of the boldest imagination—an imagination fully controlled by taste. The most captious critic could find no flaw in this production.

"The Minister's Black Veil" is a masterly composition of which the sole defect is that to the rabble its exquisite skill will be *caviare*. The *obvious* meaning of this article will be found to smother its insinuated one. The *moral* put into the mouth of the dying minister will be supposed to convey the *true* import of the narrative; and that a crime of dark dye (having reference to the "young lady"), has been committed, is a point which only minds congenial with that of the author will perceive.

"Mr. Higginbotham's Catastrophe" is vividly original and managed most dexterously.

"Dr. Heidegger's Experiment" is exceedingly well imagined, and executed with surpassing ability. The artist breathes in every line of it.

"The White Old Maid" is objectionable, even more than the "Minister's Black Veil," on the score of its mysticism. Even with the thoughtful and analytic, there will be much trouble in penetrating its entire import.

"The Hollow of the Three Hills," we would quote in full, had we space;—not as evincing higher talent than any of the other pieces, but as affording an excellent example of the author's peculiar ability. The subject is commonplace. A witch subjects the Distant and the Past to the view of a mourner. It has been the fashion to describe, in such cases, a mirror in which the images of the absent appear; or a cloud of smoke is made to arise, and thence the figures are gradually unfolded. Mr. Hawthorne has wonderfully heightened his effect by making the ear, in place of the eye, the medium by which the fantasy is conveyed. The head of the mourner is enveloped in the cloak of the witch, and within its magic folds there arise sounds which have an all-sufficient intelligence. Throughout this article also, the artist is conspicuous—not more in positive than in negative merits. Not only is all done that should be done, but (what perhaps is an end with more difficulty attained) there is nothing done which should not be. Every word *tells,* and there is not a word that does *not* tell. . . .

In the way of objection we have scarcely a word to say of these tales. There is, perhaps, a somewhat too general or prevalent *tone*—a tone of melancholy and mysticism. The subjects are insufficiently varied. There is not so much of *versatility* evinced as we might well be warranted in expecting from the high powers of Mr. Hawthorne. But beyond these trivial exceptions we have really none to make. The style is purity itself. Force abounds. High imagination gleams from every page. Mr. Hawthorne is a man of the truest genius. We only regret that the limits of our Magazine will not permit us to pay him that full tribute of commendation, which, under other circumstances, we should be so eager to pay.

The Philosophy of the Short-Story

II

The difference between a Novel and a Novelet is one of length only: a Novelet is a brief Novel. But the difference between a Novel and a Short-story is a difference of kind. A true Short-story is something other and something more than a mere story which is short. A true Short-story differs from the Novel chiefly in its essential unity of impression. In a far more exact and precise use of the word, a Short-story has unity as a Novel cannot have it.[1] Often, it may be noted by the way, the Short-story fulfils the three false unities of the French classic drama: it shows one action, in one place, on one day. A Short-story deals with a single character, a single event, a single emotion, or the series of emotions called forth by a single situation. Poe's paradox[2] that a poem cannot greatly exceed a hundred lines in length under penalty of ceasing to be one poem and breaking into a string of poems, may serve to suggest the precise difference between the Short-story and the Novel. The Short-story is the single effect, complete and self-contained, while the Novel is of necessity broken into a series of episodes. Thus the Short-story has, what the Novel cannot have, the effect of "totality," as Poe called it, the unity of impression.

Of a truth the Short-story is not only not a chapter out of a Novel, or an incident or an episode extracted from a longer tale, but at its best it impresses the reader with the belief that it would be spoiled if it were made larger, or if it were incorporated into a more elaborate work. The difference in spirit and in form between the Lyric and the Epic is scarcely greater than the difference between the Short-story and the Novel; and the "Raven" and "How we brought the good news from Ghent to Aix" are not more unlike the "Lady of the Lake" and "Paradise Lost," in form and in spirit, than the "Luck of Roaring Camp," and the "Man without a Country," two typical Short-stories, are unlike "Vanity Fair" and the "Heart of Midlothian," two typical Novels.

Another great difference between the Short-story and the Novel lies in the fact that the Novel, nowadays at least, must be a love-tale, while the Short-story need not deal with love at all. Although there are to be found by diligent search a few Novels which are not love-tales—and of course "Robinson Crusoe" is the example that swims at once into recollection—yet the immense majority of Novels have the tender passion either as the motive power of their machinery or as the pivot on which their plots turn. Although "Vanity Fair" was a Novel without a hero, nearly every other Novel has a hero and a heroine; and the novelist, however unwillingly, must concern himself in their love-affairs. . . .

While the Novel cannot get on easily without love, the Short-story can. Since love seems to be almost the only thing which will give interest to a long story, the writer of Novels has to get love into his tales as best he may, even when the subject rebels and when he himself is too old to take any delight in the mating of John and Joan. But the Short-story, being brief, does not need a love-interest to hold its parts together, and the writer of Short-stories has thus a greater freedom; he may do as he pleases; from him a love-tale is not expected.[3]

But other things are required of a writer of Short-stories which are not required of a writer of Novels. The novelist may take his time; he has abundant room to turn about. The writer of Short-stories must be concise, and compression, a vigorous compression, is essential. For him, more than for any one else, the half is more than the whole. Again, the novelist may be commonplace, he may bend his best energies to the photographic reproduction of the actual; if he show us a cross-section of real life we are content; but the writer of Short-stories must have originality and ingenuity. If to compression, originality, and ingenuity he add also a touch of fantasy, so much the better.

In fact, it may be said that no one has ever succeeded as a writer of Short-stories who had not ingenuity, originality, and compression; and that most of those who have succeeded in this line had also the touch of fantasy. But there are not a few successful novelists lacking, not only in fantasy and compression, but also in ingenuity and originality; they had other qualities, no doubt, but these they had not. If an example must be given, the name of Anthony Trollope will occur to all. Fantasy was a thing he abhorred; compression he knew not; and originality and ingenuity can be conceded to him only by a strong stretch of the ordinary meaning of the words. Other qualities he had in plenty, but not these. And, not having them, he was not a writer of Short-stories. Judging from his essay on Hawthorne, one may even go so far as to say that Trollope did not know a good Short-story when he saw it.

I have written "Short-stories" with a capital S and a hyphen because I wished to emphasize the distinction between the Short-story and the story which is merely short. The Short-story is a high and difficult department of fiction. The story which is short can be written by anybody who can write at all; and it may be good, bad, or indifferent; but at its best it is wholly unlike the Short-story. In "An Editor's Tales" Trollope has given us excellent specimens of the story which is short; and the narratives which make up this book are amusing enough and clever enough, but they are wanting in the individuality and in the completeness of the genuine Short-story. Like the brief tales to be seen in the British monthly magazines and in the Sunday editions of American newspapers into which they are copied, they are, for the most part, either merely amplified anecdotes or else incidents which might have been used in a Novel just as well as not.

Now, it cannot be said too emphatically that the genuine Short-story abhors the idea of the Novel. It neither can be conceived as part of a Novel, nor can it be elaborated and expanded so as to form a Novel. A good Short-story is no more the synopsis of a Novel than it is an episode from a Novel. A slight Novel, or a Novel cut down, is a Novelet: it is not a Short-story. Mr. Howells's "Their Wedding Journey" and Miss Howard's "One Summer" are Novelets,—little Novels. Mr. Anstey's "Vice Versa," Mr. Besant's "Case of Mr. Lucraft," Hugh Conway's "Called Back," Mr. Julian Hawthorne's "Archibald Malmaison," and Mr. Stevenson's "Strange Case of Dr. Jekyll and Mr. Hyde" are Short-stories in conception although they are without the compression which the Short-story requires. . . .

III

It is to be noted as a curious coincidence that there is no exact word in English to designate either *vers de société* or the Short-story, and yet in no language are there better *vers de société* or Short-stories than in English. It may be remarked also that there is a certain likeness between *vers de société* and Short-stories: for one thing, both seem easy to write and are hard. And the typical qualifications of each may apply with almost equal force to the other: *vers de société* should reveal compression, ingenuity, and originality, and Short-stories should have brevity and brilliancy. In no class of writing are neatness of construction and polish of execution more needed than in the writing of *vers de société* and of Short-stories. The writer of Short-stories must have the sense of form, which has well been called "the highest and last attribute of a creative writer." The construction must always be logical, adequate, harmonious.

Here is a weak spot in Mr. W. H. Bishop's "One of the Thirty Pieces," the fundamental idea of which—that fatality awaits every successive possessor of every one of the coins once paid to Judas for his betrayal of Jesus—has genuine strength, not fully developed in the story. But other of Mr. Bishop's stories—the "Battle of Bunkerloo," for instance—are admirable in all ways, conception and execution having an even excellence. Again, Hugh Conway's "Daughter of the Stars" is a Short-story which fails from sheer deficiency of style: here is one of the very finest Short-story ideas—the startling and fascinating fantasy that by sheer force of will a man might have been able to draw down from the depths of the sky a lovely astral maid to share his finite human life—ever given to any mortal, but the handling is at best barely sufficient. To do justice to the conception would tax the execution of a poet. We could merely wonder what the tale would have been had it occurred to Hawthorne, to Poe, or to Theophile Gautier. An idea logically developed by one possessing the sense of form and the gift of style is what we look for in the Short-story.

But, although the sense of form and the gift of style are essential to the writing of a good Short-story, they are secondary to the idea, to the conception, to the subject. Those who hold, with a certain American novelist, that it is no matter what you have to say, but only how you say it, need not attempt the Short-story; for the Short-story, far more than the Novel even, demands a subject. The Short-story is nothing if there is no story to tell;—one might almost say that a Short-story is nothing if it has no plot,—except that "plot" may suggest to some readers a complication and an elaboration which are not really needful. But a plan—if this word is less liable to misconception than "plot"—a plan a Short-story must have, while it would be easy to cite Novels of eminence which are wholly amorphous—for example, "Tristram Shandy."

Whatever its length, the Novel, so Mr. Henry James told us not long ago, "is, in its broadest definition, a personal impression of life." The most powerful force in French fiction today is M. Emile Zola, chiefly known in America and England, I fear me greatly, by the dirt which masks and degrades the real beauty and firm strength not seldom concealed in his novels; and M. Emile Zola declares that the novelist of the future will not concern himself with the artistic evolution of a plot: he will take *une histoire quelconque,* any kind of a story, and make it serve his purpose,—which is to give elaborate pictures of life in all its most minute details.

It is needless to say that the acceptance of these stories is a negation of the Short-story. Important as are form and style, the subject of the Short-story is of more importance yet. What you have to tell is of greater interest than how you tell it. . . . As a Short-story need not be a love-story, it is of no consequence at all whether they marry or die; but a Short-story in which nothing happens at all is an absolute impossibility.

Perhaps the difference between a Short-story and a Sketch can best be indicated by saying that, while a Sketch may be still-life, in a Short-story something always happens. A Sketch may be an outline of character, or even a picture of a mood of mind, but in a Short-story there must be something done, there must be an action.[4] Yet the distinction, like that between the Novel and the Romance, is no longer of vital importance In the preface to the "House of the Seven Gables," Hawthorne sets forth the difference between the Novel and the Romance, and claims for himself the privileges of the romancer. Mr. Henry James[5] fails to see this difference. The fact is, that the Short-story and the Sketch, the Novel and the Romance, melt and merge one into the other, and no man may mete the boundaries of each, though their extremes lie far apart. With the more complete understanding of the principle of development and evolution in literary art, as in physical nature, we see the futility of a strict and rigid classification into precisely defined genera and species. All that is needful for us to remark now is that the Short-story has limitless possibilities: it may be as realistic as the most prosaic novel, or as fantastic as the most ethereal romance.

VII

The Short-story should not be void or without form, but its form may be whatever the author please. He has an absolute liberty of choice. It may be a personal narrative, like Poe's "Descent into the Maelstrom" or Mr. Hale's "My Double, and how he Undid me"; it may be impersonal, like Mr. Frederick B. Perkins's "Devil-Puzzlers" or Colonel J. W. De Forest's "Brigade Commander"; it may be a conundrum, like Mr. Stockton's insoluble query, the "Lady or the Tiger?" it may be "A Bundle of Letters," like Mr. Henry James's story, or "A Letter and a Paragraph," like Mr. Bunner's; it may be a medley of letters and telegrams and narrative, like Mr. Aldrich's "Margery Daw"; it may be cast in any one of these forms, or in a combination of all of them, or in a wholly new form, if haply such may yet be found by diligent search. Whatever its form, it should have symmetry of design. If it have also wit or humour, pathos or poetry, and especially a distinct and unmistakable flavour of individuality, so much the better.[6] But the chief requisites are compression, originality, ingenuity, and now and again a touch of fantasy. Sometimes we may detect in a writer of Short-stories a tendency toward the over-elaboration of ingenuity, toward the exhibition of ingenuity for its own sake, as in a Chinese puzzle. But mere cleverness is incompatible with greatness, and to commend a writer as "very clever" is not to give him high praise. From this fault of supersubtlety, women are free for the most part. They are more likely than men to rely on broad human emotion, and their tendency in error is toward the morbid analysis of a high-strung moral situation.

VIII

The more carefully we study the history of fiction the more clearly we perceive that the Novel and the Short-story are essentially different— that the difference between them is not one of mere length only, but fundamental. The Short-story seeks one set of effects in its own way, and the Novel seeks a wholly distinct set of effects in a wholly distinct way. We are led also to the conclusion that the Short-story—in spite of the fact that in our language it has no name of its own—is one of the few sharply defined literary forms. It is a *genre*, as M. Brunetière terms it, a species, as a naturalist might call it, as individual as the Lyric itself and as various. It is as distinct an entity as the Epic, as Tragedy, as Comedy. Now the Novel is not a form of the same sharply defined individuality; it is—or at least it may be—anything. It is the child of the Epic and the heir of the Drama; but it is a hybrid. And one of the foremost of living American novelists, who happens also to be one of the most acute and sympathetic of American critics, has told me that he was often distracted by the knowledge of this fact even while he was engaged in writing a novel.

In the history of literature the Short-story was developed long before the Novel, which indeed is but a creature of yesterday, and which was not really established in popular esteem as a worthy rival of the drama until after the widespread success of the Waverley Novels in the early years of the nineteenth century. The Short-story also seems much easier of accomplishment than the Novel, if only because it is briefer. And yet the list of the masters of the Short-story is far less crowded than the list of the masters of the longer form. There are a score or more very great novelists recorded in the history of fiction; but there are scarcely more than half a score Short-story writers of an equal eminence.

From Chaucer and Boccaccio we must spring across the centuries until we come to Hawthorne and Poe almost without finding another name that insists upon enrolment. In these five hundred years there were great novelists not a few, but there was no great writer of Short-stories. A little later than Hawthorne and Poe, and indeed almost contemporaneous with them, are Mérimée and Turgenef, whose title to be recorded there is none to dispute. Now at the end of the nineteenth century we find two more that no competent critic would dare to omit,—Guy de Maupassant and Rudyard Kipling.

---

[1] In a letter to a friend, Stevenson lays down the law with his usual directness: "Make another end to it? Ah, yes, but that's not the way I write; the whole tale is implied; I never use an effect when I can help it, unless it prepares the effects that are to follow; that's what a story consists in. To make another end, that is to make the beginning all wrong. The denouement of a long story is nothing, it is just 'a full close,' which you may approach and accompany as you please—it is a coda, not an essential member in the rhythm; but the body and end of a short-story is bone of the bone and blood of the blood of the beginning." *Vailima Letters,* Vol. I, p. 147.

[2] See his essay on "The Philosophy of Composition," to be found in the sixth volume of the collected edition of his works, prepared by Messrs. Stedman and Woodberry.

[3] In an essay on "The Local Short-story" contributed to the *Independent* for March 11, 1892, Colonel T. W. Higginson points out the disadvantages the novelist labours under when he knows that his work is to be published in instalments; and he declares that this possible serial publication "affords the justification of the short-story. For here, at least, we have the conditions of perfect art; there is no sub-division of interest; the author can strike directly in, without preface, can move with determined step toward a conclusion, and can—O highest privilege!—stop when he is done. For the most perfect examples of the short-story—those of De Maupassant, for instance—the reader

feels, if he can pause to think, that they must have been done at a sitting, so complete is the grasp, the single grasp, upon the mind. This completeness secures the end; they need not be sensational, because there is no necessity of keeping up a series of exciting minor incidents; the main incident is enough. Around the very centre of motion, as in a whirlwind, there may be a perfect quiet, a quiet which is formidable in its very response. In De Maupassant's terrific story of Corsican vengeance, "Une Vendetta," in which the sole actor is a lonely old woman who trains a fierce dog so that he ultimately kills her enemy, the author simply tells us, at the end, that this quiet fiend of destruction went peacefully home and went to sleep. *Elle dormit bien, cette nuit-là.* The cyclone has spent itself, and the silence it has left behind it is more formidable than the cyclone.''

[4] This difference is considered briefly by Mr. F. B. Perkins in the characteristically clever preface to the volume of his ingenious Short-stories, which takes its title from the first and best—"Devil-Puzzlers'' (New York: G. P. Putnam's Sons).

[5] In the narrow but suggestive biography of Hawthorne contributed to Mr. John Morley's "English Men of Letters.''

[6] In a chatty and somewhat uncritical paper on the "Rise of the Short-story'' contributed by Mr. Bret Harte to the "International Library of Famous Literature'' and published also in the *Cornhill Magazine* for July, 1899, we find the assertion that the secret of the American Short-story is "the treatment of characteristic American life, with absolute knowledge of its peculiarities and sympathy with its methods, with no fastidious ignoring of its national expression, or the inchoate poetry that may be found hidden even in its slang; with no moral determination except that which may be the legitimate outcome of the story itself; with no more elimination than may be necessary for the artistic conception, and never from the fear of the fetish of conventionalism.'' This is cleverly phrased; but it is open to the obvious objection that it is not so much an adequate definition of the Short-story as a form as it is a defence of the special kind of Short-story Mr. Bret Harte himself had chosen to write.

JAMES COOPER LAWRENCE

A Theory of the Short Story

More than seventy years ago Edgar Allan Poe, in reviewing a volume of Hawthorne's tales, said some things about the short story that have been quoted by practically every man who has written upon the subject since. After discussing the technique of the novel, Poe declared:

> The ordinary novel is objectionable from its length, for reasons already stated in substance. As it cannot be read at one sitting, it deprives itself, of course, of the immense force derivable from *totality*. Worldly interests intervening during the pauses of perusal modify, annul, or counteract, in a greater or less degree, the impressions of the book. But simple cessation in reading would of itself be sufficient to destroy the true unity. In the brief tale, however, the author is enabled to carry out the fullness of his intention, be it what it may. During the hour of perusal the soul of the reader is at the writer's control. There are no external or extrinsic influences—resulting from weariness or interruption.

In this statement Poe has given us the two distinguishing characteristics of all true short stories which set them apart in a class by themselves as a distinct literary type—brevity and the necessary coherence which gives the effect of totality. The only limitation upon the development of the type which can be established beyond question is the physical inability or unwillingness of the average reader or listener to keep his mind on any one topic for any great length of time. The limits to human patience are not very different today from what they were before the flood. A man will listen just so long to a story or read just so many pages and then the spell is broken; his mind demands a change of diet, and the effect of the story is lost. Every extraneous statement, every unnecessary word, must be eliminated in order to bring the tale within the bounds of patience. And any tale which fails to meet these fundamental requirements of brevity and coherence is not a true short story.

This negative statement eliminates a large mass of published matter from the field of our consideration and relieves us from the necessity of attempting to find a justification for that apparently inexcusable thing, an intended short story which is not short.

Further than this, Poe's statement not only furnishes a negative basis for telling what a short story is not, but it also offers a positive foundation upon which we can establish a definition of the short story which declares that *a short story is a brief tale which can be told or read at one sitting.*

This definition requires two things of the story: (1) that it shall be short and (2) that it shall possess coherence sufficient to hold the reader's or listener's unflagging interest from beginning to end. The terms of the definition are of necessity relative. It is, of course, impossible to draw a hard and fast line and say that any story which contains less than so many hundred words is short, while a tale which contains one word more than the allotted portion is long. The personal equation entering into the problem also renders it impossible to establish any fixed measure of the degree of coherence which is required to hold a reader's or listener's unflagging attention.

The more we look into the matter the more evident it becomes that the limits and distinguishing characteristics of the short story as we know it today are the limits and distinguishing characteristics of the spoken story as it has existed from the beginning of time. It is frequently possible to read at one sitting a story which is not brief, but it would be a physical impossibility to *tell* at one sitting any story of this sort so as to hold the unbroken interest of a group of listeners. Human impatience insists that a spoken story shall be brief and to the point; and no better line of demarcation than this can be found to set off the literary type with which we are concerned from its brethren, the novel and the novelette.

If we accept the test of brevity and coherence which this definition proposes, the only question which arises is as to its adequacy. Are brevity and coherence to be accepted as the sole distinguishing marks of a literary type? Or is it necessary to introduce some further limitations which will render our conception of the short story more concrete?

Poe, in his criticism already quoted, maintained that in order to produce a true short story an author must not only make his tale short and to the point, but must also fashion it with deliberate care so that it will produce a *single effect;* and this statement has been accepted with more or less unquestioning faith by practically every man who has written authoritatively upon the short story since Poe's time.

Brander Matthews[1] declares that "the short story is the single effect."

Professor Bliss Perry,[2] while rejecting many of Mr. Matthews's conclusions, agrees with him that the short story of the nineteenth century is set off from those that preceded it by the "new attitude of the contemporary short-story writer toward his material, in his conscious effort to achieve under certain conditions a certain effect."

Professor Canby[3] says that "Poe succeeded in his work by fixing the attention upon the climax of his story, so that the reader sees, feels, thinks of the 'unique effect' of the story and of nothing else. If the modern short story has a technique, here it is; if it is an invention, Poe invented it."

It is only natural that the way in which these men make a fetish of "effect" should lead us to inquire whether, after all, this striving to produce a single foreseen impression is the only manner in which the coherence essential to a true short story can be secured?

Even a casual consideration of the subject presents objections to the "effect" theory of the short story. If, as Professor Matthews declares, "the short story *is* the single effect," then most certainly such tales as *The Scarlet Letter* must be classed as short stories in violation of all of the canons of brevity; and if this cannot be done, the single effect definition will have to be modified. Dr. William J. Dawson[4] holds that the true short story treats "of one incident and only one,"· and Professor Matthews says that: "The short story fulfills the three false unities of the French classic drama: it shows one action, in one place, in one day." If these statements are accepted, ninety percent of the tales that are commonly regarded as short stories will have to be put in some other class of literature. The question naturally arises, what are we going to do with Kipling's *The Man Who Would be King,* which deals with four distinct episodes in as many different places, or with a story like Björnson's *The Father,* which covers a whole lifetime? The answer which suggests itself is that instead of trying to make every sort of tale a separate literary type, it may be easier and more satisfactory to attempt to frame a comprehensive definition of the short story which by its nature will be inclusive instead of exclusive.

Coming back for a moment to a consideration of the statement that the only way in which coherence in a short story can be secured is by striving to produce a single foreseen effect, it is altogether probable that even Professor Matthews would experience some difficulty in pointing out the single effect which Mr. Stockton aimed to produce with *The Griffin and the Minor Canon,* or which "Q" had in mind when he wrote *John and the Ghosts.* And the statement which applies to these tales of fancy would probably also hold true in a consideration of those tales whose sole purpose is to give a plain unvarnished statement of the facts in the case, without giving the slightest thought to any one particular effect which those facts may produce. In this class would come such narratives as the Biblical story of Joseph, Björnson's stories of Norwegian peasant life, and most of Kipling's soldier stories.

The best of these stories of fancy and fact are just as coherent as any tale ever told by Poe or de Maupassant with the idea of producing a single effect; and every one of them has just as much right to the name "short story" as is possessed by any other tale. The short story frequently deals with more than one incident, and does not by any means always produce a single foreseen effect.

These facts would seem to lead to the conclusion that any attempt to limit the definition of a short story beyond the statement that it is "a brief tale which can be told or read at one sitting," is for our purposes inadvisable, if not impossible.

The acceptance of this definition as it stands renders unnecessary any such efforts at classification as Mr. Matthews's rather futile attempt to distinguish between the "Short-story" (spelled with a hyphen and a capital S), "the story which is merely short," "the brief tale," and "the sketch"; and leaves us free to include all short stories under one heading for study as a literary type.

For those who insist upon some further subdivision of the great inclusive short story group, it will then be possible to classify short stories in the following manner:

First, as to substance,

A—Stories of Fact.

B—Stories of Fancy.

Second, as to form,
    A—Stories told *historically*.
    B—Stories told *dramatically*.
    C—Stories told *didactically*.

In the telling of a tale, what is not fact is fancy. Of course, the two classifications frequently overlap. Elements of fancy are found in fact narratives, while fanciful tales are constructed upon foundations of fact. It is possible, however, to throw all short stories into one group or the other in accordance with the element which makes up the substance of the story. Fact stories appear every day in the newspapers and in the narratives which make up the record of the historian. Stories of fancy have existed from the earliest time as one expression of man's desire to take himself occasionally far from the world of hard and inescapable facts. This classification brings us back to the basic truth in the child's division of his world into one part "really truly" and one part "let's pretend."

After short stories have been grouped as stories of fact or stories of fancy, another classification suggests itself based upon the way in which the stories are told. A story of fact or a story of fancy may be told in any one of three ways—historically, dramatically or didactically. The same story may be told in three different ways. The man using the historical narrative method seeks primarily to convey the impression that here is the matter-of-fact story of things just as they happened. The man using the dramatic method seeks a single effect; while the didactic method involves as the chief consideration, the effort to teach a lesson.

In the light of this classification it would appear that those who undertake to define the short story as "the single effect" are clearly striving to make a part greater than the whole.

All of these men whose opinions on the short story we have been considering regard the short story as distinctly a nineteenth-century type of literature, as a literary form which was first successfully employed by Poe and his French contemporaries. As a matter of fact, even the briefest consideration of the history of literature should be sufficient to convince us that the short story, far from being a distinctive product of the nineteenth century, is the oldest form of literature, from which all other literary types, with the exception of the lyric and the critical essay, have developed in the course of time.

Oral tradition begins with the first human family; and it is to this first oral tradition that we look for the genesis of the short story. Anthropologists assure us that primitive man was endowed with substantially the same imagination, pride in achievement, curiosity, and love of excitement and novelty which characterize the average man today. These are the attributes upon which the story-telling faculty depends; and hence we reach the conclusion that ever since human nature has been constituted as it is now men have been telling stories.

Professor Bliss Perry says:[5]

> Story-telling is as old as the day when men first gathered around a camp-fire or women huddled in a cave. The study of comparative folk-lore is teaching us every day how universal is the instinct for it. Even were we to leave out of view the literature of oral tradition, and take the earlier written literature of any European people—for instance, the tales told by Chaucer and some of his Italian models—we should find these modern characteristics of originality, ingenuity, and the rest in almost unrivaled perfection, and perhaps come to the conclusion of Chaucer himself, as he exclaims in whimsical despair, "There is no new thing that is not old."

As far back as research carries us in the history of any people, we find a well defined oral literature. Scholars of every nationality[6] in studying the epic and the ballad have traced for us the steps that mark the growth of the early national literatures. We find the great epics, the *Chanson de Roland,* the *Nibelungenlied,* Beowulf, the Odyssey, and the Iliad, developing from ballad cycles, centering about national heroes, which are shown to have rested upon lesser ballad groups dealing with separate achievements of these heroes, which, in their turn, can be, at least theoretically, split up into their component parts—single isolated ballads.

With the processes of association, selection, and elimination by which the innumerable ballad groups and cycles which merged to form the epics were brought together, we are not concerned; but it will further the object of our inquiry to bear in mind the fact that the early ballads, which were merely short stories in rhythmical form, rested ultimately upon a basis of prose narrative—oral short stories.

M. Leon Gautier, in the introduction to his monumental work on the French epics,[7] accounts for the initial appearance of the lyric by declaring that the first emotions of the first man in the garden of Eden must have been such as could be expressed only in song; and in making this statement he is merely following a similar assertion found in Victor Hugo's preface to *Cromwell.* However, neither Gautier nor Hugo goes so far as to maintain that the progenitors of the human race continued to talk in lyrics after the novelty of their situation wore off; and it is an historical fact that the only conversations in Eden which have been recorded were carried on in prose.

In our earliest histories we find that the art of telling stories had reached a point where the existence of fully developed cycles of spoken stories is taken as a matter of course. Tacitus refers to ''the peculiar kind of verses current among the Germans, the recital of which they call barding.'' Einhard, in his life of Charlemagne, tells how the great emperor ''had the old rude songs that celebrate the deeds and wars of the ancient kinds written out for transmission to posterity.'' And in the old Anglo-Saxon poem of *Widsith* we find references to cycles of stories centering about Attila the Hun, Chlodovech the Frank, Theodoric the Ostrogoth, Rothari the Lombard, and Gunther the Burgundian. These cycles of stories spread all over western Europe, and the written literature of the twelfth and thirteenth centuries developed out of this spoken literature.

This glimpse into the development of national literatures would seem to warrant the statement that while the epic is a national contribution to literature, and the ballad is a communal product, the short story, which in the last analysis proves to be the base of all our literature, excepting only the lyric and the critical essay, is distinctly an individual contribution.

This theory of the development of an oral literature which makes the short story a primary unit does not rest entirely upon conjecture. Oral literature is to be found today wherever there is a more or less primitive state of race culture. In Hawaii, where even an alphabet was unknown until the arrival of the missionaries in 1820, a well defined oral literature, rich in truly epic material, still survives, and it is possible to observe in that Territory at first hand the actual process of literary development suggested and outlined above. The same statement holds true in a degree of the Voodoo tales current among the Southern negroes, fragments of a great body of spoken stories brought from the African jungles.

It is much easier to produce evidence to support a theory of the antiquity of the short story as a type than it is to unearth the connecting links to make complete the chain of evidence to prove that the short story as it is known today is not only the oldest of all literary types, but had also had a continuous existence from the very beginning of time to the present day in essentially the same form as we know it now. The difficulty of this latter task is due to the fact that until comparatively recent times the short story has been to a very large extent an oral *genre,* preserved as spoken and not written literature.

The reasons for this are not hard to find. The output of ancient scribes and mediæval printers was too limited to warrant the wasting of much of their time in the preservation of short stories, which everyone told and everyone knew. Such stories and ballads as were written, or at a later date printed, were as a rule valued so lightly by the scholars of the day that no serious effort was ever made to preserve them.

In the case of the literatures of Western Europe, with which we are most familiar, the wide gap existing between written and spoken languages, taken together with the fact that only a very small portion of the population was at all familiar with the written language, tended, for centuries, to set the folk literature far apart from the literature of the scholars. The tales told in prose and verse by the people using the vulgar tongue were never considered as literature.

When the dialects of the common people became national languages the number of stories written down was greatly increased; but still it was only very rarely that any effort was made to preserve collections of tales. The attitude toward folk literature that had been built up through so many centuries could not readily be changed.

In this connection it is of more than ordinary interest to note the extent to which this popular conception of the short story as anything but literature moved Boccaccio, who thought so lightly of the *Decameron* that, although it was first given to the public in Florence in 1353, he did not submit it to Petrarch, his dearest literary friend, until after a lapse of nineteen years, in 1372.[8]

Practically no one could read, so that collections of stories, even in the popular tongue, were of little use. It was only occasionally, and then more often by a series of happy accidents than because of any recognition of merit, that the work of the masters of the short story was preserved. Nevertheless tales were told in those days just as they had been from the beginning and will be to the end; and we know that Boccaccio, Chaucer, and Rabelais, far from standing alone as exponents of their *genre,* were merely the master craftsmen in a host of story tellers. Even with our very imperfect knowledge of the periods when they lived and wrote, we are able to discover the works of long lists of forgotten lesser lights who preceded and came after them in the field of story telling. Modern students of the *Decameron* have succeeded in compiling a list of no less than twenty-eight collections of stories, the work of hundreds of authors—Greek, Latin, Oriental, Provençal, French, and Italian—from which much of the material for the immortal hundred tales was derived, while the list of immediate followers and imitators of Boccaccio is even more formidable than the array of his predecessors. These few early works which are still known to present-day scholars are, of course, but fragments of the great body of oral short stories which existed during the twenty centuries or more that they represent.

The tremendous growth in the numbers of the reading public and the corresponding development of periodicals during the past two centuries, and particularly in the last one hundred years, has brought about the transformation of the short story from a spoken to a written type of literature. The great public, which was formerly satisfied to have its stories told to it, has become literate, and now reads for itself.

However, the attitude of the scholars of the Middle Ages, who regarded the short story as an undignified excrescence upon the body of literature, unworthy of recognition or preservation, still persists in some quarters today.

Having considered past and present conditions as they bear upon the general theory of the antiquity and continuous existence of the short story, it behooves us to examine the specific evidence which justifies the statement that the short story of the nineteenth century is in no essential way different from the tales which preceded it by a thousand years or more.

The declaration is frequently made that Poe created a new literary type when he laid down his rules for the short story. But Poe's rules applied only to one class of short stories, those told to produce a single effect. Professor Matthews, Professor Perry, and their followers, in accepting Poe's dictum, have treated one class of short stories as if they constituted the whole body of short-story literature; and, therefore, it is only necessary for us, in considering their declaration that the short story as we know it today is essentially a nineteenth-century product, to look up the antecedents of the tale that is told to produce a single effect. Is it possible that this one class of stories has developed so recently as to warrant the statement that it belongs exclusively to the nineteenth and twentieth centuries?

If the search back to the beginnings of things, through the cycles of medieval tales to the ballads which have been preserved as the oldest fragments of the great body of prehistoric oral literature, reveals not merely one method of telling stories or two, but every type of the short story, we have reason to believe that every type of the short story was to be found even in the earliest tales of all, the prose narratives from which the ballads developed.

There can be no question as to the antiquity of historical and didactic methods of story telling, and the examples of ''effect'' stories in the most primitive literatures are numerous enough to warrant the conclusion that such tales have almost, if not quite, as ancient a lineage as the other forms of the short story.

There is not a literature known to modern research which does not contain ghost stories told to produce a single effect. The intensely dramatic story upon which Bürger founded his ballad of *Lenore* is found in the very earliest popular poetry of England, in different parts of Germany, in the Slavic countries, and in one form or another all over Western Europe. For compression, speed, and the skill with which a single effect is produced, this grim, primeval tale as it is told in the old ballads bears the same stamp of superlative excellence which is placed on the best product of Poe's pen.

The old Germanic ballad of Tannhäuser, published in the Arnim and Brentano collection of *Volkslieder*, is another example of the antiquity of the ''effect'' story. The *coup de théâtre* at the end of the story is just the sort of thing that we find in the work of the masters of the short story in the nineteenth century. Still another example of this same thing is to be found in the old English ballad of *Lord Randall:* and many pages would be required to give a complete list of the ''effect'' stories which might be selected from collections of English and German ballads alone, without any consideration of other literatures presenting the same features.

In Boccaccio and his imitators and in the numerous collections of tales brought into Europe from the Orient we find all of the essential variations of the story told to produce a single effect, along with tales told in accordance with the other methods of narration.

As the scope of the investigation becomes wider, it becomes more and more evident that as far back as it is possible to trace literary forms every type of the short story is to be found. The ''effect'' story has always persisted as a recognized mode of literary expression.

When the development of periodicals and newspapers created a demand for the printed short story, this form made its appearance along with the others. Poe, Pushkin, and Mérimée were all producing it at the same time; and the wide dissemination of Poe's dictum and of the rules of the successful French realists, through the newly established periodicals and other products of the constantly improving printing-press, led to the wave of over-emphasis of the "effect" story which is still with us.

The facts and theories which have been cited above would seem to offer a pretty solid basis for the conclusion that the short story as it is known in the nineteenth and twentieth centuries is not a new form of literature, but is rather the elementary literary type, whose essential characteristics have remained unchanged throughout all the ages.

However, if the essentials of the short story are today what they were in the beginning, and if there is really nothing new or distinctive in striving to attain a given effect, the question arises, what is to be done with Professor Matthews's theory of the evolution of the short story, with Professor Perry's statement that the attitude of the modern story-teller toward his material is different from that of his forerunners, and with the numerous other authoritative utterances which treat the short story as a new literary type brought into being by Poe and his contemporaries early in the nineteenth century? What explanation is to be offered for the difference which exists between the stories which de Maupassant and Boccaccio told with the idea of producing a single effect, or between a story of horror as it is set forth in one of Poe's narratives and as it is told in an old ballad?

In order to account for and explain this difference we must first determine what it is, wherein it is to be found. If the best stories of today are put side by side with those of four hundred or four thousand years ago, the old stories and the new ones not only fall together into the classes enumerated above, but also prove to be alike in methods of treating plot, setting, and characters, and are on a plane of absolute equality so far as unity of action, originality, and ingenuity are concerned. The fundamental characteristics of the best short stories today are the features that have characterized the best stories of all time.

The only difference between modern short-story technique and that of the Middle Ages is a verbal one. The only development that can be traced is not an improvement in any distinctive essential of the art of story-telling, but is merely a general development in the knowledge of words and the ability to use them, which affects the framing of wills and the formulation of official documents much more vitally than it does the telling of tales. The average short-story writer today can be a better craftsman than the man who told tales a thousand years ago, solely because he has better tools of expression at his command.

Extensive vocabularies are a product of the printing-press. The early short stories were told by men with comparatively few words at their command; and if the study of modern tales reveals in some instances a greater compression and a more realistic atmosphere than is to be found in the old stories, these things may be ascribed to the superior verbal equipment of the modern writer, which enables him to use exactly the right word in the right place, where his predecessor, piling up phrase upon phrase, could only approximate his meaning. Such development of the short story as there has been is due very largely to the development of the dictionary; and there would seem to be reason for holding that this narrow ground is the only one upon which any kind of an evolutionary study of the short story can be based.

The final test of a theory of the sort set forth in the preceding pages, after all historical requirements have been met, is its application to present conditions. During the generation that has elapsed since 1870 five men have stood out above all others as masters of every form of the short story. These five men—Alphonse Daudet, Rudyard Kipling, Robert Louis Stevenson, Frank R. Stockton, and Sir Arthur Quiller-Couch—have not attempted to restrict their genius to any one channel, but have written fact stories and tales of fancy, telling these stories historically, dramatically, or didactically with impartial and unfailing skill. These men have, of course, their distinctive traits, their individual strong points and weaknesses; but they are alike in their conception of the fundamental characteristics of the short story.

The instinct for story-telling exists in substantially the same form in every race; all men recognize and insist upon the simple limitations of brevity and coherence; and hence, in this field of literature more than in any other, it is possible for an artist to produce masterpieces whose appeal, in spite of national lines and racial characteristics, is truly universal. The best short stories are not essentially French, English, Italian, or American, but are a part of the world's anthology.

1. *Philosophy of the Short Story*, p. 17.
2. *A Study of Prose Fiction*, p. 304.
3. *The Short Story in English*, p. 233.
4. *The Modern Short Story*—North American Review 190: 802.
5. *A Study of Prose Fiction*, p. 302.
6. Notably Grimm and Paul in Germany. Child in England, and Gautier and those who have supported and opposed his theories in France.
7. *Les Epopées Françaises*, T. I., p. 3.
8. cf. Boccaccio's *Decameron* (Bohn). Notes by W. K. Kelly, pp. 541 ff.

The Modern Short Story: Retrospect

The history of the novel is short: covering only, if we date its invention from Richardson, a period of two hundred years. The history of the short story, through its phases of myth and legend, fable and parable, anecdote and pictorial essay, sketch, and even down to what the crudest provincial reporter calls "a good story," cannot be measured. The account in Genesis of the conflict between Cain and Abel is a short story; the parable of the Prodigal Son is a short story, and in itself a masterpiece of compression for all time; the stories of Salome, Ruth, Judith, and Susannah are all examples of an art that was already old, civilized, and highly developed some thousands of years before the vogue of *Pamela*. At what date, then, shall we begin an examination of its history? The paradoxical answer is that the history of the short story, as we know it, is not vast but very brief. "The short story proper," says Mr. A. J. J. Ratcliff, "that is, a deliberately fashioned work of art, and not just a straightforward tale of one or more events, belongs to modern times";[1] "the short story is a young art," says Miss Elizabeth Bowen, "as we know it, it is a child of this century";[2] to this I shall only add an earlier judgment of my own that "the history of the English short story is very brief, for the simple reason that before the end of the nineteenth century it had no history.''[3] It is therefore with this aspect of the short story, the development of the last hundred years—more pointedly still of the last forty or fifty years—that the present volume will deal.

It is clear, in that case, that there are many things with which it will not deal. Of two thousand years of story evolution only one-twentieth will be examined, and of that remaining twentieth only a part dissected. Dickens wrote short stories, but as far as the present survey goes he could well have saved his ink; Defoe, Meredith, Thackeray, and many other English novelists of the eighteenth and nineteenth centuries also wrote short stories, but they recall too often the dish hashed up from the left-overs of the joint; Henry James wrote short stories, but it is the influence rather than the achievement of his art that will be examined; Kipling wrote short stories, but their value will seem of less account than that of comparatively little-known names such as A. E. Coppard, Katherine Mansfield, V. S. Pritchett, Dorothy Edwards, Katherine Ann Porter, Malachi Whitaker, H. A. Manhood, Sean O'Faoláin, and others; James Joyce wrote *Ulysses,* but here at any rate *Dubliners* will seem of greater importance; Somerset Maugham will be accounted a better writer than Kipling, in some ways his nearest prototype, but a poorer writer than Joyce, whose impregnable reputation rests on one solitary, delicate, and long unwanted volume. O. Henry will be regarded just as one in the succession of those many American short story writers who created the most important indigenous tradition outside nineteenth-century Russia. And so on. Constantly throughout the survey of the modern story one is struck by the fact that the reputation is often of less importance than the art; the unknown, unprofessional writer appears with a fine, even a great, story; the voice speaks once and is silent; but by this isolated achievement the frontiers of the short story may be pushed forward a significant fraction, and the flexibility of the art shown, once again, to be infinite.

The basis of almost every argument or conclusion I can make is the axiom that the short story can be anything the author decides it shall be; it can be anything from the death of a horse to a young girl's first love affair, from the static sketch without plot to the swiftly moving machine of bold action and climax, from the prose poem, painted rather than written, to the piece of straight reportage in which style, colour, and elaboration have no place, from the piece which catches like a cobweb the light subtle iridescence of emotions that can never be really captured or measured to the solid tale in which all emotion, all action, all reaction is measured, fixed, puttied, glazed, and finished, like a well-built house, with three coats of shining and enduring paint. In that infinite flexibility, indeed, lies the reason why the short story has never been adequately defined.

Many definitions have been, and always are being, attempted. Wells defined the short story as any piece of short fiction that could be read in half an hour. Poe, sometimes acclaimed its modern originator, declared that "in the whole composition there should be no word written, of which the tendency, direct or indirect, is not to one pre-established design." Tchehov held that a story should have neither beginning nor end, but reminded authors that if they described a gun hanging on the wall on page one, sooner or later that gun must go off. Mr. John Hadfield describes the short story as "a story that is not long."[4] The late Sir Hugh Walpole, in a moment of truly remarkable perception, asserted that "a story should be a story: a record of things happening, full of incident and accident, swift movement, unexpected development, leading through suspense to a climax and a satisfying dénouement."[5] Jack London declared that it should be "concrete, to the point, with snap and go and life, crisp and crackling and interesting." Miss Elizabeth Bowen, rightly wary of the concrete definition, says, "the first necessity of the short story, at the set out, is *necessariness*. The story, that is to say, must spring from an impression or perception pressing enough, acute enough, to have made the writer write."[6] The late E. J. O'Brien, to whom the short story in Britain and America owes an unpayable debt, holds that "the first test of a short story, in any qualitative analysis, is the measure of how vitally compelling the writer makes his selected facts or incidents."[7] Mr. Ellery Sedgewick, who pounced on the genius of Hemingway's *Fifty Grand* when that story had been rejected by half the editors of America, holds that "a story is like a horse race. It is the start and finish that count most."[8] Finally, Mr. A. E. Coppard bases the whole theory of his work on the essential difference between a story, as something which is written, and a tale, as something which is told.

All of these definitions have one thing in common. None of them has a satisfactory finality; none defines the short story with an indisputable epigrammatic accuracy which will fit all short stories. For Tchehov, the craftsman, beginning and end do not matter; for Mr. Sedgewick, the editor, beginning and end are everything. Yet both are right. Mr. Hadfield's definition will fit a thousand stories yet fail to account satisfactorily for *Death in Venice, Family Happiness,* or *The Gentle-*

man from San Francisco. Sir Hugh Walpole's definition will do admirably for a work by O. Henry but fails miserably on application to Tchehov's *The Darling,* Mrs. Malachi Whitaker's *Frost in April,* or the unpredictable sketches of Mr. Saroyan. One does not measure the beauty of landscape with a tape measure. Jack London's demand for a concoction with "snap and go and life" is a perfect answer for those who like whisky, but it will be lost on those whose taste has been educated to the bouquet of Turgenev or James Joyce's *The Dead.* It is only when Mr. Ellery Sedgewick asserts, in his extremely perceptive essay written for American schools, "So it is that the short story has become all sorts of things, situation, episode, characterization, or narrative—in effect a vehicle for every man's talent,"[9] that we come back again to the sensible conclusion that the short story, whether short or long, poetical or reported, plotted or sketched, concrete or cobweb, has an insistent and eternal fluidity that slips through the hands.

This is, and has always been, my own view. The impression that the short story has something of the indefinite and infinitely variable nature of a cloud is one which sooner or later must be forced on anyone who not only reads, but attempts to break down analytically, the work of writers differing so vastly as Turgenev and Hemingway, Sherwood Anderson and O. Henry, George Moore and Stephen Crane, Kipling and Katherine Mansfield. Is the cumulus or the cirrus more beautiful? The thunder-cloud or the flotilla of feathers? The calm blue and white of noon, or the savagery of sunset? There is no definition, no measure, which will aptly contain the structure, effect, and beauty of them all. As the sky is not made of bricks, so it is worth remembering that stories are not put together with plumb-line and trowel.

There is one other thing which these many and varied definitions all have in common. All omit to point out the advantages of elasticity, in both choice of character and use of time, which the short story holds over the novel. The novel is predominantly an exploration of life: reflecting and describing in some form the impact, entanglement, fruition, destruction or fulfilment of human emotions and desires. "Characters begin young; they grow old; they move from scene to scene, from place to place," said Virginia Woolf.[10] This development of character, this forward movement of time, have always been and perhaps always will be the pulse and nerve of the novel. But in the short story time need not move, except by an infinitesimal fraction; the characters themselves need not move; they need not grow old; indeed there may be no characters at all. A novel without characters would be a tiresome affair; but a novel with characters who never spoke a word would surely be more tiresome still. Yet many a good short story has characters who never open their lips. A novel whose characters were never named, whose location and time were never stated, might well impose on its readers a strain that they would justifiably refuse to bear. Yet many a short story has characters which bear no more marks of identification than the anonymous and universal label of "boy" or "girl," "man" or "woman," "the traveller" or "the commercial traveller," "the barmaid" or "the soldier," and no more topographical exactitude than "the street," "the field," "the room," or any seashore between Brighton and Botany Bay.

"The Novel," said Edward Garnett, "can be anything according to the hands which use it"—a truth far more widely applicable to the short story. For the short story remains plastic, and continues to increase its plasticity, as long as human nature remains the infinitely plastic and variable thing it is. In the 'nineties Kipling was writing of India from a viewpoint that was so popular and so widely endorsed that it might well have seemed, to the Empire-drunken Britisher of the day, to give the only right and proper view; in 1940 young native Indian writers have something to say of their own country from a viewpoint so unsuspected, so unheard of, and so real that Kipling seems guilty of nothing but plain falsification. Again in the 'nineties, when O. Henry was performing elaborate conjuring tricks with an amazing collection of comic human paraphernalia and the result was accepted with the same universal applause as Kipling had enjoyed, who could have guessed that fifty years later a young American-Armenian named Saroyan would demonstrate how a conjuring trick could be performed without any human paraphernalia at all, but with only a pair of eyes, a typewriter, and a handkerchief to dry his tears?

In its various stages of development the short story has frequently been compared with some other literary form, sometimes with some artistic form outside literature. It is thus declared to have affinities with the drama; with the narrative ballad; with the lyric and the sonnet. In the last thirty years it has shown itself, as in fact much other writing has, to be pictorial rather than dramatic, to be more closely allied to painting and the cinema than to the stage. Mr. A. E. Coppard has long cherished the theory that short story and film are expressions of the same art, the art of telling a story by a series of subtly implied gestures, swift shots, moments of suggestion, an art in which elaboration and above all explanation are superfluous and tedious. Miss Elizabeth Bowen advances the same idea:

> The short story . . . in its use of action is nearer to the drama than to the novel. The cinema, itself busy with a technique, is of the same generation: in the last thirty years the two arts have been accelerating together. They have affinities—neither is sponsored by a tradition; both are, accordingly, free; both, still, are self-conscious, show a self-imposed discipline and regard for form; both have, to work on, immense matter—the disoriented romanticism of the age.[11]

This is strikingly true. Indeed the two arts have not only accelerated together but have, consciously or not, taught each other much. The scrap of dirty paper blown by wind along the empty morning street, a girl sewing, on a railway station, the tear in her lover's jacket and he hiding it by holding up a suitcase, a mother staring dumbly at her returned gangster son—these tiny moments, seen as it were telescopically, brightly focused, unelaborated and unexplained, stamp swiftly on the mind the impressions of desolation, embarrassed love, or maternal despair. Each moment implies something it does not state; each sends out a swift brief signal on a certain emotional wave-length, relying on the attuned mental apparatus of the audience to pick it up.

That audience, it seems to me, becomes of increasingly greater importance; but more important still, I feel, becomes the attitude of writer or director towards that audience. Are its powers of reception and perception to be consistently underestimated? In a process of underestimation what happens? At the extreme a writer takes a character and describes not only his physique, his weight, his moustache and glasses, but also his clothes, his manner, and his mannerisms, his taste in food and drink, all in minute detail—in order to eliminate any possibility, it seems, of his being confused with the clothes-prop.

This, a century ago, and indeed with some writers for long afterwards, was the accepted convention. Dickens, artist though he was, played throughout novel after novel, with gusto and brilliance, this game of underestimating the reader: so much so that he not only described every character by the system of catalogue but, in many cases, and because he was often writing a serial story that was to be read in parts, reissued that catalogue after an interval in which he judged the reader might have forgotten what goods were for sale.

This was all very well, and in many cases delightful fun, in a novel of 200,000 words; but to apply the same method to the short story was rather like dressing a six-months-old baby in a top-hat and fur coat, with the inevitable result—suffocation. Hence, I think, the languishing of the short story in England throughout the first three-quarters of the nineteenth century, when no single writer applied to it a technique different from that of the novel; and its gradual emergence, accelerated during the last thirty years, as a separate form addressed to a reader who was presumed to be able to take many previously elaborated things such as physical descriptions for granted.

The evolution of the short story may therefore, I think, have something to do with the evolution of the general reader. We must be wary of condemning Dickens, when it would be more just, perhaps, to condemn an age more confined to compartments of class, place, and prejudice than our own. Dickens, often publishing a novel in monthly parts, found it necessary to devote some hundreds of words, and if necessary repeat those words a month later, to a single character. In 1920 Sherwood Anderson remarked simply that "she was a tall silent woman with a long nose and troubled grey eyes"; in 1930 Mr. Ernest Hemingway in a moment, for him, of unusual expansion, said, "He wore a derby hat and a black overcoat buttoned across his chest. His face was small and white and he had tight lips. He wore a silk muffler and gloves." In 1940 Mr. V. S. Pritchett writes, "He had a cape on, soaked with rain, and the rain was in beads in his hair. It was fair hair. It stood up on end."

Anderson took up fourteen words, Mr. Hemingway thirty-one, Mr. Pritchett twenty-six. Between Dickens and Mr. Pritchett, then, something has happened. Is it only the evolution of the short story? May it not also be, perhaps, the parallel evolution of the reader? Education, travel, wider social contact, the increased uniformity of life, dress, and manners have made us all familiar with things that were once remote enough to need to be described. Today all of us have seen Sherwood Anderson's woman, the tragic, anonymous representative of a whole inarticulate class; we have seen Mr. Hemingway's tough with the black overcoat and bowler hat; we know Mr. Pritchett's type with its fair hair that stands up on end. The widening of social contact, among other things, has relieved these three writers, and their generation, of an oppressive obligation. It is no longer necessary to describe; it is enough to suggest. The full-length portrait, in full dress, with scenic background, has become superfluous; now it is enough that we should know a woman by the shape of her hands.

In this way the short story can be seen not as a product evolved by generations of writers united in a revolutionary intention to get the short story more simply, more economically, and more truthfully written, but as something shaped also by readers, by social expansion, and by what Miss Bowen calls "peaks of common experience." For there has not been, and rarely is, any such united revolution among writers. Writers work, die, and leave legacies. Other writers draw on those inheritances, as Katherine Mansfield did on Tchehov's, and in turn leave others. But in their turn, too, readers live and perhaps succeed in raising, by an infinitely small fraction, the level of common experience and artistic receptivity. To that level the short story must adjust itself.

1. A. J. J. Ratcliff: ed. *Short Stories by H. G. Wells* (2 volumes, Nelson)
2. Elizabeth Bowen: *The Faber Book of Modern Stories* (Faber)
3. H. E. Bates: "The Short Story" (*Lovat Dickson's Magazine and Story,* New York)
4. John Hadfield: ed. *Modern Short Stories* (Everyman)
5. J. W. Marriott: ed. *A Modern Anthology of Short Stories* (Nelson)
6. Elizabeth Bowen: ed. *Faber Anthology of Modern Stories* (Faber)
7. E. J. O'Brien: ed. *The Best Short Stories: 1918 et seq.* (Cape)
8. Sedgewick and Dominovitch: ed. *Novel and Story* (Atlantic Monthly Press)
9. Sedgewick and Dominovitch: ed. *Novel and Story* (Atlantic Monthly Press)
10. Virginia Woolf: *The Leaning Tower* (Folios of New Writing, ed. John Lehmann, Hogarth Press)
11. Elizabeth Bowen: *Faber Book of Modern Stories* (Faber)

MARY ROHRBERGER

The Short Story: A Proposed Definition

Short narrative fiction is as old as the history of literature; short narrative *prose* fiction is as old as the history of prose fiction. But the short story, as we know it today, is the newest of literary genres. Something happened to the short tale early in the Nineteenth Century to cause Brander Matthews later in the century to proclaim the birth of a new genre characterized by brevity, a closely wrought texture, freedom from excrescence, and a unity of effect. The origins of the new form are to be found in the writings of Irving, Gogol, Poe, and Hawthorne. Since Poe was the first to theorize upon the kind of tale then being written and to attempt to define it, the definition is as old as the form. In itself, there is nothing wrong with a definition that has not been revised or subjected to much examination in better than a hundred years, as long as the definition is valid. But the definition that we have is something of a problem. Its terms are too broad; its diction imprecise.

Consider, for example, the word "brevity." How brief is brief? There is as much difference in length between a three page story and a thirty page story as between a thirty page story and a three hundred page story. Obviously "brief" is a relative term, applying more to the limits of the author's conception than to any actual page length. Faulkner's "A

Rose for Emily" is shorter than "Wash," but we call them both short stories. And *Madame Bovary* is no less a novel because it runs to some three hundred and fifty pages than, say, *Crime and Punishment,* which is more than twice as long.

And the other terms—"closeness of texture," "freedom from excrescence," "unity of effect"—can apply to all art forms. Beauty is often defined as the harmony of parts in a whole, and a large number of literary theorists take the idea of the organic whole as a standard for judgment.

The idea that a short story deals with a single character in a single action is useful but not always applicable. Short story after short story belies the limitation to a single protagonist. Lawrence's "The Horse-Dealer's Daughter" and "The Prussian Officer" have dual protagonists, and in Faulkner's "Dry September" there are at least three. Granted, most stories do deal with a single protagonist, but so do many novels.

It seems better to define the short story in terms of its overall purpose and structure, and this is what I have tried to do. Beginning with an examination of Hawthorne's literary theory and noticing the clear relationship between what Hawthorne thought literature should be and what his stories were, then moving to the literary theory and a selection of stories by representative modern masters of the form, I find similarities which seem to me to be useful.

The short story derives from the romantic tradition. The metaphysical view that there is more to the world than that which can be apprehended through the senses provides the rationale for the structure of the short story which is a vehicle for the author's probing of the nature of the real. As in the metaphysical view, reality lies beyond the ordinary world of appearances, so in the short story, meaning lies beneath the surface of the narrative. The framework of the narrative embodies symbols which function to question the world of appearances and to point to a reality beyond the facts of the extensional world.

There is, however, a group of stories which does not fit the definition that I propose. They are brief, closely wrought, and unified, but they do not have the depth or complexity provided by a symbolic structure. These stories I categorize separately under the title of simple narrative. The structure of the simple narrative is as different from the structure of the short story as the structure of the prose romance is from the structure of the novel. Since there are already two categories for long prose fiction, it seems reasonable to suggest two categories for short fiction, particularly since there is greater similarity between the short story and the prose romance than there is between the short story and the novel or the short story and the simple narrative.

Given the distinction that I make, the evaluation of short fiction should be easier and more valid, and evaluation I take to be the purpose of criticism.

The Lonely Voice

"BY THE HOKIES, there was a man in this place one time by the name of Ned Sullivan, and a queer thing happened him late one night and he coming up the Valley Road from Durlas."

That is how, even in my own lifetime, stories began. In its earlier phases storytelling, like poetry and drama, was a public art, though unimportant beside them because of its lack of a rigorous technique. But the short story, like the novel, is a modern art form; that is to say, it represents, better than poetry or drama, our own attitude to life.

No more than the novel does it begin with "By the hokies." The technique which both have acquired was the product of a critical, scientific age, and we recognize the merits of a short story much as we recognize the merits of a novel—in terms of plausibility. By this I do not mean mere verisimilitude—that we can get from a newspaper report— but an ideal action worked out in terms of verisimilitude. As we shall see, there are dozens of ways of expressing verisimilitude—as many perhaps as there are great writers—but no way of explaining its absence, no way of saying, "At this point the character's behavior becomes completely inexplicable." Almost from its beginnings the short story, like the novel, abandoned the devices of a public art in which the storyteller assumed the mass assent of an audience to his wildest improvisations—"and a queer thing happened him late one night." It began, and continues to function, as a private art intended to satisfy the standards of the individual, solitary, critical reader.

Yet, even from its beginnings, the short story has functioned in a quite different way from the novel, and, however difficult it may be to describe the difference, describing it is the critic's principal business.

"We all came out from under Gogol's 'Overcoat'" is a familiar saying of Turgenev, and though it applies to Russian rather than European fiction, it has also a general truth.

Read now, and by itself, "The Overcoat" does not appear so very impressive. All the things Gogol has done in it have been done frequently since his day, and sometimes done better. But if we read it again in its historical context, closing our minds so far as we can to all the short stories it gave rise to, we can see that Turgenev was not exaggerating. We have all come out from under Gogol's "Overcoat."

It is the story of a poor copying clerk, a nonentity mocked by his colleagues. His old overcoat has become so threadbare that even his drunken tailor refuses to patch it further since there is no longer any place in it where a patch would hold. Akakey Akakeivitch, the copying clerk, is terrified at the prospect of such unprecedented expenditure. As a result of a few minor fortunate circumstances, he finds himself able to buy a new coat, and for a day or two this makes a new man of him, for after all, in real life he is not much more than an overcoat.

Then he is robbed of it. He goes to the Chief of Police, a bribe-taker who gives him no satisfaction, and to an Important Personage who merely abuses and threatens him. Insult piled on injury is too much for him and he goes home and dies. The story ends with a whimsical description of his ghost's search for justice, which, once more, to a poor copying clerk has never meant much more than a warm overcoat.

There the story ends, and when one forgets all that came after it, like Chekhov's "Death of a Civil Servant," one realizes that it is like nothing in the world of literature before it. It uses the old rhetorical device of the mock-heroic, but uses it to create a new form that is neither satiric nor heroic, but something in between—something that perhaps finally transcends both. So far as I know, it is the first appearance in fiction of the Little Man, which may define what I mean by the short story better than any terms I may later use about it. Everything about Akakey Akakeivitch, from his absurd name to his absurd job, is on the same level of mediocrity, and yet his absurdity is somehow transfigured by Gogol.

> Only when the jokes were too unbearable, when they jolted his arm and prevented him from going on with his work, he would bring out: "Leave me alone! Why do you insult me?" and there was something strange in the words and in the voice in which they were uttered. There was a note in it of something that roused compassion, so that one young man, new to the office, who, following the example of the rest, had allowed himself to mock at him, suddenly stopped as though cut to the heart, and from that day forth, everything was as it were changed and appeared in a different light to him. Some unnatural force seemed to thrust him away from the companions with whom he had become acquainted, accepting them as well-bred, polished people. And long afterwards, at moments of the greatest gaiety, the figure of the humble little clerk with a bald patch on his head rose before him with his heart-rending words "Leave me alone! Why do you insult me?" and in those heart-rendering words he heard others: "I am your brother." And the poor young man hid his face in his hands, and many times afterwards in his life he shuddered, seeing how much inhumanity there is in man, how much savage brutality lies hidden under refined, cultured politeness, and my God! even in a man whom the world accepts as a gentleman and a man of honour.

One has only to read that passage carefully to see that without it scores of stories by Turgenev, by Maupassant, by Chekhov, by Sherwood Anderson and James Joyce could never have been written. If one wanted an alternative description of what the short story means, one could hardly find better than that single half-sentence, "and from that day forth, everything was as it were changed and appeared in a different light to him." If one wanted an alternative title for this work, one might choose "I Am Your Brother." What Gogol has done so boldly and brilliantly is to take the mock-heroic character, the absurd little copying clerk, and impose his image over that of the crucified Jesus, so that even while we laugh we are filled with horror at the resemblance.

Now, this is something that the novel cannot do. For some reason that I can only guess at, the novel is bound to be a process of identification between the reader and the character. One could not make a novel out of a copying clerk with a name like Akakey Akakeivitch who merely needed a new overcoat any more than one could make one out of a child called Tommy Tompkins whose penny had gone down a drain. One character at least in any novel must represent the reader in some aspect of his own conception of himself—as the Wild Boy, the Rebel, the Dreamer, the Misunderstood Idealist—and this process of identification invariably leads to some concept of normality and to some relationship—hostile or friendly—with society as a whole. People are abnormal insofar as they frustrate the efforts of such a character to exist in what he regards as a normal universe, normal insofar as they support him. There is not only the Hero, there is also the Semi-Hero and the Demi-Semi-Hero. I should almost go so far as to say that without the concept of a normal society the novel is impossible. I know there are examples of the novel that seem to contradict this, but in general I should say that it is perfectly true. The President of the Immortals is called in only when society has made a thorough mess of the job.

But in "The Overcoat" this is not true, nor is it true of most of the stories I shall have to consider. There is no character here with whom the reader can identify himself, unless it is that nameless horrified figure who represents the author. There is no form of society to which any character in it could possibly attach himself and regard as normal. In discussions of the modern novel we have come to talk of it as the novel without a hero. In fact, the short story has never had a hero.

What it has instead is a submerged population group—a bad phrase which I have had to use for want of a better. That submerged population changes its character from writer to writer, from generation to generation. It may be Gogol's officials, Turgenev's serfs, Maupassant's prostitutes, Chekhov's doctors and teachers, Sherwood Anderson's provincials, always dreaming of escape.

> "Even though I die, I will in some way keep defeat from you," she cried, and so deep was her determination that her whole body shook. Her eyes glowed and she clenched her fists. "If I am dead and see him becoming a meaningless drab figure like myself, I will come back," she declared. "I ask God now to give me that privilege. I will take any blow that may fall if but this my boy be allowed to express something for us both." Pausing uncertainly, the woman stared about the boy's room. "And do not let him become smart and successful either," she added vaguely.

This is Sherwood Anderson, and Anderson writing badly for him, but it could be almost any short-story writer. What has the heroine tried to escape from? What does she want her son to escape from? "Defeat"—what does that mean? Here it does not mean mere material squalor, though this is often characteristic of the submerged population groups. Ultimately it seems to mean defeat inflicted by a society that has no sign posts, a society that offers no goals and no answers. The submerged population is not submerged entirely by material considerations; it can also be submerged by the absence of spiritual ones, as in the priests and spoiled priests of J. F. Powers' American stories.

Always in the short story there is this sense of outlawed figures wandering about the fringes of society, superimposed sometimes on symbolic figures whom they caricature and echo—Christ, Socrates, Moses. It is not for nothing that there are famous short stories called "Lady Macbeth of the Mtsensk District" and "A Lear of the Steppes" and—in reverse—one called "An Akoulina of the Irish Midlands." As a result there is in the short story at its most characteristic something we do not often find in the novel—an intense awareness of human loneliness. Indeed, it might be truer to say that while we often read a familiar novel again for companionship, we approach the short story in a very different mood. It is more akin to the mood of Pascal's saying: *Le silence éternel de ces espaces infinis m'effraie.*

I have admitted that I do not profess to understand the idea fully: it is too vast for a writer with no critical or historical training to explore by his own inner light, but there are too many indications of its general truth for me to ignore it altogether. When I first dealt with it I had merely noticed the peculiar geographical distribution of the novel and the short story. For some reason Czarist Russia and modern America seemed to be able to produce both great novels and great short stories, while England, which might be called without exaggeration the homeland of the novel, showed up badly when it came to the short story. On the other hand my own country, which had failed to produce a single novelist, had produced four or five storytellers who seemed to me to be first-rate.

I traced these differences very tentatively, but—on the whole, as I now think, correctly—to a difference in the national attitude toward society. In America as in Czarist Russia one might describe the intellectual's attitude to society as "It may work," in England as "It must work," and in Ireland as "It can't work." A young American of our own time or a young Russian of Turgenev's might look forward with a certain amount of cynicism to a measure of success and influence; nothing but bad luck could prevent a young Englishman's achieving it, even today; while a young Irishman can still expect nothing but incomprehension, ridicule, and injustice. Which is exactly what the author of *Dubliners* got.

The reader will have noticed that I left out France, of which I know little, and Germany, which does not seem to have distinguished itself in fiction. But since those days I have seen fresh evidence accumulating that there was some truth in the distinctions I made. I have seen the Irish crowded out by Indian story-tellers, and there are plenty of indications that they in their turn, having become respectable, are being out-written by West Indians like Samuel Selvon.

Clearly, the novel and the short story, though they derive from the same sources, derive in a quite different way, and are distinct literary forms; and the difference is not so much formal (though, as we shall see, there are plenty of formal differences) as ideological. I am not, of course, suggesting that for the future the short story can be written only by Eskimos and American Indians: without going so far afield, we have plenty of submerged population groups. I am suggesting strongly that we can see in it an attitude of mind that is attracted by submerged population groups, whatever these may be at any given time—tramps, artists, lonely idealists, dreamers, and spoiled priests. The novel can still adhere to the classical concept of civilized society, of man as an animal who lives in a community, as in Jane Austen and Trollope it obviously does; but the short story remains by its very nature remote from the community—romantic, individualistic, and intransigent.

But formally as well the short story differs from the novel. At its crudest you can express the difference merely by saying that the short story is short. It is not necessarily true, but as a generalization it will do well enough. If the novelist takes a character of any interest and sets him up in opposition to society, and then, as a result of the conflict between them, allows his character either to master society or to be mastered by it, he has done all that can reasonably be expected of him. In this the element of Time is his greatest asset; the chronological development of character or incident is essential form as we see it in life, and the novelist flouts it at his own peril.

For the short-story writer there is no such thing as essential form. Because his frame of reference can never be the totality of a human life, he must be forever selecting the point at which he can approach it, and each selection he makes contains the possibility of a new form as well as the possibility of a complete fiasco. I have illustrated this element of choice by reference to a poem of Browning's. Almost any one of his great dramatic lyrics is a novel in itself but caught in a single moment of peculiar significance—Lippo Lippi arrested as he slinks back to his monastery in the early morning, Andrea Del Sarto as he resigns himself to the part of a complaisant lover, the Bishop dying in St. Praxed's. But since a whole lifetime must be crowded into a few minutes, those minutes must be carefully chosen indeed and lit by an unearthly glow, one that enables us to distinguish present, past, and future as though they were all contemporaneous. Instead of a novel of five hundred pages about the Duke of Ferrara, his first and second wives and the peculiar death of the first, we get fifty-odd lines in which the Duke, negotiating a second marriage, describes his first, and the very opening lines make our blood run cold:

> That's my last Duchess painted on the wall,
> Looking as if she were alive.

This is not the essential form that life gives us; it is organic form, something that springs from a single detail and embraces past, present, and future. In some book on Parnell there is a horrible story about the death of Parnell's child by Kitty O'Shea, his mistress, when he wandered frantically about the house like a ghost, while Willie O'Shea, the complaisant husband, gracefully received the condolences of visitors. When you read that, it should be unnecessary to read the whole sordid story of Parnell's romance and its tragic ending. The tragedy is there, if only one had a Browning or a Turgenev to write it. In the standard composition that the individual life presents, the storyteller must always be looking for new compositions that enable him to suggest the totality of the old one.

Accordingly, the storyteller differs from the novelist in this: he must be much more of a writer, much more of an artist—perhaps I should add, considering the examples I have chosen, more of a dramatist. For that, too, I suspect, has something to do with it. One savage story of J. D. Salinger's, "Pretty Mouth and Green My Eyes," echoes that scene in Parnell's life in a startling way. A deceived husband, whose wife is out late, rings up his best friend, without suspecting that the wife is in the best friend's bed. The best friend consoles him in a rough-and-ready way, and finally the deceived husband, a decent man who is ashamed of his own outburst, rings again to say that the wife has come home, though she is still in bed with her lover.

Now, a man can be a very great novelist as I believe Trollope was, and yet be a very inferior writer. I am not sure but that I prefer the novelist to be an inferior dramatist; I am not sure that a novel could stand the impact of a scene such as that I have quoted from Parnell's life, or J. D.

Salinger's story. But I cannot think of a great storyteller who was also an inferior writer, unless perhaps Sherwood Anderson, nor of any at all who did not have the sense of theater.

This is anything but the recommendation that it may seem, because it is only too easy for a short-story writer to become a little too much of an artist. Hemingway, for instance, has so studied the artful approach to the significant moment that we sometimes end up with too much significance and too little information. I have tried to illustrate this from "Hills Like White Elephants." If one thinks of this as a novel one sees it as the love story of a man and a woman which begins to break down when the man, afraid of responsibility, persuades the woman to agree to an abortion which she believes to be wrong. The development is easy enough to work out in terms of the novel. He is an American, she perhaps an Englishwoman. Possibly he has responsibilities already—a wife and children elsewhere, for instance. She may have had some sort of moral upbringing, and perhaps in contemplating the birth of the child she is influenced by the expectation that her family and friends will stand by her in her ordeal.

Hemingway, like Browning in "My Last Duchess," chooses one brief episode from this long and involved story, and shows us the lovers at a wayside station on the Continent, between one train and the next, as it were, symbolically divorced from their normal surroundings and friends. In this setting they make a decision which has already begun to affect their past life and will certainly affect their future. We know that the man is American, but that is all we are told about him. We can guess the woman is not American, and that is all we are told about her. The light is focused fiercely on that one single decision about the abortion. It is the abortion, the whole abortion, and nothing but the abortion. We, too, are compelled to make ourselves judges of the decision, but on an abstract level. Clearly, if we knew that the man had responsibilities elsewhere, we should be a little more sympathetic to him. If, on the other hand, we knew that he had no other responsibilities, we should be even less sympathetic to him than we are. On the other hand, we should understand the woman better if we knew whether she didn't want the abortion because she thought it wrong or because she thought it might loosen her control of the man. The light is admirably focused but it is too blinding; we cannot see into the shadows as we do in "My Last Duchess."

She had
A heart—how shall I say?—too soon made glad,
Too easily impressed; she liked whate'er
She looked on, and her looks went everywhere.

And so I should say Hemingway's story is brilliant but thin. Our moral judgment has been stimulated, but our moral imagination has not been stirred, as it is stirred in "The Lady With the Toy Dog" in which we are given all the information at the disposal of the author which would enable us to make up our minds about the behavior of his pair of lovers. The comparative artlessness of the novel does permit the author to give unrestricted range to his feelings occasionally—to *sing;* and even minor novelists often sing loud and clear for several chapters at a time, but in the short story, for all its lyrical resources, the singing note is frequently absent.

That is the significance of the difference between the *conte* and the *nouvelle* which one sees even in Turgenev, the first of the great storytellers I have studied. Essentially the difference depends upon precisely how much information the writer feels he must give the reader to enable the moral imagination to function. Hemingway does not give the reader enough. When that wise mother Mme. Maupassant complained that her son, Guy, started his stories too soon and without sufficient preparation, she was making the same sort of complaint.

But the *conte* as Maupassant and even the early Chekhov sometimes wrote it is too rudimentary a form for a writer to go very far wrong in; it is rarely more than an anecdote, a *nouvelle* stripped of most of its detail. On the other hand the form of the *conte* illustrated in "My Last Duchess" and "Hills Like White Elephants" is exceedingly complicated, and dozens of storytellers have gone astray in its mazes. There are three necessary elements in a story—exposition, development, and drama. Exposition we may illustrate as "John Fortescue was a solicitor in the little town of X"; development as "One day Mrs. Fortescue told him she was about to leave him for another man"; and drama as "You will do nothing of the kind," he said.

In the dramatized *conte* the storyteller has to combine exposition and development, and sometimes the drama shows a pronounced tendency to collapse under the mere weight of the intruded exposition—"As a solicitor I can tell you you will do nothing of the kind," John Fortescue said. The extraordinary brilliance of "Hills Like White Elephants" comes from the skill with which Hemingway has excluded unnecessary exposition; its weakness, as I have suggested, from the fact that much of the exposition is not necessary at all. Turgenev probably invented the dramatized *conte*, but if he did, he soon realized its dangers because in his later stories, even brief ones like "Old Portraits," he fell back on the *nouvelle*.

The ideal, of course, is to give the reader precisely enough information, and in this again the short story differs from the novel, because no convention of length ever seems to affect the novelist's power to tell us all we need to know. No such convention of length seems to apply to the short story at all. Maupassant often began too soon because he had to finish within two thousand words, and O'Flaherty sometimes leaves us with the impression that his stories have either gone on too long or not long enough. Neither Babel's stories nor Chekhov's leave us with that impression. Babel can sometimes finish a story in less than a thousand words, Chekhov can draw one out to eighty times the length.

One can put this crudely by saying that the form of the novel is given by the length; in the short story the length is given by the form. There is simply no criterion of the length of a short story other than that provided by the material itself, and either padding to bring it up to a conventional length or cutting to bring it down to a conventional length is liable to injure it. I am afraid that the modern short story is being seriously affected by editorial ideas of what its length should be. (Like most storytellers, I have been told that "nobody reads anything longer than three thousand words.") All I can say from reading Turgenev, Chekhov, Katherine Anne Porter, and others is that the very term "short story" is a misnomer. A great story is not necessarily short at all, and the conception of the short story as a miniature art is inherently false. Basically, the difference between the short story and the novel is not one of length. It is a difference between pure and applied storytelling, and in case someone has still failed to get the point, I am not trying to decry applied storytelling. Pure storytelling is more artistic, that is all, and in storytelling I am not sure how much art is preferable to nature.

Nor am I certain how one can apply this distinction if one can apply it at all. In trying to distinguish between Turgenev's novels and *nouvelles,* Dmitry Mirsky has suggested that the *nouvelles* omit conversations about general ideas which were popular in the nineteenth-century Russian novel. I have tried to assimilate this to my own vague feelings on the subject by suggesting that this is merely another way of saying that the characters in the *nouvelles* were not intended to have general significance. In a marvelous story like "Punin and Baburin," the two principal characters seem to have no general significance at all as they would have been bound to have had they been characters in a novel. In fact when they do appear in a novel like "On the Eve" they have considerable general significance, and the reader is bound to take sides between them. The illegitimate defender of human liberty and the gas-bag poet are not people we take sides with. We sympathize and understand, all right, but they both remain members of a submerged population, unable to speak for themselves.

Even in Chekhov's "Duel," that fantastic short story which is longer than several of Turgenev's novels, the characters are too specific, too eccentric for any real generalization, though generalized conversations are strewn all over the place. We look at Laevsky and Nadyezhda Fyodorovna as we look at Punin and Baburin, from outside, with sympathy and understanding but still feeling, however wrongly, that their problems are their own, not ours. What Turgenev and Chekhov give us is not so much the brevity of the short story compared with the expansiveness of the novel as the purity of an art form that is motivated by its own necessities rather than by our convenience.

Is the Short Story Necessary?

Elizabeth Janeway, the chairman of this panel, is the author of several highly successful novels and one of American's best-known essayists and critics. Mrs. Janeway is president of The Authors Guild of America.

ELIZABETH JANEWAY: Welcome to *The Writer's World*. We're going to talk about short stories. We are lucky to have three panelists with us who write short stories extremely well, but who also write novels.

Many novelists begin when young by writing short stories, but they are apt to be seduced away by that larger form, the novel, and to relinquish the art and perhaps lose the skill. Let me introduce our three panelists who have maintained their ability to write the short story while also writing excellent novels.

Shirley Hazzard was born in Sydney, Australia, and educated at the Queenwood Ladies' College in Sydney. Rarely are women writers also officially stamped as ladies.

Shirley has lived in the Far East and in New Zealand, and now lives in New York with her husband, Francis Steegmuller. For ten years she worked with the United Nations. She is a contributor to *The New Yorker,* and her first short-story collection, called *Cliffs of Fall and Other Stories,* appeared in 1963. In January of 1966, she published that lovely book, *The Evening of the Holiday.*

John Cheever was born in Quincy, Massachusetts. He too has written considerably for *The New Yorker,* and for other magazines as different as *The Saturday Evening Post.* His novels, *The Wapshot Chronicle* and *The Wapshot Scandal* are, I'm sure, well known to you, and he has published a number of short-story collections: *The Housebreaker of Shady Hill; Some People, Places, and Things That Will Not Appear in My Next Novel*—a lovely title; *The Brigadier and the Golf Widow.*

Harry Mark Petrakis was born in St. Louis, and now lives in Chicago with his wife and three children, and he is the author of three novels: *Lion at My Heart, The Odyssey of Kostas Volakis,* and most recently, *A Dream of Kings.* His collection of short stories, *Pericles on 31st Street,* was one of the final contenders for the National Book Award in 1965.

Some writers confine themselves to short stories or almost do so. Kipling was one. Chekhov did it in the field of narrative fiction. His longer works were dramas. Perhaps we can best come down to talking about short stories by quoting from a most distinguished writer of short stories, and only short stories, our near contemporary, Frank O'Connor, who died only recently.

Let me offer for our panel some of Mr. O'Connor's thoughts on the short story. I'm not sure that I agree with all of them. I doubt that the panelists do.

"From the very beginning," wrote Frank O'Connor in his book *The Lonely Voice,* "the short story has functioned in a quite different way from the novel." As an example, he takes Gogol's famous story, "The Overcoat," and points out that in this story there occurs the first appearance in fiction of the little man. From this, he goes on to suggest that, while the novel must offer the reader a character with whom to identify himself, this is not true of the short story.

"The novel," Frank O'Connor says, "presupposes a normal society, while the short story does not. The modern novel has been called the novel without a hero, but the short story has never had one.

"In the short story at its most characteristic," he says, "there is something that we do not often find in the novel, an intense awareness of human loneliness. Instead of a hero, a short story offers a submerged population—Gogol's officials, Turgenev's serfs, Maupassant's prostitutes, Chekhov's doctors and teachers, Sherwood Anderson's provincials—always dreaming of escape.''

John, do you agree?

JOHN CHEEVER: No, not at all, no. We always say that the short story was born, of course, with Gogol, and then came out from under "The Overcoat.'' The short story was extremely efficient in dealing with the bureaucracies of Petrograd, Paris, and still is with Moravia's Rome. This is the obsessive thing. A man desires a pair of yellow boots, and he will make love to a number of women, and murder a number of men in order to get his pair of yellow boots.

This I think was great in the 1860s. It was perhaps the birth *not* of the short story, because we have, of course, *The Decameron* which is a collection of short stories, but rather of the *modern* short story. I think that what O'Connor was speaking of has vanished into thin air—the problem of the single man in a bureaucratic society who desires a single object, usually not a woman—has totally gone from our comprehension. The responsibilities of the short story, of course, at this point are much broader than that.

MRS. JANEWAY: O'Connor seems to believe or to suggest that the short story differs from the novel because in the novel the reader finds someone with whom to identify. In the short story, he feels, characters are seen from outside. Does this seem to you true, Shirley?

SHIRLEY HAZZARD: Well, I don't know offhand. I can't think of all of the examples I'm sure exist that would refute Mr. O'Connor immediately. I agree rather with John, that it was something which perhaps seemed enormously true to him when he was saying these things, but some of them seem to me very questionable. The idea that a certain form of art *began with somebody* seems to me very strange, because, after all, a story, whether written or spoken, has always existed.

Stories have always been told; probably it was the first kind of literary self-expression, if you can call it that, that existed on the earth. It's what you tell to a child to make it go to sleep; and to adults to make them wake up, a little later.

MR. CHEEVER: It's what you tell yourself in a dentist's office while you're waiting for an appointment. The short story has a great function, it seems to me, in life. Also, it's the appeasement of pain, in a very special sense—in a stuck ski lift, a sinking boat, a dentist's office, or a doctor's office—where we're waiting for a death warrant. Where you don't really have long enough for a novel, you do the short story. I'm very sure that, at the very point of death, one tells oneself a short story—not a novel.

MRS. JANEWAY: Do you think then there is always someone speaking in a short story? Does it come out of the tale? Mr. Petrakis? How do you feel? Your characters are perhaps closer to the old world and the world of the bardic tale than are those of our other participants.

HARRY MARK PETRAKIS: Perhaps closer to what Frank O'Connor himself called the storytelling as a public art.

MRS. JANEWAY: Yes.

MR. PETRAKIS: Since I lecture and read my stories before colleges and clubs, I feel strongly the relationship of the short story to the art of drama. But, I would like to take just a moment if I can to make a momentary digression, because there may be those in the audience who are perhaps wondering what I am doing here with Mr. Cheever and Miss Hazzard. I am here this evening because I have not published in *The New Yorker*.

I am also from Chicago, and I am very grateful that my microphone is connected. Now what was the question?

MRS. JANEWAY: Where do you feel the short story came from, Mr. Petrakis, before it got to *The New Yorker?* Is there still a person speaking through it?

MR. PETRAKIS: Oh, I think very definitely that there's a person speaking through it. It can be a reflective or a strident voice.

One need identify not only with characters in a novel; one can identify also with the characters in a short story. Both these forms can help us understand something of the life that goes on beneath the masks people wear with one another.

MRS. JANEWAY: Perhaps I haven't explicated O'Connor well enough. Actually, I'm simply trying to provoke you. Let me read a little bit more.

"If the novelist takes a character of any interest and sets him up in opposition to society, and then, as a result of the conflict between them, allows his character either to master society, or be mastered by it, he has done all that can be reasonably expected of him."

Now, perhaps, we are still back in the nineteenth century, John.

MR. CHEEVER: I should say yes.

MRS. JANEWAY: Back with the old-fashioned novel.

MR. CHEEVER: Yes, Frank O'Connor was back with Stendhal. Yes, of course he's with Stendhal.

MRS. JANEWAY: I think that one of O'Connor's points is still a valid distinction between the novel and the short story: "The element of time is the novelist's greatest asset, the chronological development of character or incident is an essential form, as we see it in life, and the novelist flouts it at his peril. For the short story writer, there is no such thing as essential form. His frame of reference can never be the totality of a human life, and he must be forever selecting the point at which he can approach it, and each selection he makes contains the possibility of a new form, as well as the possibility of a complete fiasco."

Time is certainly present in the traditional novel. In the short story is it less so?

MR. CHEEVER: No, I don't think time is actually important and I can't think of an important novel or series of novels in which time, chronological time, is not totally violated. This includes *War and Peace*, as well as *À la recherche du temps perdu*. It seems to me . . . I'm here to defend the short story, right?

MRS. JANEWAY: Yes.

MR. CHEEVER: A rather difficult task, but it seems to me that one of the things that the short story has done is to keep the novel on its mettle. The novel is essentially massive, and is always reviewed as though it were something immense, although it might be eight hundred pages of trifling humbug. Also, it seems to me that the short story has done a good deal to invigorate poetry, because there have been decades in my lifetime when the short stories written in this country have been much more precise, much more penetrating, and much briefer than the poetry one reads.

The short story, among its other virtues, has more or less kept the novel and poetry working. Both forms are generally acceptable.

In some ways the short story is still something of a bum; but it has to be very lively or it doesn't pass.

MRS. JANEWAY: How do you know when you're writing a short story and not a novel?

MISS HAZZARD: I was going to ask that question, because I wonder really whether one does think to oneself, "I'm now sitting down to write a short story." If I can go back a little bit, the subject is, "Is the Short Story Necessary?" I was thinking about that, because, after all, the interesting thing about any work of art is that nobody can *prove* that it's necessary. It's more, one might say, essential. It's of our essence, it's what makes our experience coherent to us. We can't say that we will be any different if art didn't exist, and yet we know that we would be. And I think what's rather endearing about the short story is that nobody *can* show that it's necessary, but that it must be necessary—I assume we're talking of things of quality—it must be necessary to the writer. If it is to be successful, or to have any endurance, then it must be a form that happened *because* the writer had something to say that fitted into that particular form.

After all, writers are not a bureaucracy, not yet anyway, and they don't have to fall into any classification. They don't have to write a short story because that's an accepted form, or because it keeps the novel on its mettle, or makes poetry seem too long, or something of that sort. I don't think it "serves a useful purpose." If an artist writes something with a useful purpose in mind, and it succeeds as a work of art, then it succeeds in spite of his useful purpose, I rather think. It might succeed in some other way as well, but art needs no justification other than itself. It seems to me that must be essential, but the fact that it's in short-story form must be incidental to what the writer has to say.

I don't think that one should necessarily confine what one has to say into a short story or necessarily prolong it to make a novel. One selects the form most appropriate to what one has to say.

MR. CHEEVER: It's a very deep impulse actually. To write at all is a very deep impulse, and it's rather like falling in love. You don't say that I'm going to fall in love for three months, or I'm going to fall in love for two weeks.

But these are your deepest intuitions, your deepest drives, and may have a duration which is determined by an endless chain of contingencies.

MR. PETRAKIS: I find myself agreeing more with Mr. Cheever and Miss Hazzard than I do with Frank O'Connor here. I think though, that he must be given his due, because before I knew that you were going to quote, Mrs. Janeway, from Mr. O'Connor, I read his book on the short story, and I too felt it a very spirited defense of the short story. Like John, I'm here to defend the short story.

I think O'Connor was comparing short stories with novels which assume the guise of chronological time merely to show this basic difference—that in the novel you have a great deal more liberty with time, and that you can chronologically begin to establish the great rhythms of time. You could start with the fact that, at a given time, a man was born, and you could follow him forward through adolescence, into maturity, into marriage, to the birth of his children, through perhaps all the various aberrations which unleash themselves upon him during his life.

Whereas, the short story, by necessity, becomes an episode of selected incident. You move into it at a given time. You move into it at a given place. You are not given the liberty which you have in the novel, and you must catch the character "at a point," I believe O'Connor says, "of crisis in his life." Once the story is finished, his life is not going to be quite the same again. The greatness of the short story lies in this marvelous zeroing in. One thinks of a television camera at a football game, and thinks of the novel in terms of a camera panning the whole field, and all the players, and all of a sudden moving in on the individual play, and on the twisted, frenzied face of one of the players, the end, or the quarterback.

This, it seems to me, in terms of the conflict involved anyway, would be the difference between the novel and the short story. Each has its function, each its place; and yet as a short-story writer myself, I have an endearment for this moment of capture, this moment of revelation.

MRS. JANEWAY: According to A. E. Hotchner, in his book on Hemingway—it's really a fascinating book; the amount that Hotchner believed of what Hemingway told him is absolutely fabulous—one of the things that Hemingway told him—and this I think might possibly be true; I offer it to the panel—was that he never sat down to write a novel, but that his novels all grew out of short stories. Does this happen to you, panel? Do you know when you start something whether or not it's going to be a novel or a short story? Or, do you simply start and have it tell you on the way? Shirley?

MISS HAZZARD: I think to a certain extent it tells on the way. I think very often one does have, in advance, an idea of the scope. But I agree with Mr. Petrakis to a great extent about the crisis, and the incident that evokes a larger measure of life. Whereas a novel, I think, could be said to be a large measure of life that evokes a still larger one.

I think, however, that there are many exceptions to this, and that perhaps it's something easier to say than to sustain. I was thinking just now of the great short story of Joyce's, "The Dead," which does turn on a moment of crisis, which does deal with an incident you might say, and which leaves a person's life changed. The central figure's life is changed, and yet in a way the story does evoke the whole of experience. It does deal as completely with life, and with as large a scope, as any novel. One does have the whole football field wrangling and writhing as you were saying.

It's not at all that he has bitten off less than he could chew. It isn't that at all. He has sought to compress it in some tremendously artistic and ingenious way. Of course it's quite a long story, but it's by no means a novel. Nobody could call it a short novel. It's a long short story.

MRS. JANEWAY: That's a fascinating difference. O'Connor points out—and he's, I'm afraid, a bit of a straw man, but at least let me quote him once more because this is really almost a matter of fact— "Chekhov's long short story, 'The Duel,' is longer than some novels that we accept as novels." In other words, length has really little to do with—or not all to do with it. Something else gets into this. There is something different about the short story. I'm particularly fascinated by it, because I've lost the ability to write short stories myself. I did write them for a while, and I've tried since then, but I find that I've gotten used to novel size. I'm a little like that Victorian husband who spoke of the deep peace of the double bed in marriage, after the hurly-burly of the chaise longue; the novel is like that wonderful double bed, and I can't seem to get back on the chaise longue.

I think this is a matter of clumsiness. Writers of short stories have a special and delicate skill, the ability to pick up just the right nexus, the right situation which will illuminate the patch of the universe that they want to explore.

John, when you begin a short story, do you foresee its end? That is, do you see it complete and as a whole when you begin?

MR. CHEEVER: No more, Elizabeth, than I foresee the end of a love affair.

When Shirley mentioned "The Dead," of course, it was like striking it great. This is one of the great things. It's not a great short story. It's one of the great works that we have, great works of man, and some of the Chekhov stories are equally beautiful. As a matter of fact, the whole history of the short story, even though it's rather threadbare at this point, is great as far as understanding what other—

No, when I start a short story—but really I'm rather a retired short-story writer—I think I've written only three in the last two years; I used to write something like twelve a year. No, I do think that if it is good, it is perhaps the most intense form of writing that I've ever had any experience with. And the last story I wrote that I liked—I felt as though it had been written out of my left ventricle—I thought, "I don't want to write any more short stories, because you *don't* fool around."

The novelist, especially the German novelists in the late twenties and some American novelists now, approach the reader as though he were a ground feeder. If you've ever fished—when you fish a ground feeder, you hook him in the mouth. You start by saying, "She was raped on Thursday," and then there's a fairly interesting chapter, and then all sorts of horseradish and things come in; but the reader of the novel will go on and on and on, for something like three or four hundred pages, sometimes eight hundred pages.

With a short story, you have to be in there on every word; every verb has to be lambent and strong. It's a fairly exhausting task, I think.

MISS HAZZARD: Still I don't think it ought to look as though it's "all done by hand" though, if you know what I mean.

MR. CHEEVER: But it *is* done by impulse.

MISS HAZZARD: By impulse, yet with care—

MR. CHEEVER: No, I'm speaking of it impulsively; but when you are working on it, you can't—I'm sure you can't—walk past the room in which the manuscript lies without having a coronary thrombosis.

MRS. JANEWAY: Whereas, with novels there's the feeling that, isn't it nice, there's a large thing there which I can put everything in.

MR. CHEEVER: Everything?

MRS. JANEWAY: Yes, everything.

MR. CHEEVER: Sometimes, too much?

MRS. JANEWAY: Sometimes indeed, John. But specifically, sections of *The Wapshot Scandal* appeared in *The New Yorker* as separate stories. I read them there with delight, but when the book appeared, and I read them as part of the book, I found almost all of them strengthened by being read in context. Did you write them as stories first?

MR. CHEEVER: No, this was entirely a commercial expedient. I've, as you know, a family, and a very demanding family, and it's virtually impossible for me to support myself writing novels. And it's virtually impossible for me to support myself writing short stories, also.

MRS. JANEWAY: It's actually almost impossible for anyone to support himself by writing.

MR. CHEEVER: So I've hit on the expedient of publishing novels piecemeal. At the moment, I don't have to do it anymore, but that's the way it worked out. *The New Yorker* was very gallant with *The Chronicle,* in printing "Leander's Journal" and so forth. I would much sooner not do it that way; but that's the only way I've been able to do it.

MRS. JANEWAY: Well, I thought they stood up very well as stories. But as I say, I liked them better in their setting.

MR. CHEEVER: It was nice of you to mention it.

MRS. JANEWAY: There was a little explosion about finding out whose briefcase it was that had got lost on that terrible plane flight.

MR. CHEEVER: My sense is to always put the chapter in a novel precisely where it belongs, and then take it out.

MRS. JANEWAY: Yes?

MR. CHEEVER: And sell it. But I know exactly where it belongs before I sell it to someone else.

MR. PETRAKIS: This evening will have been my first opportunity to talk to Mr. Cheever and Miss Hazzard, who I think are marvelous short-story writers. And I think it very interesting, for instance, that Miss Hazzard mentions "The Dead," which is one of Joyce's later stories, and, I think, very effective inasmuch as it foreshadows Joyce the novelist. He does a short story, and yet he does in the short story, in "The Dead," that which suggests the great scope and the great panorama of *Ulysses,* which is to come, and *A Portrait of the Artist as a Young Man.*

I, too, have had difficulty in the last few years with the writing of the short story. I do them now with considerably more burden than before. I'm grateful to the short story, because I came to the novel through the short story. I think there are many contemporary novelists who would have gained a great deal by working at the short story first. I am thinking among others of Ruark and Wallace and Robbins, who write great, bulky, exhaustive novels, from which you could cut pages and pages.

Perhaps for this reason I will not be able to write a long, eight-hundred-page novel, because having come to the novel through the short story, I try to write that which is essential. And yet, after three novels, I too feel the difficulty now of going back to the short story. I think this is significant, and probably true of a good many novelists.

The early Irwin Shaw stories, for instance, are tremendously more effective as short stories than some of the short stories that Shaw has done recently; and I don't know just why this should be. It's an area of great interest to me because, as John suggested as well, it affects my family's ability to eat, and my capacity to pay the rent; so I'd be interested in some further development along this area.

MR. CHEEVER: Wallace couldn't have written a short story on pain of death.

MISS HAZZARD: You said before that it was just on the pain of death that one *would* write a short story.

MR. CHEEVER: Oh, Shirley! Shaw has written some marvelous short stories. He belonged to a particular era—it was up to and through the war. The fact that his novels aren't as appealing, I think, doesn't reflect either on the short story or the novel.

MRS. JANEWAY: No, it reflects on his talent.

MR. CHEEVER: It seems to me, as a matter of fact, that I've rather gotten us off the track. The short story is a particularly acute form with a very intense emotional spectrum. This is its only life. It doesn't go on making raspberry jam, or reporting the yacht races and so forth.

MRS. JANEWAY: Some of them do though.

MR. CHEEVER: Ah, but they shouldn't.

MISS HAZZARD: Those *aren't* necessary!

MR. CHEEVER: It's really a very rare form, and as I've said earlier, not only is it an exceptionally penetrating form of communication, it also keeps the rest of literature at heel.

MISS HAZZARD: Yes. I don't know if I understand properly, but I don't regard the short story as necessarily a training for the novel. I don't think of it as a form of discipline, like being trained in sail in the days of steamships.

MR. CHEEVER: No, no.

MR. PETRAKIS: Perhaps I should have clarified this. I think the short story exists in and for itself. I have great affection for it. I would have preferred to have written poetry, but I could not, and since I have not felt myself qualified to write poetry, I wrote the short story, which I believe comes as close to poetry as anything can. I think, in addition to this, it can be a training ground for a novelist in that it forces him to eliminate that which is unnecessary and ponderous. There are novels in which you can spend three pages on a man's moving up in an elevator, discussing trivialities with the elevator operator. I don't think the short-story writer, trained in the discipline of the short story, trained in the discipline of the incident and the revelation, will permit himself to fall into this trap.

MRS. JANEWAY: Is it a matter of compression then? Novels come in different sizes. I'd rather use that word, I think, than length. Do stories come in different sizes, too? Are some of them tighter, but bigger?

MR. CHEEVER: When you define a short story, I think it's as if you were defining any piece of fiction at all. One should say that it's not a short story; it's a short narrative. Then there's the modern short story, which begins with Gogol—and I do think we do have the modern short story—and is inclined to be rather short. It deals, as in Gogol's "Overcoat," with a whole new spectrum of self-understanding, and also with bureaucracy which is actually what the story coped with, and the phobias of that particular society.

No, there's no length. Katherine Anne Porter has written short stories that run—what? Twenty-five pages?

MRS. JANEWAY: At least.

MR. CHEEVER: And Salinger—some of his best stories are rather long. But the impulse—There is a spontaneity, an impetuosity involved, I think, that one doesn't have in the novel.

MR. PETRAKIS: Isn't this what O'Connor was talking about in a way, when he said that he was a lyrical writer? John. Your reference to the intense emotional spectrum of the short story must have been O'Connor's feeling—that he worked this way, lyrically and explosively, and that he could never envisage himself maintaining this kind of emotional intensity over the span of a novel, so that he had to work in the realm of the short story.

MR. CHEEVER: Yes, exactly.

A. L. BADER

The Structure of the Modern Short Story

ANY teacher who has ever confronted a class with representative modern short stories will remember the disappointment, the puzzled "so-what" attitude, of certain members of the group. "Nothing happens in some of these stories," "They just end," or "They're not real stories" are frequent criticisms. An examination of the reviews of the yearly O'Brien anthologies as well as of the collections of leading short-story writers discloses a similar attitude on the part of many professional critics. Sometimes the phrase "Nothing happens" seems to mean that nothing significant happens, but in a great many cases it means that the modern short story is charged with a lack of narrative structure. Readers and critics accustomed to an older type of story are baffled by a newer type. They sense the underlying and unifying design of the one, but they find nothing equivalent to it in the other. Hence they maintain that the modern short story is plotless, static, fragmentary, amorphous—frequently a mere character sketch or vignette, or a mere reporting of a transient moment, or the capturing of a mood or nuance—everything, in fact, except a story.

These charges, it seems to me, are not borne out by an examination of representative modern short stories. In this article I shall compare and analyze a number of stories, old and new, in an endeavor to demonstrate that the modern short story does have structure, that is, a basic design or skeletal framework; that this structure is essentially the same as that of the older story; and that what is frequently taken to be lack of structure is the result of various changes in technique.

The older type of story is the story of traditional plot. By a story of traditional plot I do not necessarily mean what has come to be known as "the plot story," although the latter is one example of the type. I mean any story (1) which derives its structure from plot based on a conflict and issuing in action; (2) whose action is sequential, progressive, that is, offers something for the reader to watch unfold and develop, usually by means of a series of complications, thus evoking suspense; and (3) whose action finally resolves the conflict, thus giving the story "point." The structure of traditional plot stories is essentially dramatic; somewhere near the beginning of the story the reader is given a line of progression to follow—a clear statement of the conflict, or a hint of it, or sometimes merely a sense of mystery, of tension, or a perception that a conflict exists although its nature is not known—and from this point on he follows the action to a crisis and a final resolution. There is a geometrical quality to plot structure of this type; just as a proposition is stated, developed by arguments, and finally proved, so a conflict is stated at the beginning of a story, developed by a series of scenes, and resolved at the end. The test for unity of such a structure is simple: Each scene, incident, and detail of the action not only must bear a direct relation to the conflict and its resolution but must also carry its share of significance at the particular point in the progression that it occupies. Thus the reader's sense of unity, of having watched something develop to the point of completion, is derived from the writer's focusing upon conflict and the eventual resolution of conflict.

Obviously, stories of traditional plot are capable of considerable variation; plot is not necessarily a strait jacket, as in the formula story, and it is only one of the elements of complete short-story form. Hence plot may be the dominant element in a story, or again it may be subordinated to elements such as character, theme, or atmosphere. Conflict may be of two fundamental types: external conflict, in which a character struggles against a tangible obstacle, and internal conflict, or conflict within a character. Also, there are wide differences as to how soon the conflict is made apparent to the reader and how much of it he is allowed to understand early in the story.

Jack London's "Love of Life" is a convenient example of the story in which plot is dominant and external. A prospector in the Far North, deserted by his partner and without food and ammunition, successfully overcomes the threat of death by starvation, exposure, and the attack of wild animals. The conflict here is between man and the forces of nature; it is apparent early in the story, and it is the focus of the reader's attention throughout. The action is progressive or sequential—consisting of a series of incidents, each a minor conflict in itself. The resolution occurs when the man reaches safety, and only when the outcome is no longer in doubt is the story completed. A second example, Sarah Orne Jewett's "A White Heron," shows character dominant over plot. A nine-year-old girl, a lover of nature, is asked by a young ornithologist to reveal the haunts of the white heron in order that he may secure a specimen for his collection, but the girl refuses. The conflict is internal, between the girl's love for the beautiful bird and her desire to make the young man happy and win for her grandmother the reward he offers. The conflict, however, does not make its appearance until the mid-point of the story, since the first half is given over to characterization on which the resolution of the conflict eventually turns. Yet, despite its differences, the story conforms to the same structural pattern of traditional plot that the London story exemplifies. All that is claimed for plot here is that it furnishes the skeletal structure of the older type of story, whether it be a so-called "atmosphere story" like "The Fall of the House of Usher," a psychological story like "Markheim," or a story of theme like "Ethan Brand."[1]

By contrast the modern story frequently seems to be without narrative structure and, as was stated earlier, has been called plotless, fragmentary, and amorphous. Certainly there is evidence to show that the modern writer has attempted to break away from traditional plot. Plot, he feels, is unreal, artificial. Sherwood Anderson's remarks on plot in *A Story-teller's Story* are typical: "'The Poison Plot' I called it in conversation with my friends as the plot notion did seem to me to poison all story-telling. . . . In the construction of these stories there was endless variation but in all of them human beings, the lives of human beings, were altogether disregarded. . . . it was certain there were no plot short stories in any life I had known anything about." The same belief in the antipathy between plot and realism is seen in a challenging article by Bonaro Overstreet: "The nineteenth century story teller was a master of plot. The twentieth century fellow, seeing that life was not made up of neatly parcelled collections of incidents, took his rebel stand.''[2]

Now, it seems to me that statements such as these are not so much protests against plot as against the misuse of plot. Fundamentally, they are protests against plot based on formulas and their "deceptive sentimentalizing of reality,"[3] which the writers find artificial. Yet plot is not necessarily artificial. Conflict, the basis of plot, is the very stuff of life, whether the individual writer tends to see it within the mind or in the external world. The kind of conflict the writer chooses, and the method by which the conflict is developed, may vary, and should vary, from story to story according to the individual aims of the writer; but the resultant plot need not illustrate the platitudes and mechanical patterns of the formula stories. And the fact is that modern stories which presumably satisfy their authors on the score of realism do exhibit the traditional structure of conflict, action, and resolution. The charges of plotlessness, or loose, invertebrate structure, that have been made against the modern story seem to me to be better explained by changes in modern technique.

Chief among these changes are the stricter limitation of subject and the method of indirection. The modern writer's desire for realism causes him to focus upon a limited moment of time or a limited area of action in order that it may be more fully explored and understood. One result is that he frequently finds a story in material which would yield nothing to an earlier writer. Naturally he makes little use of plot complication, because he regards plot complication as artificial, and doubly so if the subject is limited. More important than this limitation of subject, however, is the marked emphasis upon indirection, which seemingly stems as much from the pervasive modern desire for subtlety as from the realistic ideal. To suggest, to hint, to imply, but not to state directly or openly—this is a favored contemporary technique. The method is well described by L. A. G. Strong: "The modern short story writer is content if, allowing the reader to glance at his characters as through a window, he shows them making a gesture which is typical: that is to say, a gesture which enables the reader's imagination to fill in all that is left unsaid. Instead of giving us a finished action to admire, or pricking the bubble of some problem, he may give us only the key-piece of a mosaic, around which, if sufficiently perceptive, we can see in shadowy outline the completed pattern."[4] In other words, as will be apparent in the following analyses, the reader must supply the missing parts of the traditional plot in many modern stories.

A case in point is William March's "A Haircut in Toulouse" from his collection *Some Like Them Short:*

> A veteran of World War I meets an old war comrade, Bob Decker, at a Legion reunion in France. Decker, grown stout and middle-aged, appears ridiculous in a flamboyant costume of gold-braided, bell-bottomed trousers, white silk blouse, wide crimson sash, and sombrero. He tells his friend a story that he has never told to anyone else. After the war, in Toulouse, he went to a French barber shop where his attempts to explain to the barber that he wanted "clippers on the neck but nothing off the top" were misunderstood; and out of sheer inability to protest further, he submitted to having his hair curled. To his surprise, he liked the result; it "brought out something in me that I didn't even know was there before." But almost immediately he reflected that if he appeared at his barracks with his hair curled, he would never live down the resulting ridicule. He then picked up the clippers and sheared a path through the curls on his head, forcing the barber to complete the job, while inwardly he lamented his lack of freedom to do as he wished.
>
> At the conclusion of this narrative, Decker's wife and twelve-year-old daughter join the friends. After the introductions, Mrs. Decker apologizes for her husband's costume and adds, "All the boys from his Post are dressed just like he is." But the daughter says, "Don't you think Daddy looks *silly* dressed that way?" For a moment "the expression in his eyes must have been the same as it was when he picked up the French barber's clippers; but it passed almost at once and he smiled. . . ." He draws the child to him and says mildly, "Don't you suppose Daddy knows that as well as you do?"

If the synopsis is momentarily puzzling, so is the story, because the method is that of indirection. The writer's aim here is to depict a conflict within a character, to let us see within a man, to catch a glimpse of what is individual in him, even though it is usually hidden from the world. Decker, seemingly a conformist, secretly desires to individualize himself, to play the beau, to flout the conventions in the matter of dress, but he fears public ridicule. Some fifteen years before the time of the story, he yielded to his fear of ridicule when he sheared off his curled hair; and he has continued to yield. Now, because all the members of his post have chosen a flamboyant costume for the reunion, he can appear in a way that delights him, but beneath his gay exterior—and that is the real point of the story—lies the unhappy awareness of his own absurd appearance, and it is brought to a focus by his daughter's remark and his reply: "Don't you suppose Daddy knows that as well as you do?"

Once understood, the story is seen to possess the traditional elements of narrative structure. There is a conflict, the conflict is not immediately apparent to the reader, and it is the chief aim of the writer to make the reader see and understand it in order that he may understand the man Decker. It is made apparent by action, but here the story departs sharply from the traditional technique. There are two seemingly unrelated scenes—one in the barber shop at Toulouse, the other in the hotel lobby when the wife and daughter appear. The seeming lack of relationship is deliberate; the emphasis is not upon the sequence of the scenes, their progression, or what has been called earlier their geometrical quality. Rather it is upon their meaning. The aim of a story of this kind is a perceived relationship. Given, in L. A. G. Strong's language, the parts of a mosaic, the reader must find the pattern. The ''key-piece'' of the mosaic is the statement: ''. . . the expression in his eyes must have been the same as it was when he picked up the French barber's clippers''; and when at the very end of the story Decker says, ''Don't you suppose Daddy knows that as well as you do?'' the reader's mind should, in a moment of illumination, connect the two statements as well as supply what is omitted. The omissions, of course, are clear statements of what Decker's internal conflict is, and the fact that he has been repeatedly frustrated by convention.

Finally, the story satisfies the third requirement of plot structure in that the action resolves the conflict. Here again the method is indirect; the resolution is by implication. Instead of being taken into Decker's mind by the writer, we are given two objective statements, one about the look in the man's eyes and the other what he says. Having furnished the reader with the requisite hints, the writer stops. The suggestion is that *this time* Decker hoped to satisfy his own desire to dress as he wished as well as to escape ridicule. But his daughter's remark has recalled him unhappily to the reality of a world of conventional judgment, and the immediate conflict is resolved when once more he recognizes frustration. It is, of course, true that the story derives much of its power from its ability to project the reader's imagination beyond the limits of the story, to make him see that Decker's life has included many such experiences and that presumably his frustration will continue to the end of his life. Also it should be observed that in a story of this type the resolution and moment of perception are practically simultaneous and that the emotion is evoked principally at the end when the reader understands the situation.

Such a story, then, may be said to have the traditional elements of structure. Its principle of unity is that of the perceived relationship; each incident contributes to the perception of that relationship, there is an ordered arrangement of the parts, and no one incident can be omitted without destroying the unity and hence the meaning of the whole. Obviously, such a story puts demands upon both writer and reader. The suggestions and implications must be nicely calculated to reveal neither too little nor too much, and the reader must be alert to seize upon what is given and construct from it the desired pattern of meaning.

A second example of the modern type of story is John O'Hara's "Are We Leaving Tomorrow?" from his collection *Files on Parade:*

> A young couple, Mr. and Mrs. Campbell from Montreal, are staying at a resort hotel in the States. They keep a good deal to themselves, although Mrs. Campbell, "a pleasant, friendly little woman," has nodding acquaintance with some of the other guests. Quite by chance they meet Mr. and Mrs. Loomis in the hotel bar and talk small talk over their drinks. We learn that "Mrs. Campbell was almost gay that afternoon." Mr. Campbell, however, has said nothing.
>
> One evening, after a movie shown by the hotel management, Mr. Loomis insists on buying the Campbells a drink. When he gives his order, Campbell tells the waiter to bring the bottle, and, after a moment's incredulity, Mr. Loomis confirms the order. The talk is idle gossip of movie stars, and Campbell, drinking steadily, is curiously aloof; but, as the Loomises feel this and address their remarks to him, he begins to respond in an exaggerated way, nodding before it is time to nod and saying, "Yes, yes, yes," very rapidly. Then he tells a story. "It had in it a priest, female anatomy, improbable situations, a cuckold, unprintable words, and no point." The Loomises, shocked and embarrassed, say "Good night" and leave.
>
> Mrs. Campbell, who has lowered her eyes all during her husband's story, now says, "I wonder if the man is still there at the travel desk. I forgot all about the tickets for tomorrow." Her husband asks, "Tomorrow? Are we leaving tomorrow?" Her answer is "Yes," and she gets up to see about the tickets.

Here again both story and synopsis may offer momentary difficulty. Yet the "key-piece" of the mosaic has been provided by the writer. Linked to a chronic alcoholic who is offensive when drunk, Mrs. Campbell spends her life taking him from one resort to another. What happens in the story, it is suggested, is the repetitious pattern of their lives. Arrived at a new hotel, they at first remain aloof, but after a time Mrs. Campbell's natural friendliness causes her to speak and nod to other guests. Sooner or later, presumably by chance, they are brought into social relationships with others, Mr. Campbell reveals himself for what he is, and his wife feels the necessity of moving on, of "leaving tomorrow."

Aside from the fact that the story is not as compressed in time as March's "A Haircut in Toulouse," it shows generally similar characteristics. First of all, there is conflict in the story—an immediate conflict between Mr. and Mrs. Campbell, but, from a broader point of view, a conflict between Mrs. Campbell's desires for normal social companionship and the social mores which she can never satisfy because of her husband's character. As in the March story, the conflict is not immediately apparent to the reader, although the whole point of the narrative is to make him understand it and, by understanding it, sympathize with Mrs. Campbell. Again, the conflict is revealed through action which is not sequential in the dramatic sense but which has as its aim a perceived relationship. There are four scenes: the opening picture of the Campbells as mere spectators at the hotel; the chance meeting with the Loomises; the second meeting with the Loomises when Campbell tells his story; and the final scene with its moment of illumination when we perceive the entire situation and behind it the pattern of the Campbells' lives. The "key-piece" is Mrs. Campbell's "Yes," to her husband's question, "Tomorrow? Are we leaving tomorrow?" It is at this point that all previous scenes and details, when the requisite omissions are supplied, fall into a pattern of meaning. In this case the principal omissions concern the Campbells' past; the reader must see that what occurs in the story has occurred many times before. Finally, the immediate conflict is resolved when it becomes apparent that Mrs. Campbell has failed once more to achieve her desire; but, as in the March story, the resolution and moment of perception are simultaneous, the emotion is evoked at the end, and the basic conflict is not resolved, since Mrs. Campbell's life will probably continue to be a series of "leaving tomorrow's."

Another way of demonstrating the existence of structure in such a story is to re-form the parts into the conventional dramatic pattern. The story could begin, for example, by showing the Campbells arriving at a new resort. Next we might learn what Mrs. Campbell's problem is, how she longs for social companionship, and how frequently she has tried to make just such a new start as she is making when the story opens. After the first chance meeting with the Loomises, she would build her hopes anew, only to have them dashed by her husband's conduct at the second meeting with the Loomises. The ending would be the same—a reference to tickets and to leaving tomorrow. If the story were written according to the dramatic pattern, the traditional structure of conflict, sequential action, and resolution would stand forth clearly. The reader, knowing the situation early in the story, would follow the action principally to learn the outcome; the question would be: Will Mrs. Campbell succeed or fail? As the story is actually written, however, an understanding of the situation, that is, the conflict, and the outcome or resolution are reached simultaneously. Yet the elements of narrative structure are present, despite the different pattern.

Thus, it seems to me, the modern short story demonstrates its claim to the possession of narrative structure derived from plot. Basically, its structure is not very different from that of the older and more conventional type of story, but its technique is different, and it is this difference in technique that is frequently mistaken for lack of structure by readers and critics.

1. The surprise-ending story is only a seeming exception. While it is true that in stories such as Aldrich's ''Marjorie Daw'' and those of O. Henry the *real* story is hidden until the end, the reader nevertheless follows a conflict in the form of a progression of scenes and incidents, and the surprise ending merely contributes a new understanding to the progression and resolution of the conflict.

2. Bonaro Overstreet, ''Little Story, What Now?'' *Saturday Review of Literature,* XXIV (November 22, 1941), 4.

3. Warren Beck, ''Art and Formula in the Short Story,'' *College English,* V (November, 1943), 59. Professor Beck demonstrates convincingly that the formula story is basically the story of sentimental platitude.

4. L. A. G. Strong, ''The Story: Notes at Random,'' *Lovat Dickson's Magazine,* II (March, 1934), 281–82.

THEODORE A. STROUD

A Critical Approach to the Short Story

VIEWED in any reasonable perspective, all approaches to literature result in oversimplification, in that they fix upon one aspect as the most rewarding to explore. There are several questions which imaginative works seem almost inevitably to evoke; yet the very act of phrasing the questions exalts one critical position and places the others at a disadvantage. Furthermore, the critical approach that each teacher prefers is largely determined by accidents of personality or training. However disturbing this conclusion may be, it is almost forced upon us as our views are challenged on every side by colleagues whose intelligence and powers of discrimination we respect.

Unfortunately, whenever we seek to make students conscious of a variety of critical approaches, more difficulties emerge. Not only do we feel pressed for time, but we lack assurance of what would constitute a sampling of other approaches. If we persist, we tend to leave students convinced of the sterility of other views, since the insights worthy of a critical position come only to its enthusiastic practitioners.

Some of these problems, at least, can be solved if teachers can exchange interpretations of frequently reprinted stories in a form that can be used for class discussion, together with an explanation of the principles being applied. This study is a contribution to that goal. It is directed toward answering *one* of the basic critical questions about fiction—namely, what approach will most adequately explain why the author begins where he does, includes what he does, and ends as he does? I am convinced that most stories have a pattern, which, once formulated, permits us to appreciate how the parts fit into one whole. Such an inquiry seems logically prior to, and hardly less important than, any of the other basic issues. But my conclusions are tenable only if others find the analyses illuminating and the distinctions applicable to other stories.

At the present time "plot" has become a pejorative term, reserved for stories intended to evoke a simple kind of suspense. Prestige attaches instead to the stories which have a "theme," preferably discernible as a system of symbols and not as an explicit moral. Writers are viewed as determining what to include or exclude with the incalculable intuition of a somnambulist; all rational concern with unity and plot is dismissed as likely to mislead the readers. How did such a climate of opinion ever develop? Let us digress momentarily to speculate about the reasons.

Although the tale had been a prominent oral genre for centuries, it was only in the eighteenth century that an expanding audience gave its written form any real impetus. But what the period gave with one hand it took away with the other, for narrative literature (even the novel) steadily lost in prestige. The semantic parallel of this shift was that the word "poet," which had previously signified the writers of narratives (especially tragedy and epic), came to refer primarily to lyricists. The new genre recouped its fortunes, however, with the theory and practice of E. A. Poe, who promoted the idea of selecting episodes and words which contributed to a single mood and thus permitted the short story to compete with the Victorian lyric.

In a few generations the lyric began to emphasize images and symbols, and many short-story writers came to feel that Poe's influence was stifling the genre. Coincidentally several Russian writers were brilliantly illustrating the potentialities of the "primitive" folk tale, with its apparent looseness. Instead of returning to the nature of the narrative and reconsidering the implications of its form, the leaders of the revolt more or less consciously sought to prove that the short story could excel the lyric "at its own game"—namely, in organizing symbols to produce "pure poetry" (the modern equivalent of Longinian sublimity). One can hardly censure them for seeking to usurp the throne of the lyric poet. But there is reason to suppose that the effort was rather sporadic, that most writers were at the same time conscious of the potentialities of narratives. Has this desire to excel the lyric poet resulted in stories without self-justifying parts? If so, the tendency is encouraged by critics who view the episodes of a "serious" story as little more than pretexts for distributing, and even obscuring, a set of symbols. In another vein, Malraux insists that modern writers no longer consider the work as an object but rather as a "stake" signalizing the fact that some restless genius has explored a new area of the human mind.

In the face of such critical opinions, anyone should hesitate to generalize about the kinds of unity he expects to find in modern stories. Instead he may treat stories, lyrics, and plays indifferently as reflecting certain universal traits of language used for emotive purposes. Or he may focus on the "strategies" of the writers or on the system of impulses directing their choice of materials, as Kenneth Burke chooses to do. But Burke also observes that a work of art "survives as an objective structure, capable of being examined in itself"; and this line of inquiry is the one we have chosen to pursue. Variations in audience reaction and possible shifts in the intention of the writer seriously complicate any effort to treat the work as an artificial object. But the effort seems worth while if we can avoid the necessity, on the one hand, of lumping together such disparate genres that statements about their structure must be disappointingly vague and, on the other, of building hypotheses about the author's impulses upon our inferences about the work.

Obviously, what the reader sees first about a work is its words and then the minor organizing principles of syntax, of logical discourse, and of narrative episodes. Ultimately, he discerns its principle of organization, not in a relatively few half-concealed symbols scattered throughout the episodes, but in the power the total story has to affect its readers' feelings, not accidentally, but as human beings who share part of the author's culture. A story inevitably impresses different readers in diverse ways; it occasionally stirs up obsessions which paralyze the critical faculties. If not, we can distinguish between our accidental reactions to a story (Isn't this character like my mother? That incident reminds me of my neighbors! Such filthy language!) and the reactions which the writer had a right to expect (What is that character *really* like? What will happen to him next? How ironical to have that happen to him right now!) By further minimizing reactions to single episodes or minor characters in a story, we come to recognize the power of the story as a whole, as a mingling of some degree of anxiety and relief, pathos and frustration, amusement and self-satisfaction, or other compatible reactions. Perhaps the most striking reassurance that we have validly formulated the emotional impact of the story is the accompanying glimpse of its unity and completeness.

From this analysis of our impression, which may be viewed as the end of the story, should evolve a way of correlating the means, that is, the successive units of narration, dialogue, description, or commentary which combine to impart that unique pleasure. Primarily, the concern is with discerning the pattern in the work, why apparently irrelevant episodes are included, or some events expanded and others telescoped, rather than with an estimate of its excellence. But there is no escaping the implication that the pleasure natural to fictitious narratives somehow depends upon a feeling of completeness. If so, a story that defies analysis as a whole is artistically defective—whatever the merits of its various parts.

Many present-day stories seem disconnected or chaotic, but we need only to penetrate beneath the surface or the mode of presentation to recognize integrating principles. The occasional story which seeks to reflect the chaos of our times by means of utter irrelevancies has chosen a plausible, but probably a self-defeating, artistic principle.

II

In most of the stories today, as in previous centuries, the completeness results from the units or episodes in a story being combined to make credible a "change" in one of the characters. And all the episodes in such stories, upon consideration, appear to bear upon this change, either as weakening or as strengthening his resistance to becoming a person perceptibly different from what he was in the beginning. The changes may be roughly characterized as taking place either in the character's moral traits (the psychologists might call them "behavior patterns") or in his attitude toward himself or others. In previous centuries a third change, in the fortune or estate of the person, was rather commonly employed to interlink the events, but today such stories are largely limited to pulp magazines. This is not to imply that the central characters in serious stories today never face disaster, but the concern is ordinarily not with their ultimate prosperity or prestige but with what effect the threat will have on their personalities. Only rarely are adventure stories conceived in a form sufficiently complex to deserve analysis. Exceptions include such well-known stories as Crane's "The Open Boat" and Jack London's "To Build a Fire."

The other types of change present a bewildering picture, with all their overlapping and combination. Obviously, some change in attitude must accompany any moral variation; sometimes changes in sentiment have moral consequences, such as the change from antipathy to affection in conventional love stories. Some of the changes which serve to configure the incidents in a story may seem far less significant than the one from dislike to love, at least when they are viewed as phenomena in real life. But fiction has the power, as it constructs a microcosm in which the characters live and of which they form the ingredients, to endow with significance what would otherwise be trivial changes. If readers often fail to see this aspect of stories, it may be because their interests and training have led them to look elsewhere. Some idea of the pattern thus described may be gathered from the following analysis of Katherine Mansfield's very brief story, "Miss Brill."

At the beginning, Miss Brill is mildly happy because she is able to compensate for her lack of companionship by her faculty for personifying a fur neckpiece and her ability to participate vicariously in the activities of strangers she observes. Superficially, the story is merely one of her visits to the park on Sunday afternoons, except that she is disturbed by a fortuitous insult. Yet almost from the first, the details (composed of her observations except for one almost imperceptible action on her part) have an order about them which grows believably out of her imaginative reactions. We are permitted to witness how, with subtle logic, her sensations begin to coalesce in a new impression of her surroundings: the band performing showily under the influence of a larger audience (the opening of the season), her regular seat on a bench (reserved), her skill at converting random conversations into drama, and her unsatisfied craving to participate. Having thus revealed the traits underlying her behavior, her impressions evolve at an even faster pace: the spectacular nature of the kaleidoscopic crowds (a sharp contrast to the regular audience), the scenery viewed as a stage drop, the pantomimic interplay of the strollers (each with its appropriate musical theme).

Born of this flux is her notion that the park is a stage, and, instantaneously, that she and the "regular audience" are part of the performance.

In her imagination, details facilely slide into place to carry out the analogy, and happiness overwhelms her in the impression of "belongingness." But a necessary concomitant is pride, betraying her into a momentary but positive commitment of vital significance. For this woman—expert at "listening as though she didn't listen"—is now so self-confident, so blissful in her delusion that her lonely monotony is dramatically purposeful, so pleased that a hero and heroine had materialized to confirm her interpretation of the scene, that she "prepared to listen" with a "trembling smile."

The crushing rebuff she receives is evidently accidental, but the minute episodes somehow appear to be sequential or related as cause and effect. Her every perception contributes to her emotional state and in some fashion promises her happiness, yet makes probable her final misery. It would be difficult to find a better illustration of how a writer should seek to make the episodes of his stories come about unexpectedly, and yet in retrospect seem probable.

Our initial awareness of Miss Brill's precarious balance between sadness and happiness prepares us for the concatenation of events which destroys that balance and permits the pitiful irony of the variant of "Pride goeth before a fall." Thus, at the end, even inanimate objects have the power to make her unhappy; she has been permanently relegated to the "dark little rooms or even—cupboards."

Are the critics who view this story as a "portrait in miniature" giving us any clue to its real nature? No matter how often they speak of it as a masterpiece, I maintain that they are not. If the story were longer, the critics would probably have assumed that it is organized by a "theme." For there is a tendency today among critics and teachers to find "themes" everywhere and, thereby, to credit the author with a desire to inculcate some form of morality. A typical example is the recent analysis of Hemingway's "The Short, Happy Life of Francis Macomber" as having for its theme "the final victory of Man over Death" (West and Stallman's *The Art of Modern Fiction,* pp. 260 ff.). The theme is said to be "adequately embodied in the action . . . and properly intensified by the other elements." But this view distracts us from the actual way in which the details of the story interlock to change a personality. Macomber's act of cowardice has consequences which evoke his inner resources to triumph over those who feel superior and thus ironically to bring about his death. But what he really triumphs over is his fear, not death; nor is death the cause of his victory, even though the particular form death takes here makes it a consequence of his victory, a confirmation, and a source of irrevocability. Other forms of death might be plausible—for example, at the claws of a wounded animal—but could never give a pattern to the events.

Before we consider the small fraction of stories that are actually organized as arguments, however, let us continue the analysis of what it means for a story to be organized around a change.

It must be recognized that several characters in a story may change incidentally, but ordinarily only one changes as a *result* of a concatenation of stimuli which constitute the parts of the story. Sometimes two characters are related as undergoing reciprocal changes; so that, for instance, the happiness of one requires misery for the other. Sometimes even more: Gorki's 'Twenty-six and One" is a rare example of a story in which a large group is treated as a single personality undergoing a change. But further distinctions and qualifications are necessary if the reader is to identify the various pleasures such stories may afford. For, ordinarily, recognizing that a change is critical is tantamount to discovering the "plot." Only then do we rationally comprehend the emotions vaguely produced as we read the story for the first time.

One distinction concerns the possible variations in our attitude toward the central character. As soon as the other characters in a work establish the mores of his world, we tend to wish him good or bad fortune in varying degrees. Our urge to mete out punishment may be fervent, as toward Midge in Lardner's "The Champion," who victimizes defenseless and innocent people. An almost equally vicious character, such as Farrington in Joyce's "Counterparts," may excite relatively little fervor if his associates seem only slightly less vicious. The deserts of some characters are neatly balanced, or our good wishes are called for merely by their helplessness or immaturity. Ordinarily, our attitude is determined by what the character wants for others, viewed in the context of how others treat him.

In order to obtain the pleasure intended by a story, we must judge by similar signs how much weight to give the events which appear to the recipient as distressing or satisfying, insulting or complimentary. In farces, death is amusing, in some stories a look of contempt may cause permanent damage. Also we must infer his responsibility for what he does and undergoes, the amount of ignorance involved in his actions, from the quality of the little world he inhabits—not from real life analogues, unless the words so direct us. An instance in point is the occasional criticism of Lardner's "Haircut" because the mentally deficient Paul is incapable of planning a successful murder. He is part of a world, however, in which cruel practical jokes seem inextricably connected with, if not exactly the product of, stupidity. How appropriate it is, then, that the weakest member of that society should somehow perpetrate the grimmest practical joke of all!

Another distinction in the character of "change" stories evolves from the relation between the central character and the events. At one extreme the central character is active, in that he primarily determines what is to happen next and seems to control even the accidents. In such stories the opening establishes the hero's goal and hints at some alternatives. And in his surge toward a goal, the central figure will either guide his fortunes safely through a crisis or shape the events ironically to bring about his misery or destruction. Such a quasi-tragic figure is Kendall (in Lardner's "Haircut"), who is responsible for the episodes which constitute his revenge and thus for inciting his own murder. Moreover, he is in the ironical position of having contributed greatly to the popular feeling in the town that Paul cannot be held mentally responsible for the deed. The barber thus comes to be the perfect narrator: he exhibits the kind of thinking that would have made it futile for Doc Stair to report the shooting as murder.

One further brief example: Once Davidson (in Maugham's "Rain") is conscious of Sadie's profession, he unmistakably shapes the events to his will. His self-destruction is ironically due to the fact that he eliminates from the prostitute all signs of sex (that is, the trappings and gestures against which a Puritan upbringing would condition him) and thus makes it credible for him to succumb to his sexual urges—at the very moment when he feels he has succeeded in eliminating a symbol of evil. Here again we may observe the appropriateness of McPhail as narrator, for in the first half of the story he establishes enough moral authority and objectivity to outweigh the powerful religious symbols cloaking Davidson's personality. That function accomplished, he lets Davidson take the stage as a tragic protagonist.

Incidentally, our comments on these two stories have for the first time raised questions about the function of narrators. If in this study no systematic distinction is made between the change being represented and the technique of representing it, the assumption is that one cannot discern the nature of a particular plot without partly accounting for the method of presentation. In fact, the validity of a hypothesis about the plot can often be tested by its implications for the choice of narrator or point of view.

III

In contrast to these "active" heroes, a far more popular type of short story is built around a passive character, to whom all the episodes *appear* as accidents. Here the events can no longer be linked as cause and effect; instead, they seem to be introduced to disturb the emotional balance of the central character and thus to facilitate a certain kind of change in him. In such stories the "hero" moves from ignorance to knowledge about himself or others, even though what he comes to "know" may be manifestly false. Since initially he has no goal, except some vague desire to be happy or secure, he obviously will not determine what is to happen next or do anything more than react to the situations as they arise. It is no accident that many such stories center around children or adolescents, for their receptive passivity is both credible and dramatic.

In analyzing such stories, we need to recognize the interplay of means and ends. The traits of the central figures serve as a means to make the "change" probable, but the "change" is a means to the total effect. The minor characters are means either to show the major figure for what he really is or to strip him of his defenses against the "change." Images, figures, symbols, may reflect what the character is becoming, or they may be that which he comes to know. Thus, for example, when the boy in Wallace Stegner's "Butcher Bird" is driven to see that the shrike symbolized all that disturbed him in his father, his attitude toward his father correspondingly changes from respect to loathing. His mother and the other characters serve to produce a susceptibility to the symbol. Again, in Robert Penn Warren's "Christmas Gift," it is irrelevant to ask whether the storekeeper is the kind of person who would give the boy candy (although the action should not violate our impression of the storekeeper). It is appropriate if it somehow has an emotional impact on the boy and contributes to his climactic change of attitude, implied by his action of giving candy to the doctor.

Kenneth Burke holds that whenever a story is essentially tragic, destiny seems to "bring about a representative kind of accident which belongs with the agent's particular kind of character." But why, it seems pertinent to ask, cannot incidents seem to "belong" in any story?

Observe, for example, the opening of Steinbeck's "The Leader of the People": the hero is a self-centered boy, vaguely rebelling against authority and intensely bored with his surroundings. Isn't there something peculiarly appropriate about the accidental arrival of his grandfather, who exemplifies romance to the boy and boredom to his parents? My contention is that pattern is aesthetically preferable to random order and is ordinarily discernible in stories which we hear praised as having a character who "burst the bonds" of the plot. Furthermore, if irony is characteristic of the most satisfying patterns, it may be evoked by arranging the events so that one or more of them appear to reinforce the character's original state of mind, only later to undermine it. An apparent compliment, for instance, may seem to strengthen a hero's confidence in himself, only to have him recognize it later as hypocritical when his self-respect is in the balance.

This view may be further tested and illustrated by an analysis of William Faulkner's "Delta Autumn." Readers of the story tend to stress Roth's love affair or its racial implications and to view McCaslin as a mouthpiece for the author's views. But only when we recognize him as the passive central character on whom the events converge will the story cease to be a series of passages having merely symbolic or dramatic merit.

For the story to achieve its proper effect, we must first know what is to be changed. Thus the opening events lead us to credit McCaslin with such impressive virtues as integrity, patriotism, humanity, and prudence—all revealed in the context of a traditional hunting trip. At first puzzled by the way his grandnephew is being taunted, McCaslin is further upset by having Roth challenge him as once Socrates was challenged by Thrasymachus: "It's only because folks happen to be watching him that a man behaves at all." In his eloquent rejoinder, McCaslin momentarily becomes a surrogate for the Creator, full of compassion for erring men. His conception of a God of hunters forces grudging admiration even from his associates.

Later he lies in bed recalling how at the beginning of adolescence he was consecrated to this God in a quasi-religious ceremony and how later he rejected a family inheritance as a protest against the sins of his society. Gradually the years have freed him from that bitterness and from physical passion as well; and now he achieves an Olympian detachment in his reflections on "this puny evanescent clutter of human sojourn."

But of such thoughts is fashioned the sin of pride. The term "hubris" might be preferable, for the attitude springs from real virtues. His feelings of righteous indignation toward Roth for his affair with a Negro woman deserves our approbation. But a few hours later when she mysteriously arrives, the feeling betrays him into assuming that she is a culprit bound over to his judgment. It makes him incapable of realizing that, symbolically, she is a doe come voluntarily to participate in a perverted version of his own "religious ceremony": there can be no other plausible explanation if she scorns the money and has no delusions about Roth's marrying her. She admits her guilt readily, then regains the initiative by charging McCaslin with having caused Roth's moral degeneration. A moment later McCaslin is catapulted by his horror of miscegenation into senile bitterness, into the gift-bribe of the hunting horn, and into advice worthy of Roth himself. Momentarily, at least, his belief in the inherent dignity of the Negro is undermined by his passion. At this point her triumph is complete, and she expresses it magnificently: "Old man, have you lived so long and forgotten so much that you don't even remember anything you ever knew or felt or even heard about love?" The irony is that he *had* known the night before when he was speaking to the hunters: ". . . at that instant the two of them [man and woman] together were God."

How much he suffers for having denied love and thus having betrayed his deepest religious convictions is revealed by indirection in the final paragraphs. Twice we have phrases suggesting a kind of death (with "grieving rain" outside) and reminding us of Roth's insult: "Where have you been all the time you were dead?" But the most significant inferences about his mood of self-hatred are to be drawn from the italicized jeremiad. The passage restates a topic frequently in his thoughts the day before, but now he pronounces judgment with such intensity as to imply that he includes himself in the total depravity of what God created. Thus, at the end, when the hunters are hurrying to conceal Roth's latest crime of doe-killing, we are hardly surprised to see McCaslin recognize this symbolic confirmation but remain inert. Literally and symbolically, he has made his last hunting trip.

One final illustration of a "change" story deserves inclusion because it exhibits how neatly one symbol may give the episodes of a story almost an organic synthesis. In Dorothy Parker's "Big Blonde," a widely reprinted story, the author makes no pretense to subtlety in establishing the character of Hazel as vain, subnormal, and craving social approval. Even the events are blurred in telling to resemble their impress on her mind. But one incident is significantly not blurred: ". . . a big, scarred horse pulling a rickety express wagon crashed to his knees before her. The driver swore and screamed and lashed the beast insanely, bringing the whip back over his shoulder for every blow, while the horse struggled to get a footing on the slippery asphalt. A group gathered and watched with interest." Even with her imperfect grasp of reality, she dimly realizes that the incident is symbolic. And with the failure of her suicide attempt, the realization of her true status becomes complete: she at last identifies herself with "a long parade of weary horses and shivering beggars, and all beaten, driven, stumbling things." To anyone interested in part-whole relationships, the lashing she witnesses is far more than a figurative hint of the narrator's attitude toward Hazel: one has merely to conjure up the implications of this symbol to grasp the unity of the parts, their mutual appropriateness. If she is equivalent to a draft horse, then this is the story of her becoming immeasurably weary as her vitality wanes, flinching at the very thought of pressing her feet against the ground. In this same context, all the men are drivers, their identity of no consequence. Even the physician is identified as a driver by his initial appearance on the scene with a mistress. And he is to be identified with the driver lashing the fallen horse to its feet when he "plunged his thumbs into the lidded pits above her eyeballs, and threw his weight upon them." The parallelism of the climax is inescapable: the driver deprives Hazel of her only means of escape.

IV

Many short stories, however, are not organized around a change. We are justified in stressing this pattern chiefly because a search for it will often disclose an alternative one. Of the various possibilities, one might think first of stories in which the events almost cry out for a change in the central character, but none occurs; for example, Stevenson's "A Lodging for the Night" or Silone's "Mr. Aristotle." Another group would include stories which are hybrids, part essay, part fiction. An example is Proust's "Filial Sentiments of a Parricide," in which the narrator is stimulated by the ironic juxtaposition of a letter and a news story to speculate about the disturbing paradoxes encompassed by a human soul.

In still another type of story one character is central, but the change is in the reader, not the character. For the reader is confronted with the puzzling inconsistency in the traits of the character or is somehow induced to conjecture about the motives underlying his behavior. The narrator may carry the reader along with him from ignorance to knowledge, or he may merely collect the data from which the reader infers an answer. In either instance, we can establish this movement as a pattern only when it accounts for all the episodes and even for the choice of the narrator. Thus in Chekhov's "The Darling," a vegetative woman is oddly charming and self-sacrificing. At the very end she suddenly comes into focus as a psychological vampire because of the boy's complaint in his dream: "I'll give it to you. Get away. Quit your scrapping." Here alone can we find the explanation of Chekhov's selection of data: loss of a father, death of two husbands, departure of a lover, and acquisition of a "son." (Note how Chekhov almost systematically canvasses the possibilities of her relations to males.)

Somewhat comparable in form is Eudora Welty's story, "A Worn Path." From almost the beginning we become curious about the "long way" which this ancient Negro woman feels impelled to travel. At every turn we catch glimpses of her poetic hallucinations, her hypnotic determination, and her instinctive benignity and shrewdness, sharpened rather than blurred by her senility. The trip becomes a mysterious pilgrimage, and the traits of her personality will not fall into place until we learn her motive for this oft repeated trip. Out of his simple cynicism, the hunter who rescues her offers us a false but plausible lead: she "wouldn't miss going to town to see Santa Claus." This conjecture seems confirmed by her efforts to pocket the nickel he drops, so that only the fantastic quality that her consciousness imparts to the scenes keeps his remark from poisoning our anticipation. She arrives, and we are still kept in suspense by her senility. As she receives the medicine for her grandson, she acts to recall our suspicion of her cupidity. Then the suspicion is ironically reversed. The pattern of her personality revealed and even confirmed by her selfless use of the money, we rest content in our admiration, buoyed up by echoes of legendary quests—even the Holy Grail.

In a different category are the "theme" stories, the ones we can validly describe as being patterned in a certain way because of the author's desire to enrich our moral perceptiveness. Sometimes (but not nearly so often as many readers suppose) a set of symbols does actually body forth a moral concept. They may give the story an allegorical cast, as in Katherine Anne Porter's "Flowering Judas," in which the report of a nightmare reveals to us, if not to the heroine, how her rejection of *all* forms of love is a betrayal of the life-principle itself. (Note again the apparent exhaustion of the possibilities; this feature frequently appears in stories *not* patterned by a "change.") A vaguely comparable use of dreams occurs in Italo Svevo's "The Sparrows": in his waking hours the hero writes an apologia for his pointless existence in fables about sparrows but only in his sleep mourns his sparrow-like frustrations.

It is very natural and even profitable to extract some more or less explicit comment on human nature from a story and assume that the story exists for the sake of the comment. The result is often unfortunate, however, in that (1) the story is left a pastiche of arbitrarily connected parts, and (2) the writer is shown to lack ingenuity, for almost anyone could invent a situation which would more adequately support the thesis. How can a writer hope to convince us, for instance, that all men have their price unless his exhibit is a man shown as unlikely to accept a bribe? And in a longer story this writer might well pretend to exhaust the possibilities: several persons of widely differing ages or estates must yield to bribery before the story "proves" its thesis. An effective illustration of how all men (represented by four men of varied professions), when Western civilization has blown itself up, will miss the culture unutterably more than the comforts is found in Van Tilburg Clark's "The Portable Phonograph." Similarly, in Peter Taylor's "Their Losses," three elderly southern women are introduced as representatives of a vanishing social class. The initial parallelism of their circumstances at first seems too pat, but it soon becomes appropriate for these three people, whose diverse ways of life are converging on extinction, to be traveling to or from a funeral. The friction generated by their being thrown together, as their train travels through scenes equally symptomatic of a decaying era, leads them to reveal their otherwise suppressed despair.

Categories other than the ones described are to be found, as well as various hybrids. But by means of these schematic distinctions, it should be possible to discern the unique pattern which accounts for the details of a story. Perhaps the teacher should again be cautioned about his concern with the moral intention of an author. The dogmatist judges all stories according to his own standard and tends to read a moral into any story he likes. Other teachers fall quite plausibly into the position that *any* moral concept will serve as the basis for good stories, so long as it convinces the reader of its sincerity. The writer's capacity to produce memorable characters and events depends, they imply, on the sincerity of his belief in a theme. Since men may dedicate their lives to a cause, however, and still not promote it by stories that "ring true," this view ends by substituting one mystery (What are valid signs of sincerity?) for another (Why is the work satisfying?).

Once the teacher can resist looking at the parts of a story as signs of the author's philosophy, or even of his sincerity, he must still develop a capacity for dismissing his personal concept of reality—that is, if he is to discern a pattern (or any defections from it). The world of the story may be ruled by sex—or be completely devoid of the sex drive. Neither frame of reference seems realistic, but either may become artistically necessary to the structure and its end product. Actually, if we may return to the opening distinction, it may be naive to believe that people change or, on the other hand, to suppose that they have enough stability in their traits to make a change significant. The signs of change in flesh-and-blood persons are so fallible that any view whatever can be documented. In a world of fiction, however, the audience approaches the ideal status of knowing the truth about (1) the character's initial behavior pattern, with special attention to areas under fire; (2) his reaction to significant stimuli and their cumulative effect; and (3) any variations in his personality. That this information is often suspensefully delayed or gradually revealed is granted, but the complete story, with relatively few exceptions, permits trustworthy inferences on all these points.

Yet here is no intention of suggesting that readers should ignore questions of verisimilitude, morality, or any other issue which will enrich their social impulses or increase their understanding of human motives. My only contention is that, *whenever* the inquiry turns to part-whole relationships in stories, other issues are both irrelevant and misleading; for a simultaneous concern with structure *and* values will continue the impression that many serious stories are composed of arbitrarily related episodes, highly uneven in dramatic worth and symbolic significance.

NORMAN FRIEDMAN

What Makes a Short Story Short?

The truth is that, just as in the other imitative arts one imitation is always of one thing, so in poetry the story, as an imitation of action, must represent one action, a complete whole. . . . Now a whole is that which has a beginning, middle, and end. A beginning is that which is not itself necessarily after anything else, and which has naturally something else after it; an end is that which is naturally after something itself, either as its necessary or usual consequent, and with nothing else after it; and a middle, that which is by nature after one thing and has also another after it.

—Aristotle, *Poetics,* Chs. 7 and 8.

Although the short story as a literary type gets a fair share of attention in classroom texts and writer's handbooks, it is still—tainted by commercialism and damned by condescension—running a poor fourth to poetry, drama, and novel-length fiction in the books and journals devoted to serious theoretical criticism. It is in the hope of making a beginning toward the evaluation of the short story as a worthy and noble art that I should like to attempt a frontal attack upon its basic problem—that of its shortness.

But it is not a question merely of defining "shortness," of fixing the upper and lower limits in terms of the number of words a work of fiction should have in order to be called a short story. Common sense tells us that, although the exact dividing lines cannot—and need not—be determined, we can pretty well distinguish, apart from marginal cases, between long, short, and medium fiction. We will not argue, then, about length in strictly quantitative terms, for most of us know what a short story is and can pull down from our shelves at a moment's notice a dozen anthologies containing stories of varying lengths—all called "short." To haggle over the borderlines is almost always fruitless, and that is one very good reason for not trying. I will simply assume without proof that the examples discussed in this paper as specimens of the type are indeed commonly regarded as short stories.

Nor is it a question of defining a different form, if by form we mean, as we usually do, certain materials unified to achieve a given effect, for the materials and their organization in a short story differ from those in a novel in degree but not in kind. To say, as has frequently been done, that short is distinguished from long fiction by virtue of its greater unity is surely to beg several questions at once. A fossil survivor of Poe's aesthetic, this notion confuses wholeness with singleness, unity with intensity. If unity implies that all the parts are related by an overall governing principle, there is certainly no reason why a short story should have more unity than a novel, although it may naturally have fewer parts to unify—a matter we shall examine in due course.

Nor may we say that a short story cannot deal with the growth of character, as has also been frequently done, or that it focuses upon culminations rather than traces developments, because the simple fact is that many stories do portray a character in the process of changing—Hemingway's "The Short Happy Life of Francis Macomber," for example, or Faulkner's "Barn Burning." Similarly, there is no reason why a story cannot deal with a change in thought, as in Steele's "How Beautiful With Shoes," or with a change in fortune, as in Fitzgerald's "Babylon Revisited." (Of course, some stories *are* static, and we shall discuss them below.) Nor may we say that stories are more commonly organized around a theme than novels, for some are, as Shirley Jackson's "The Lottery," and some are not, as Edith Wharton's "The Other Two." A story may arouse suspense and expectation, pity, repugnance, hope, and fear, just as a novel may, and may resolve those emotions in a complete and satisfying way, just as a novel may.[1]

There is, of course, much truth in the approaches we have just touched upon, but none of them manages to include enough of the actual possibilities to be finally useful. Surely short stories contain fewer words than novels, but that measure is a misleading one because it centers on symptoms rather than causes; surely short stories may make a more singular impact upon the reader, but that is an effect having to do with questions other than simply unity as such; and just as surely a novel may deal at greater length with dynamic actions than a story, but there are ways in which a story may handle changes within its own sphere. Most of these principles, in brief, are too prescriptive. In order to understand how and why a short story gets to be short, therefore, I would like to propose a way of answering these questions which will apply to all examples of the type without prescribing beforehand what the characteristics of that type should be.

A story may be short, to begin with a basic distinction, for either or both of two fundamental reasons: the material itself may be of small compass; or the material, being of broader scope, may be cut for the sake of maximizing the artistic effect. The first reason has to do with distinctions as to the *object of* representation, while the second with distinctions as to the *manner* in which it is represented. We will thus discuss the size of the action (which may be large or small, and is not to be confused with the size of the *story,* which may be short or long), and its static or dynamic structure; and then the number of its parts which may be included or omitted, the scale on which it may be shown, and the point of view from which it may be told. A story may be short in terms of any one of these factors or of any combination, but for the sake of clarity and convenience we shall discuss them separately and give cross-references where necessary.

Elder Olson has provided us with a useful set of terms for discussing the question of size with some degree of clarity and precision.[2] A *speech,* he says, contains the continuous verbal utterance of a single character in a closed situation; the speaker is either talking to himself without interruption (soliloquy), or, if there are others present they neither reply nor make entrances and exits while he speaks (monologue). This is the kind of action shown in most short poems commonly called "lyric," as in Marvell's "To His Coy Mistress," for example, or Keats's "On First Looking Into Chapman's Homer," and many many others. A *scene* includes the continuous chain of utterance engendered between two or more speakers as one replies to the other (dialogue) in a closed situation, while an *episode* contains two or more such scenes centering around one main incident. A *plot,* finally, is a system of two or more such episodes. And a short story may conceivably encompass an action of any such size.

Naturally, a large action, such as the plot of *Great Expectations,* although unified in terms of its overall size, will contain smaller subactions, such as speeches, scenes, and episodes, unified in terms of *their* particular sizes; and these smaller subactions may be and often are detachable for certain purposes, as when an episode, for example, is extracted from a larger work for inclusion in an anthology. Actions of different sizes, that is to say, dovetail the smaller into the larger. The point is, however, that a speech, scene, or episode which is designed in itself to serve as the unifying basis of a single complete work must be fully independent, whereas in a larger work it is only partially so, necessarily containing elements binding it to what has gone before and what is to come after.

Why an author makes a certain initial choice regarding size we can only guess, except that he probably senses that he has a whole and complete action in itself and that this will suffice as a basis for separate treatment. This is a matter, then, of the original conception, and all that we can say is that a writer chooses to treat actions of different sizes because he feels, either by habit or deliberate choice or intuition or some combination, that any given one embodies all that is relevant to his purpose. An action of any given size, then, may be whole and complete in itself, and the smaller the action, the shorter its presentation may be.

The relevant parts of an action which is whole and complete, therefore, include those incidents which are needed to bring about and then display whatever necessary or probable consequences the writer wants to show his protagonist enacting or undergoing, and such other incidents as may be useful in casting these in their proper light. The size of that action, then, will depend upon what he wants his protagonist to do or suffer and upon how far back, correspondingly, he must go in the protagonist's experience to find those causes which are both necessary and sufficient to motivate and make credible that action. Clearly, a dynamic action will call into play a larger number of causes than a static one, and a more inclusive change will require a longer chain of causes than a less inclusive one. An action of whatever size is thus whole and complete whenever the delicate interlinkage of causes and effects encompasses whatever is enough to make that action both understandable and likely.

The speech is best suited, obviously, to render a single moment or a brief succession of moments in any given chain of cause and effect. An immediate response, whether static or dynamic, to an immediate stimulus is the special province of lyric poetry. In Housman's "With Rue My Heart Is Laden," for example, the speaker responds with an expression of sorrow to the fact that many of his friends are now dead, while in Frost's "Stopping By Woods" the speaker responds to the mysterious attraction of the dark and snowy woods by first yielding to their temptation and then by resisting it. In the first we have a single but complete moment of lamentation, while in the second we have a longer but equally complete succession of moments during the course of which the speaker makes up his mind about something, in the sense of choosing between alternatives. Either way, these particular actions are inherently small, and whatever is needed to make them clear and likely may therefore be encompassed in a rather short space.

As a result, such actions are rarely treated in fiction, even short fiction. We all know that the devices of the poetic art are especially capable of handling this sort of thing in an intensified manner, and that narrative prose, being especially flexible, is much more suited to larger actions where more has to be shown. I do know of two such actions in fiction, but they are the exceptions which prove the rule. Dorothy Parker's "A Telephone Call" presents a young lady in the throes of anxious anticipation as she awaits her boyfriend's belated phone call. And that is all there is to it: as far as we are concerned here, the entire story comprises her interior soliloquy as she waits for the phone to ring. E. B. White's "The Door" similarly presents practically nothing but the continuous mental states of its one and only character—presented sometimes indirectly by way of narration and sometimes directly by way of interior soliloquy—who is shown in a state of uncertainty and frustration regarding the contradictory values of modern civilization.

To present a single scene is much more feasible in short fiction, although even here pure examples are not as common as one might think. The best and clearest specimen with which I am familiar is Hemingway's "Hills Like White Elephants," which shows a young American couple waiting in an isolated train station in the valley of the Ebro for the express from Barcelona. Except for the waitress who brings them drinks, the story encompasses only the single and continuous interchange of dialogue which occurs between the man and woman as they wait. The point of this story, which deals with a static situation, is, I think, to reveal to us by degrees the causes of the girl's plight, and through that to arouse our pity. Apparently unmarried, these two are on their way to get the girl an abortion. This is not, however, the source of the story's pathos; it lies, rather, in the fact that as the conversation progresses it becomes evident that her lover has no real feeling for her and her incipient need to extend their relationship to its normal fruition. Since that is all we need to know to get this particular effect, and since it can all be done within the bounds of a single conversation, that is all Hemingway had to show to unify this particular story.

And it is done, of course, with consummate skill. We read toward the end, for example: "He did not say anything but looked at the bags against the wall of the station. There were labels on them from all the hotels where they had spent nights." From this small detail we are allowed to infer worlds about the situation of this couple—the shallowness of their relationship, its rootlessness, its transiency. This allusion to the immediate past, although not formally a part of the whole action being shown (since the causes of the pathos are shown as the scene itself progresses), helps to place the situation in its proper light in the reader's mind. And notice how artfully it has been incorporated into the fabric of the present scene itself without authorial intrusion.

The episode is an even more commonly found size in the short story—indeed, its frequency may warrant our calling it the typical sort of action dealt with by this art. Hemingway's "Ten Indians," for example, contains five scenes centered around Nick's discovery of his Indian sweetheart's infidelity, his subsequent depression, and his final forgetfulness of his sorrow. He is, after all, rather young to allow heartbreak to affect him for more than a few hours at a time. This is a dynamic action involving changes in thought and feeling, and therefore requires—other things being equal—a larger action than a single scene for the establishing of its chain of cause and effect. It does, however, all take place within the span of a few hours and each of its scenes leads up to or away from a single central incident: (1) Nick is driving home late one afternoon from a Fourth of July celebration in town with the Garners and they kid him about his Indian girlfriend; (2) they arrive at the Garners, unload the wagon, and Nick strikes out for his own home; (3) Nick is walking home; (4) his father gives him supper and tells him how he saw Prudie "having quite a time" in the woods with another boy, causing Nick to feel bad; (5) Nick goes unhappily to bed, but awakens contentedly later in the night to the sound of the wind and the waves, having forgotten his sorrow.

Thus a scene or episode requires less space in the telling, other things being equal, than the plot.

Another question regarding size is whether the action involves a change, and if so, whether that change is major or minor, and simple or complex. I hope it is clear by now that a short story may be either static or dynamic, but, as we have seen, an action which is static normally requires fewer parts than one which is dynamic and will therefore normally be shorter in the telling. That is to say, a static story simply shows its protagonist in one state or another and includes only enough to reveal to the reader the cause or causes of which this state is consequence, while a dynamic story brings its protagonist through a succession of two or more states and thus must include the several causal stages of which these states are the consequences. Thus a static story will normally be shorter than a dynamic one.

Therefore, although not all short stories are static, most static actions are likely to be found in short stories—static situations expanded and elaborated to novel-length are comparatively rare (*Mrs. Dalloway* is an example). And there is a similar general correlation between static and dynamic actions and their various sizes. To achieve in fiction a change in the protagonist in an independent speech or scene is possible but not likely, and to extend a static situation through an entire independent episode or complete plot is also possible but equally unlikely. I would say, as a rule, that most static actions comprise a scene or a small episode.

Another example of a static story, in addition to "White Elephant" already discussed, is Sean O'Faoláin's "Sinners," in which a Catholic clergyman's mental anguish over the lies of a servant girl at confession is revealed. He is first shown twitching irritably at her stories during the confession, and then crying out in positive vexation later when he happens to overhear her admitting her lies at confession to her mistress. His emotional state is announced, as it were, in the first phase of the story, and confirmed in the second phase (because of transitions there are slightly more than two scenes here). Thus the reader is made to see his frustration, and then to understand it as having ample justification. And, in order to achieve this effect, the writer showed as much as he needed, two scenes or so, and no more.

Of course, he could have continued on with this story to show us the canon going through a subsequent change in feeling for the better, in which case he would have had to introduce a whole new line of causes working in that direction, and thus could have lengthened it; but if he had merely gone on with the same sort of thing, he would have blundered in exceeding the needs of his effect. It is this effect and the amount of action required to achieve it which determine the shortness of this story, when considered in itself as an independent work.

"Francis Macomber," "Barn Burning," "How Beautiful With Shoes," "Babylon Revisited," and "The Death of Ivan Ilyich" are short stories which comprise, on the other hand, dynamic actions. In the first, a cowardly man becomes finally courageous in the face of danger; in the second, a young boy decides to oppose at last his father's vindictive destruction of their landlord's property; in the third, an ignorant mountain girl becomes aware that man can be more than an animal; in the fourth, a reformed drunkard is frustrated temporarily in his plans to regain his estranged daughter; and in the fifth, a dying man sees his empty life truthfully for the first time. But there is a difference regarding magnitude even among dynamic actions, for all but the last are minor changes, not in the sense that they are unimportant or that their consequences are not serious or far-reaching, but rather in the sense that they call into play and require for their representation only one phase of their protagonists' lives. Thus a minor change will normally require less space than a major one.

Here again there may be a general correlation between inclusiveness and the size of an action, for most minor changes will involve but an episode, while a major change will involve a complete plot. In this sense, "Ilyich" has more in common with *Great Expectations* than with the other stories just mentioned; indeed, it even covers more aspects of its protagonist's life than the Dickens novel. Some episodes, then, are static, and some are dynamic, but plots tend almost always to be dynamic. And one of the differences between a short story plot and a novel plot need not, as we shall see below, be a difference in the intrinsic size of their actions but rather in the manner in which their actions are shown. In this sense, "Ilyich" is of course much closer in length to a short story than to a novel.

On the other hand, there is no reason why an action covering several episodes may not involve merely a minor change. We have thus to distinguish, on the basis of inclusiveness, minor and major plots (and I suppose an episode may deal with a major change, but I do not think this is likely). Fitzgerald points to this distinction as he narrates the experiences of Dexter Green in "Winter Dreams": "It is with one of those denials [the mysterious prohibitions in which life indulges] and not with his career as a whole that this story deals.'' And again, toward the end of the story: ''This story is not his biography, remember, although things creep into it which have nothing to do with those dreams he had when he was young. We are almost done with them and with him now.'' Fitzgerald is saying, in effect, that this particular story finds its unity in treating only as many episodes as are required to show the reader the causes of Dexter's infatuation with Judy Jones and his subsequent disillusionment in her and the youthful possibilities she stands for in his mind, and that Dexter's other experiences (probably his business ventures and the like) are not particularly relevant thereto. He has guided himself, in consequence, largely by this original choice in matters of where to begin and end, and how much to include and omit. It is this limitation as to what phases of the protagonist's life are relevant to a given change which accounts for the shortness of this story.

The action of *The Great Gatsby,* on the other hand, although it is strikingly similar in its general outlines, because it deals with Gatsby's entire life, is a major plot. The obsession of Gatsby with Daisy and what she represents to him, that is to say, consumes all aspects of his career, and indeed costs him his very life at the end. The disillusionment of Gatsby, therefore, cannot be understood except in terms of his life as a whole, and that is why his story takes longer to tell than Dexter's. To have added Dexter's other interests to ''Winter Dreams'' would have been just as bad an artistic mistake as to have omitted Gatsby's from *The Great Gatsby:* the former would have resulted in irrelevance, while the latter would have caused a lack of clarity. Indeed, some critics of the novel have argued that it is too short even as it is to produce the requisite sense of probability or necessity in the reader, but that is quite another matter. (A rather different complaint has been raised against *For Whom the Bell Tolls,* which seems to some critics too *long* in proportion to the size of its action.)

There is a second difference regarding magnitude among dynamic actions which cuts across the one just examined between major and minor changes. A simple change brings its protagonist gradually from one state to another without reversals and is thus, since it calls into play only a single line of causation, a smaller action than a complex change, which brings its protagonist from one state into another and then into a third state opposite from the second, and which thus calls into play several lines of causation. The former, having consequently fewer parts, may be shorter in the telling.

All of the dynamic actions discussed so far are examples of the complex type, while Conrad's "An Outpost of Progress" illustrates a simple change. The moral characters of Kayerts and Carlier, weak and shallow to begin with, deteriorate swiftly and surely when brought to the acid test of prolonged and intimate contact "with pure unmitigated savagery" in the heart of Africa. If a short story can deal with the development of character, it can also deal, apparently, with its degeneration. It is interesting to contrast this story with "The Heart of Darkness," for there, in making Kurtz a paragon of moral character *before* his surrender to the abyss, Conrad set himself a much harder job. But he also achieved more vivid results, because if the fall of Kayerts and Carlier is more probable, it is also by the same token less interesting. The second story, however, is almost three times longer than the first (the great length of "The Heart of Darkness," incidentally, may also be explained in terms of its ruminative narrator—a topic to which we shall return below).

Thus, because it requires more "doing," a dynamic action tends to be longer than a static one; a major change, because it includes perforce more aspects of the protagonist's life, tends to be longer than a minor change; and a complex change, because it has more parts, tends to be longer than a simple one. But our principles must be continually qualified at every point because, as we shall see, we are dealing with a set of independent variables. A story which should be long in one way may actually be short in another; a story involving a major change, for example, which should be longer than one involving a minor change, all other things being equal, may actually turn out to be shorter because those other things are not equal.

A short story may be short, then, because its action is inherently small. But, as has been indicated, a story may encompass a larger action and still be short. If a writer has decided to show a plot, that is to say, he has a further option as to the manner in which he shall do so. And here he will be guided by his desire to maximize the vividness of his effect on the one hand, and to achieve that effect with the greatest economy of means on the other. He may decide, to begin with, that although a given part of his plot is relevant, he may best omit it and leave it to inference.

Since this question of selection can be discussed only in terms of how much of the whole action is put before the reader, and since we have defined "whole action" only generally, it behooves us to pause long enough to fill in our conceptions here. A whole action is, as we have seen, an action of a certain size—whether a speech, scene, episode, or plot—containing whatever is relevant to bringing the protagonist by probable. or necessary stages from the beginning, through the middle, and on to the end of a given situation.

The question now under examination concerns how many of these parts are actually shown to the reader and how many are merely alluded to or left to inference. In Steinbeck's "Flight," for example, a young and hitherto rather shiftless boy, as a result of his first visit alone to the city, is forced to prove himself a man—even to the point of facing death bravely. In the actual telling of the story, however, Steinbeck chose to omit the boy's trip to Monterey entirely, bringing it in only later when the boy returns and tells his mother what happened there before he sets out for the mountains.

We are dealing with a complex dynamic action: what are the parts required for a such an action to achieve its proper effect?

A complex change involves bringing the protagonist from one state to another by means of a reversal. What is required for clarity and belief, therefore, is (1) a precipitating cause to bring him into his first state, (2) a counterplot action to represent the consequences of that state, (3) an inciting cause which will serve to bring him out of the counterplot and on toward the opposite state, (4) a progressive action to represent him in the process of change; and (5) a culmination where the process is completed.[3] A simple change, as we have seen, involves bringing the protagonist from one state to another without a reversal, and therefore requires only the last three parts outlined above. And similar principles regarding selection may be applied to static actions in terms of the single states and relevant causes which they reveal.

Let us see how this scheme works for "Flight": (1) the boy is sent to Monterey for medicine by his mother; (2) he dons his father's hat and rides his father's saddle, boasting of his newfound manhood, and in Monterey drinks too much wine and gets into a fight; (3) he kills a man and must now either face the consequences like a man or run and hide "like a chicken"; (4) he returns home, tells his mother what happened, prepares himself for his journey, and suffers untold hardship for four days among the mountains; and (5) he dies finally with honor by facing, in his last extremity, his pursuers and accepting their vengeance. Most of phase two and all of three are omitted. Why?

We may say in the first place that, because probability demands that the protagonist tell his mother what happened anyway, Steinbeck simply acted in the interests of economy by avoiding repetition. That, however, is a rather mechanical explanation, although pertinent enough in its own way. More importantly, we may infer that Steinbeck intended to leave us with feelings of mingled pity and admiration for this boy as his story unfolds—pity for his suffering and death, and admiration for the noble manner in which he suffers and dies. This being the case, we may infer further that he left out most of the counterplot and the inciting incident because, in his effort to arouse our sympathies, he wanted consciously to avoid showing us his protagonist acting senselessly, without thought, and fatefully. By omitting these portions he also impresses us more vividly with the startling contrast between immaturity and maturity in his protagonist's behavior from the time he leaves in the morning till the time he returns at night. He is thus free to concentrate the greater portion of the reader's attention upon the boy's suffering and nobility rather than upon his rashness and immaturity. We must still *know,* however, what happened in Monterey, why the boy is taking to the mountains, and in what light to regard these events. And this we get from the boy's narration to his mother: the very fact that he tells her without hesitation and evasion is a sign of his real manhood. He was insulted, and so he killed before he knew what he was doing. Thus his ultimate death is made acceptable on the one hand and admirable on the other.

An instructive contrast to Steinbeck's wisdom in this matter is provided by a television adaptation of this story which I happened to see some time ago. Faced with wholly different technical problems, the television writer sought to enlarge his script not only by including those parts of the action which were left out of the original but also by elaborating upon and expanding them. The young boy was shown in Monterey—it was fiesta time and he got mixed up with a girl—and we see him getting insulted and killing his man. The fiesta allowed the insertion (intrusion would be a better word) of some dance productions as well as of some flicker of romantic interest. The flight itself was handled as honestly as possible, but even there the limitations of the medium necessitated the awkward device of having the boy talk to himself as he suffered, since he was, of course, alone and the fictional narrator was denied his function. The overall effect was distracting, to say the least: the only really relevant parts are the insult and the murder, so that the dancing and the girl, even though they were trumped up as the cause of his being insulted, simply came to nothing in terms of the rest of the story, and even with the insult and the murder it was quite upsetting actually to see our young hero draw blood; and the subsequent effort to elicit our sympathies for his suffering in the mountains was correspondingly vitiated. Perhaps because of the brevity of the original and its corresponding dependence upon narrative flexibility, the dramatized version of "Flight" was doomed from the outset.

The point to be made here is that a story may be short not because its action is inherently small, but rather because the author has chosen—in working with an episode or plot—to omit certain of its parts. In other words, an action may be large in size and still be short in the telling because not all of it is there. These gaps may be at the beginning of the action, somewhere along the line of its development, at the end, or some combination. Correspondingly, an action may be longer in the telling because more than its relevant parts are included.

Once he has decided what parts, of those which are relevant, he will include, the writer has a second option as to the scale on which he will show them. A given action, that is, may be made longer in the telling by expanding its parts, or shorter by contracting. What this implies is that, of all the things which actually "occur' or are present in a given scene—such as spoken dialogue, interior soliloquy, gesture, physical movement, clothing, and background setting—he may unfold them step by step or he may sum them up and mention only the high points. The contracted scale abstracts retrospectively from the event what is needed to advance the story and presents it in a condensed manner, while the expanded scale tries to give the illusion that the whole thing is being shown directly and in detail even as it happens. The contracted scale tends to cover a long timespan of action in a relatively short space, while the expanded scale tends to cover a short timespan in a relatively long space. And all this is, of course, actually a question of degree.

Flexibility, however, is one of the prime virtues of the fictional medium, and most narratives, whether long or short, vary the scale of presentation to suit the effect. Economy and vividness guide the writer here as before, but now the principle of proportion also comes into play. Those parts of the action which are more important than the others—and this, of course, will be related in each case to the effect intended—should naturally be emphasized by means of an expanded representation, and those which are less important should be condensed.

Although the amount of fictional time covered in the action has, as we shall see, no necessary connection with the length of its treatment, we can say that there is a general correlation, and that a writer who deals with actions covering a small timespan will normally choose the lesser magnitudes within which to work. The rule of economy tells the writer that, if the substance of his story takes place within the space of an hour, then a single scene will do the job. Likewise, if it covers several hours, a day, or a week, then an episode will be called for; and if it covers months or years, then a plot is needed. Joyce's *Ulysses,* however, reverses this correlation by expanding a single day into a full-length novel comprising many episodes, which merely emphasizes once again that we are dealing with a set of independent variables.

Tolstoy's "Death of Ivan Ilyich," on the other hand, is as good an example of a whole and full-sized plot condensed down to the length of a short story—albeit a rather long one—as can be found. It contains twelve numbered sections of varying lengths and, with some backtracking, takes its protagonist all the way from his childhood to his death in late middle age, and includes his schooling, courtship, marriage, career, and children. The whole action culminates in Ivan's first and final awareness, as he dies, of the reality of death and consequently of the hollowness of his entire life up to that point. Clearly, in order for this change to strike the reader with the proper intelligibility and force, Ivan's entire life has to be shown. The impact, that is to say, of Ivan's discovery depends for its point upon a knowledge of how his life has been lived previously and in terms of what values and attitudes.

But "Ivan Ilyich" is short (relatively) because, although the whole plot and more is shown, it is shown largely on a condensed scale. Likewise *Ulysses,* although it covers so much smaller a timespan, is so much longer because its action is expanded to the last detail (apparently).

Economy is still the general principle in these cases, however. Even though Ivan's whole life must be shown, it is of such a repetitive and shallow character (which is exactly the point, of course) that to have shown it on a full scale would have bored the reader to extinction— although Tolstoy naturally does represent the more important parts of his plot on an expanded scale. Joyce, too, did what he had to do to get his effect, although it is of an altogether different sort. Since the work turns on the ironic contrast between man as he is and man as he would be, it is exactly the meanness and triviality of daily life which Joyce must emphasize. It follows, therefore, that an almost infinite expansion serves Joyce's purpose but would have hampered Tolstoy in the achievement of his.

Another instructive contrast between the two extremes is found in comparing "Ivan Ilyich," which utilizes, as we have seen, a high degree of contraction, with "White Elephants," which is almost as expanded as a single scene between two people covering thirty minutes or so can get. And the reasons for this difference should be clear by now: Tolstoy has a large action to show, but most of it is important only as it throws light upon the final few scenes; while Hemingway has only one scene to show, and show it he does. Thus a story may be short, even if it encompasses a large action, because much of its action is best shown on a contracted scale.

We may consider, finally, how the choice of a point of view is related to the question of length.[4] If a writer decides, for example, to allow his narrator complete omniscience, then several things will naturally follow. His narrator may editorialize, as in *Tom Jones* or *War and Peace,* and this of course will add significantly to the bulk of the work. Or, given omniscience, his narrator may analyze his characters' motives and states of mind at some length, and such commentary and exposition will also increase the bulk of the work. This is the reason why Mann's "Disorder and Early Sorrow" seems to cover so much more ground at first sight than it actually turns out to encompass upon close study: although it takes almost two hours to read, it actually includes an action whose timespan runs only from afternoon to evening of one day. Because, however, the action is shown through a screen of exposition and commentary regarding the Professor's states of mind, and even though the external action itself is rarely, as a consequence, shown directly and on an expanded scale, the story—although short—is a lengthy one in proportion to the time covered in the action.

Omniscience involves, on the other hand, features favorable to brevity. That is, a narrator who exists over and above the action itself may exercise, as they say, wide discretionary powers in matters of scale and selection. Because he is bound by no "mortal" limitations, he can manipulate his material at will. Thus he may shift the scene of the action in time and place, and, more importantly for the question in hand, may omit and/or sum up parts of the action which do not merit more explicit and detailed treatment. In the long run, then, omniscience is characterized by its flexibility and is equally at home in novels and short stories alike.

A character narrator may also be given to commentary and speculation, as in Marlow in "Heart of Darkness," and this too may add to the bulk of the work. The dramatic point of view similarly, because it is committed by definition to an expanded scale, as on the stage, tends toward length. Thus, an author who chooses the dramatic method for a short story had best work with an action of small size to begin with or, dealing with a larger one, omit certain of its parts.

To sum up, a story may be short because its action is intrinsically small; or because its action, being large, is reduced in length by means of the devices of selection, scale, and/or point of view. No one can tell in advance that, if a story is short, it is short because it has a certain number of words, or because it has more unity, or because it focuses upon culmination rather than development. All we can do, upon recognizing its shortness, is to ask how and why, keeping balanced simultaneously in our minds the alternative ways of answering these questions and their possible combinations. And then we may win increased understanding and hence appreciation of the specific artistic qualities of this curious and splendid but vastly underrated art.

1. Cf. R. S. Crane, "The Concept of Plot and the Plot of *Tom Jones*," *Critics and Criticism: Ancient and Modern,* ed. R. S. Crane (Chicago, 1952) pp. 616–647; and Theodore A. Stroud, "A Critical Approach to the Short Story," *Journal of General Education,* IX (1956), 91–100. The present essay may be read as a companion to Stroud's.

2. See "An Outline of Poetic Theory," *Critics and Criticism,* pp. 546–566, esp. p. 560.

3. Similar terms and concepts are used by Paul Goodman in his *Structure of Literature* (Chicago, 1954), but in a slightly different way. I had arrived at my own position independently, before I read this brilliant but puzzling book.

4. See my "Point of View in Fiction: The Development of a Critical Concept," *PMLA,* LXX (1955), 1160–1184, for a full-length analysis of the varieties of this device.

The Short Story and the Novel

A DEFINITION of the short story as a distinct and autonomous literary *genre,* with its own special rules and laws, may well be impossible, for, among other things, the short story has an even wider sweep than the novel. It extends from the French-style *récit,* or long short story, whose characters and situations are almost those of a novel, down to the prose-poem, the sketch and the lyrical fragment. Yet when we attempt to make a rough definition of the short story we cannot help considering it in relation to its big brother, rather than in isolation: the short story is not a novel. When thus contrasted with the novel some constant characteristics do appear, and though they lack the character of laws and cannot be quoted as rules, they explain how the short story does in fact constitute a *genre* in its own right and has nothing to do with the novel or any other narrative composition of similar length.

Meanwhile it is worth noting that short story writers, accustomed as they are to expressing themselves within the limits and in accord with the rules of the *genre* however badly defined these may be, find it very difficult to write really good novels. Consider, for example, the two greatest short story writers of the end of the nineteenth century, Maupassant and Chekhov. These have both left us enormous collections of short stories which give an incomparable picture of the life in France and Russia of their time. Quantitatively speaking, Maupassant's world is wider and more varied than the world of Flaubert, his contemporary; Chekhov's more so than Dostoievsky's, his immediate predecessor. Indeed, all things considered, we can say that while Maupassant and Chekhov so to speak exhaust the variety of situations and characters of the society of their time, Flaubert and Dostoievsky are rather like those solitary birds that restlessly and loyally repeat the same significant cry. In the last analysis all they did was to write the same novel over and over again, with the same situations and the same characters.

Some centuries earlier Boccaccio, the greatest short story writer of all time, exhibited a similar variety and richness as compared with Dante. If we only had *The Divine Comedy* with its static Gothic figures carved in *bas relief* round and round the monument of the poem, we should certainly know much less than we do about the life of Florence and Italy and the Middle Ages in general. Whereas Boccaccio's depiction of it is incomparable. Unlike *The Divine Comedy,* the *Decameron* presents everything in function of a complete illustration of this life, with no end in view other than that of extolling its richness and variety.

But when Maupassant and Chekhov tried their hand at novels or even *récits* they were far less gifted and convincing than with the short story. Some of Chekhov's novel-like stories, and Maupassant's *Bel Ami,* make us think less of novels than of blown-up, lengthened and watered-down short stories—rather as some frescoes by modern paint-ers are really no more than easel paintings enlarged out of all propor-tion. In Chekhov's and Maupassant's novels and long short stories we feel the lack of that something that makes a novel, even a bad novel, a novel. Chekhov dilutes his concentrated lyrical feeling with superfluous plots lacking intrinsic necessity, while Maupassant gives us a series of disjointed pictures, seen through a telescope, and only held together by the presence of the protagonist. Indeed it is noteworthy that the very qualities that made these two great as short story writers become defects as soon as they tackle the novel. Someone may point out that we are dealing with different techniques, and Chekhov and Maupassant failed to master the technique of the novel. But this does not solve the problem, it merely states it differently. Technique is the form taken by the writer's inspiration and personality. Chekhov's and Maupassant's technique is unsuited to the novel because they could only say what they wanted to say in the short story, and not vice versa. So we are back where we started from. What is the outstanding distinction between the novel and the short story?

The principal and fundamental difference lies in the ground-plan or structure of the narrative. Of course all sorts of novels are being written, and will go on being written, with a variety of bizarre and experimental structures—which seems to give the lie to the validity of what we have just said. Nevertheless the classical novelists, those whose works have created the *genre*—men like Flaubert, Dostoievsky, Stendhal, Tolstoy, and later Proust, Joyce and Mann—go to prove that some common characteristics do exist in spite of this. The most important of these is what we could call ideology, that is the skeleton of the theme from which the flesh of the story takes its form. In other words the novel has a bone structure holding it together from top to toe, whereas the short story is, so to speak, boneless. Naturally the novel's ideology is not precise, preconstituted, or reducible to a thesis, just as the skeleton is not introduced into the human body by force when we are adults but has grown along with the body's other parts. It is this ideology that differentiates a novel from a short story and, conversely, it is the absence of bone structure that makes a short story not a novel. It is the ideology, however imprecise and contradictory it may be, with all the contradictions that are to be found in life itself (the novelist is not a philosopher, but a witness), that begets the things that make a novel a novel.

The first of these is usually called plot, or the changing succession of events that constitute the story of the novel. It can sometimes happen that the plot is an end in itself, but this is never the case with good novelists; suffice it to say that this obtains most often in detective stories where mechanical device plays the major part. With good novelists, real novelists, the plot is nothing but the sum total of the ideological themes as they conflict and merge with each other in their various ways. So the plot is made up not only of intuitions of feelings (as in the short story) but primarily of ideas expressed poetically but well defined. The plot, for example, of *Crime and Punishment* is made up of the criss-cross, the contrast, the clash and the conflicting claims of the various ideological themes presented to us by the author from the first page: the theme of Raskolnikoff, the theme of Sonia, the theme of Svidrigailoff, the theme of Marmeladoff, the theme of the judge Porphyry, and so on. All these characters are autonomous and entirely human, but they are also ideas and it is not difficult to extract from them the ideological meanings they carry, a thing it would be quite impossible to do with the characters in a short story by Chekhov or Maupassant. The plot of *Crime and Punishment* is born of these themes embodied in characters, in other words from the grandiose ground-plan of this exemplary novel which enables Dostoievsky to proceed for five hundred pages without ever giving the impression that he is either spinning out or watering down events—the impression that we get in Chekhov's longer stories and in Maupassant's novel. The twists and turns of the plot, its surprises, its contradictions, its *coups de scène,* even its *deus ex machinas,* are never due to extrinsic interventions by the author or to what we could call the inexhaustible resources of life, but to the dialectical and necessary development of the ideological themes. From one point of view nothing could be more misleading than to say that the novel competes with the civil register. It would be more accurate to say this of the short story which passes in review a large variety of characters who have individual characteristics only. The truth is that many novels compete, not with the civil register, but with a philosophical treatise or a moral essay.

Besides the plot, the quality of the characters, too, stems from the presence or absence of ideology. Andreuccio da Perugia, Boule de Suif, the boy of the steppe, are short story characters; Raskolnikoff, Julien Sorel, Madame Bovary, Prince Andrey, Bloom, Proust's 'Je', and the protagonist of Mann's *Doktor Faust* are novel characters. Those familiar with the short stories and novels in which the above-mentioned characters operate cannot fail to perceive the difference between the first group and the second. The first are caught at a particular moment, within narrow limits of time and space, and act in function of a determined event which forms the object of the short story. Whereas the second have a long, ample and tortuous development that unites biographical with ideological data, and they move in a time and space that are both real and abstract, immanent and transcendent. Characters in short stories are the product of lyrical intuitions, those in novels are symbols. Obviously a character from a novel could never be compressed within the narrow confines of a short story, just as a character from a short story could never be drawn out to the dimensions of a novel without an alteration in his nature.

So the short story is distinguished from the novel in the following ways: non-ideological characters of whom we get foreshortened and tangential glimpses in accord with the needs of an action limited in time and place; a very simple plot, even nonexistent in some short stories— when they become prose poems—and in any case one that gets its complexity from life and not from the orchestration of some kind of ideology; psychology in function of facts, not of ideas; technical procedures intended to provide in synthesis what, in the novel, needs long and extended analysis.

Of course all this has little to do with the principal qualities of the short story—I mean that indefinable and inexpressible charm of narration experienced both by the writer and the reader. An exceedingly complex charm, deriving from a literary art which is unquestionably purer, more essential, more lyrical, more concentrated and more absolute than that of the novel. Whereas, by way of compensation, the novel provides a deeper, more complex, more dialectical, more polyhedric and more metaphysical representation of reality than the short story.

So, while the short story comes near to being a lyric, the novel as we have said, is more likely to rub shoulders with the essay or the philosophical treatise.

ELIZABETH BOWEN

The Faber Book of Modern Short Stories

THE SHORT story is a young art: as we now know it, it is the child of this century. Poetic tautness and clarity are so essential to it that it may be said to stand at the edge of prose; in its use of action it is nearer to drama than to the novel. The cinema, itself busy with a technique, is of the same generation: in the last thirty years the two arts have been accelerating together. They have affinities—neither is sponsored by a tradition; both are, accordingly, free; both, still, are self-conscious, show a self-imposed discipline and regard for form; both have, to work on, immense matter—the disoriented romanticism of the age. The new literature, whether written or visual, is an affair of reflexes, of immediate susceptibility, of associations not examined by reason: it does not attempt a synthesis. Narrative of any length involves continuity, sometimes a forced continuity: it is here that the novel too often becomes invalid. But action, which must in the novel be complex and motivated, in the short story regains heroic simplicity.

An art having behind it little tradition is at once impetuous and halting, and is very affectable. Its practitioners are still tentative, watching each other: some positive and original mind is wanted to renew impetus, or to direct it. The short story as an art has come into being through a disposition to see life in a certain way. But the writer himself may stay unaware of this new disposition if he has not already seen it made evident elsewhere in art: only the rare writer does not look for a precedent. In England, the limitations of narrative prose with its *longueurs,* its conventions dangerous to truth, had appeared for a long time to be impassable: oblique narration, cutting (as in the cinema), the unlikely placing of emphasis, or symbolism (the telling use of the object both for its own sake and as an image) were unknown. The short story was once the condensed novel; it needed a complex subject and depended for merit on the skill with which condensation had been effected. The short stories of James and Hardy show, in their excellence, a sober virtuosity: they are *tours de force* by practised executants, side-issues from the crowded imagination. They show, *qua* the short story, no urgent æsthetic necessity; their matter does not dictate their form. Their shortness is not positive; it is nonextension. They are great architects' fancies, little buildings on an august plan. They have no emotion that is abrupt and special; they do not give mood or incident a significance outside the novelist's power to explore. Their very excellence made them a dead end: they did not invite imitation or advance in any way a development in the short story proper. That impetus that it needed, the English short story had to get from abroad. Rumour, the translation and easier circulation of foreign books, also a widening curiosity, brought Tchehov and Maupassant into the English view.

The influences of two foreign masters on an affectable new form have necessarily run counter to one another. Tchehov stands (or stands with us) for an emancipation of faculties, for a romantic distension of the form of the story to let in what might appear inchoate or nebulous. Maupassant stands for astringency, iron relevance. Tchehov opened up for the writer tracts of emotional landscape; he made subjectivity edit and rule experience and pull art, obliquely, its way. His work was a system of irritations beautified; he secreted over the grit inside his shell. His hero was the sub-man; he crystallized frustration, inertia, malaise, vacancy, futile aspiration, shy or sly pretentiousness. He dragged that involuntary sub-life of the spirit up into the impassive light of art. The suffering, too-intelligent and submissive bourgeois is typified in him; he came of that class which fosters its own annihilation, and which revolution cannot obliterate. He was, in art's sense, a political force in art, revolting against the aristocratic rejection of matter for manner's sake. He made his own manner, commanding it so completely as to suggest less discipline than it had—and this has, on the whole, made him a dangerous influence. He has been made to sponsor self-concern, license, fortuity.

Maupassant was the born popular writer, battered by Flaubert into austerity. His themes were simple: lust, cruelty, money and that sort of rose-pink fancy that has such a charnel underneath. He transcribed passions in the only terms possible—dispassionate understatement. There was an uninterrupted communication between his thought and his senses; his sort of erotic nearness to what he wrote of gave him a cautious language that never exceeds art. He saw life in a glare; life composed itself for him into pictures in primary colours, outlines in black chalk. His writing was energetic, ruthless, nervous and plain. Tchehov sustained with his subject a sensitive, sometimes painful, flirtation: Maupassant touched nothing of which he was not the prey. His hardness and capability made him that rare thing—the first-rate *unliterary* writer.

Till lately, Maupassant has repelled the bulk of the English, or has been read for reasons not connected with art. His work shows unhuman fire, like an animal's eye; his uncomplexity is not sympathetic. His finish appeared to have a touch of the shop about it, a faded smartness not yet fully 'period.' He had not been taught impersonality for nothing: the artist without tricks very seldom starts a school. Tchehov's cloudy detachment, charged with pity, has been more acceptable here; his deceptive looseness got him imitators. Tchehov started in England a new, a prose romanticism, romanticism of suburbs and provinces. He influenced at second-hand, through the work of Katherine Mansfield, a group of writers who did not know him directly, or only turned to him later. This group is now in turn exerting an influence, so that Tchehov may be indirectly copied by writers who do not read, or intend to read, him at all. It is arguable that, had Tchehov not been translated and first given his vogue by a few eclectics, a large body of English stories might have remained unwritten. He was a great incentive, but should not be a model. He has been devoutly and unconsciously parodied; we have suffered outpourings of minor dismay, or mediocre sentiment. From the dregs of his influence our most vital short story writers now seem to revolt.

This cult of Tchehov has had, however, its natural boundaries. The Irish Sea makes a bigger break in sentiment than the Atlantic, and Irish and American writers of the short story have—for all their differences in temper—strong common qualities. Extraverted coldness in art, objectivity, may be the fruit of a life that is, or has been lately, physically exciting or uncertain, life that is quick, rough or lived at high nervous tension, in which either sexual or political passion makes society unsafe. Precipitate feeling makes for hard form in art. The younger Irish writers have almost all carried arms; American civilization keeps the Americans, nervously, armed men: fact there overtops fantasy. There is a state of living in which events assault the imagination, stunning it: such a state of living enforces its own, a now no longer unique, literature. Amazement—involuntary and to a degree fathomed—is part of poetry. In the short story, semi-poetic, amazement is not only not fathomed but not stated; but has to be made evident. The writer must so strip fact of neutralizing elements as to return to it, and prolong for it, its first power: what was in life a half-second of apprehension must be perpetuated. The extraverted short story—bare of analysis, sparse in emotional statement—is the formula for, never the transcript of, that amazement with which poetry deals. The particular must be given general significance. Narration is bound to be exact and impassive. This method, which was Maupassant's, is now in the hands of the Irish, the Americans, some of the younger English. Liam O'Flaherty, Hemingway have perfected it. It has dangers, which are now becoming apparent—style may be too much deflated, feeling is threatened with an oversimplification that makes it savage and dull.

Properly, this collection—which invites the reader to study the development of the short story in English since, roughly, 1910, to notice its variations and watch its trend—ought to include the work of Americans. The superiority, in general, of the American short story to the British has been too eagerly claimed on the far side of the Atlantic, but this is not enough to make the claim invalid. The American level of workmanship is higher; also, to-day, from the American pen our used language starts with new vitality. The American story writer has as his matter a hybrid psychology, city life at once slick and macabre and a wide continent not yet at all fully explored by art—and he has the habit of travel. The inclusion, here, of American short stories would heighten the standard of the collection and make for a wider view. But it would mean the exclusion, to make space, of a number of English stories equally vital and serious, if not so finished in their carrying-out. Moreover, the best American writing is as positively American as French writing is French: its imposing foreignness must raise all sorts of issues not relevant to the study of English work. The English short story—however much it may have owed, initially, to abroad—must advance always inside the national limitations. Irish short stories are included because the tie between the two countries, however irksome, has made some kind of affinity, however artificial. On the Irish side, indignation has been fruitful; the long, hopeless, romantic quarrel has bred literature. And in Ireland the English language is not yet stale.

Protection in art is only justified by a fairly strong claim for the home product. Such a claim the stories here will have to substantiate. To select them was not easy. In this country, within the past fifteen years, the non-commercial or free short story—that is to say, the story unsuitable, not meant to be suitable, for the popular, well-paying magazines, and free, therefore, not to conform with so-called popular taste—has found a wider opening: it has come to have an eclectic vogue. Production in this department has consequently increased. But, unhappily, the free story is being fostered with less discrimination than good faith. It is too generally taken that a story by *being* non-commercial may immediately pretend to art. Emancipation from commercial conventions was excellent—but now a fresh set of conventions threatens to spring up and to prove as tyrannous, dangerous to living work. Too many free stories show, both in technique and subject, a desolating and nerveless similarity. The public gets slated by the free short story's promoters for not giving such stories a more grateful reception, or supporting the magazines in which they appear. But why should anyone tolerate lax, unconvincing or arty work—work whose idiom too often shows a touch of high-hat complacency? The commercial short story writer had his own, hard-learnt, competence: the new, non-commercial story, if it is to be important, should be able to make its way, any distance, on its intrinsic merits—it still has to be, in one sense or another, subsidized. Subsidy dishonours what ought to be, in the great sense, a popular art. At present, a very large number of free stories lack verisimilitude, are pompous, dissatisfying—they are not up to the mark. But what is the mark?

The mark is, the completeness, or spherical perfection, latent in any story that is projected rightly; a completeness to which any story having the germ of real life should be capable of expanding, but which too few reach—at an indefinable moment the writer's purpose slackens, or some adventitious emotion starts to deform the story. The first necessity for the short story, at the set out, is *necessariness*. The story, that is to say, must spring from an impression or perception pressing enough, acute enough, to have made the writer write. Execution must be voluntary and careful, but conception should have been involuntary, a vital fortuity. The sought-about-for subject gives the story a dead kernel, however skilfully words may have been applied: the language, being *voulu*, remains inorganic. Contrived, unspontaneous feeling makes for unquickened prose. The story should have the valid central emotion and inner spontaneity of the lyric; it should magnetize the imagination and give pleasure—of however disturbing, painful or complex a kind. The story should be as composed, in the plastic sense, and as visual as a picture. It must have tautness and clearness; it must contain no passage not æsthetically relevant to the whole. The *necessary* subject dictates its own relevance. However plain or lively or unpretentious be the manner of the story, the central emotion—emotion however remotely involved or hinted at—should be austere, major. The subject must have implicit dignity. If in the writer half-conscious awe of his own subject be lacking, the story becomes flooded with falseness, mawkishness, whimsicality or some ulterior spite. The plot, whether or not it be ingenious or remarkable, for however short a way it is to be pursued, ought to raise some issue, so that it may continue in the mind. The art of the short story permits a break at what in the novel would be the crux of the plot: the short story, free from the *longueurs* of the novel, is also exempt from the novel's conclusiveness—too often forced and false: it may thus more nearly than the novel approach æsthetic and moral truth. It can, while remaining rightly prosaic and circumstantial, give scene, action, event, character a poetic new actuality. It must have had, to the writer, moments of unfamiliarity, where it imposed itself.

The writer's imagination must operate in the world, whether factual or fantastic, that is most natural to it. The one nineteenth-century writer, in English, of the short story proper, Edgar Allan Poe, dealt almost wholly in fantasy: in England, in the same century, the much humbler F. Anstey, with a few little-known stories, followed. Since Poe's day, it has been the English rather than the Americans who have occupied the fantastic domain. Pure, objectified or projected fantasy (as opposed to private, escapist fantasy, or to *Bovaryisme*) stays, on the whole, with our older writers, or writers early in time, such as Richard Middleton, who died young by his own act. Rudyard Kipling and H. G. Wells, with some of their greatest stories, Walter de la Mare, E. M. Forster, Algernon Blackwood and M. R. James have each added to a terribly likely world, whose oddness has a super-rationality, which is waiting just at the edge of normal experience. Younger writers have, now and then, each projected his own ray into it. The fantasy story has often a literary beauty that is disarming; the one test one can apply is: does the *imagination* find this credible? Any crazy house against moonlight might, like the House of Usher, split right down to show the moon: there is assent at once, but no way to check up. Fancy has an authority reason cannot challenge. The pure fantasy writer works in a free zone: he has not to reconcile inner and outer images.

There is only one pure (or externalized) fantasy story in this book: the separate nature and problems of the fantasy story set it apart; also, the general trend of the short story has been, lately, towards inward, or, as it were, applied and functional fantasy, which does not depart from life but tempers it. Pure (as opposed to applied) fantasy has, it is true, reappeared in the apocalyptic writing of Dylan Thomas: the delirium or the dream. This may be another beginning. Up to now, however, and during most of the period this collection covers, writers have, rather, tended to explore and annotate different kinds of escape or of compensation. The retreat from fact that private fantasy offers has been as grateful in life as its variations are fascinating to art. Man has to live how he can: overlooked and dwarfed he makes himself his own theatre. Is the drama inside heroic or pathological? Outward acts have often an inside magnitude. The short story, within its shorter span than the novel's, with its freedom from forced complexity, its possible lucidness, is able, like the poetic drama, to measure man by his aspirations and dreads and place him alone on that stage which, inwardly, every man is conscious of occupying alone.

The Reading and Writing of Short Stories

1

EXPERIENCE teaches us that when we are in the act of writing we are alone and on our own, in a kind of absolute state of Do Not Disturb. And experience tells us further that each story is a specific thing, never a general thing—never. The words in the story we are writing now might as well never have been used before. They all shine; they are never smudged. Stories are *new* things, stories make words new; that is one of their illusions and part of their beauty. And of course the great stories of the world are the ones that seem new to their readers on and on, always new because they keep their power of revealing something.

But although all stories in the throes of being written seem new and although good stories are new and persist, there will always be some characteristics and some functions about them as old as time, as human nature itself, to keep them more or less alike, at least of a family; and there may be other things, undiscovered yet, in the language, in technique, in the world's body of knowledge, to change them out of our present recognition. Critics, historians, and scholars deal with these affairs—and keep good track of them—while for us, the practitioners, the writing of stories seems to simmer down—between stories—into some generalities that are worth talking about.

Between stories—yes, that's when we can talk.

I think we write stories in the ultimate hope of communication, but so do we make jelly in that hope. Communication and hope of it are conditions of life itself. Let's take that for granted, and not get sidetracked by excitement. We hope somebody will taste our jelly and eat it with even more pleasure than it deserves and ask for another helping— no more can we hope for in writing a story. Always in the back of our heads and in our hearts are such hopes, and attendant fears that we may fail—we do everything out of the energy of some form of love or desire to please. The writing of a story uses the *power* of this love or hope, of course, and not its simple, surface form such as comes out—rather nicely—in jelly-making.

During the writing of a story, all the energy we have is put to pressure and reaches a changed-over state—so as to act for the sole and concentrated purpose of making our work excellent and to the pattern of some preconceived idea we have of beauty. The diffusion of this energy will, in the long run, prevent our story from communicating, in the degree that it prevents it from being our own.

But the practical problems of the story at hand are, on the whole, minutiae. The little things that plague and absorb us in every story never let up. There, help is possible. And that they are little things explains, possibly, how it is that we can shed such problems so entirely once a story is done. Who remembers afterwards the nuisance of counting the children, or preparing the reader for the murder, or getting the moon in the right part of the sky? They aren't truly important problems, and patience is the answer—time and patience.

To get at general problems we have to go deeper—in fact, the deepest we can go—into the act of writing itself. The whole thing is subjective. All any of us can *know* about writing is what it seems like to us. It's not an imitative process.

Direct connection is all we have with short stories—reading and writing them. It is not ours to note influences, trace histories, and consider trends. We are in the thick of stories by being personally and directly concerned with them. It is from this close, unromantic, perhaps much less sure and much more passionate point of view, that we writers gaze at the art of the short story.

If we learn mostly little things from correction—from critics—do we learn the big things by doing? I think it the only way, but not an infallible way. That is, there is nothing that will guarantee our writing a better story next time than the one we have just finished. Some first stories remain a writer's best work. We work by the story—by the piece. The next story will always be a different thing. There are no two days alike—time moves. There are no two stories alike—*our* time moves. We were in one story and now we are in another—two worlds—and there are many more, though the thought neither helps nor hinders us any in the one where we now struggle.

2

How do we write a story? Our own way. Beyond that, I think it is hard to assign a process to it.

The mind in writing a story is in the throes of imagination, and it is not in the calculations of analysis. There is a Great Divide in the workings of the mind, shedding its energy in two directions: it creates in imagination, and it tears down in analysis. The two ways of working have a great way of worrying the life out of each other. But why can't they both go their ways in peace?

Let's not, to begin with, deny the powers and achievements of good criticism. That would be smug, ignorant, and blind. Story criticism can seem blind itself, when it is ingrown and tedious; on the other hand, it can see things in large wholes and in subtle relationships we should be only stupid not to investigate. It can illuminate even though, in the face of all its achievements, its business is not to tell *how*. There is the Great Divide.

I feel like saying as a friend, to beginning writers, Don't be unduly worried by the analyses of stories you may see in some textbooks or critical articles. They are brilliant, no doubt useful to their own ends, but should not be alarming, for in a practical sense they just do not bear in a practical way on writing. To use my own case, that being the only one I can rightly speak of, I have been baffled by analysis and criticism of some of my stories. When I see them analyzed—most usually, "reduced to elements"—sometimes I think, "This is none of me." Not that I am too proud to like being reduced, especially; but that I could not remember *starting* with those elements—with anything that I could so label. The fact that a story will reduce to elements, can be analyzed, does not necessarily mean it started with them—certainly not consciously. A story can start with a bird song.

Criticism, or more strictly, analysis, is an impossible way to learn how the story was written. Analysis is a one-way process, and is only good after the event. In the newsreel pictures when the dive is shown in reverse, a swimmer can come back out of the water; the splash is swallowed up, he rises in the air and is safe and dry back on the diving board. But in truth you can't come by way of analysis back to the starting point of inspiration; that's against some law of the universe, it might almost seem. I myself lack a scientific upbringing; I hear the arrow of time exists, and I feel quite certain, by every instinct, so does the arrow of creation.

Readers of Sir Arthur Eddington—who may be enjoyed even by a reader ill-equipped in science if the reader loves good literature—will remember he explains the term "entropy" as *becoming*. Our physical world is ever in the act of becoming, and not its opposite. You can't undo a dive, you can't put Humpty Dumpty together again or restore unshot the arrow to the bow. Mr. Eddington does not bother with the writing of short stories and does not say, but you can't analyze a story back to its beginning and truly find thereby what the story started out to do, what then modified and determined it, and what ever really made it a superior story and not just a good story. A story is not the same thing when it ends that it was when it began. Something happens—the writing of it. It *becomes*. And as a story becomes, I believe we as readers understand by becoming too—by enjoying.

Let's look at some short stories as writers of stories ourselves and people who like them; let's see a little how they are disposed, watch them in their motions, and enjoy them.

Luckily, we shall have none of the problems of *not* enjoying them. Putting a story in its place—we shall escape that. Putting a story in its place when its place has become the important thing means absolutely not giving over to the story. It also means taking oneself with proper seriousness, keeping close watch not to make a fool of oneself, and watching limbs, lest one go out on a few. Enjoying them, we can go out on many a limb. Yet there is really a tougher requirement for enjoying: flexibility and openness of the mind—of the pores, possibly. For heaven forbid we should feel disgrace in seeking understanding by way of pleasure.

We would be sure of this, I believe, if we asked ourselves, How would we wish a story of our own to be understood? By way of delight—by its being purely read, for the first fresh impact and the wonder attached; isn't this the honest answer? It seems to me too that almost the first hope we ever had, when we gave someone a story all fresh and new, was that the story would *read new*. And that's how we should read.

What bliss! Think how often this is denied us. That's why we think of childhood books so lovingly. But hasn't every writer the rightful wish to have his story so read? And isn't this wish implicit in the story itself? By reading secondhandedly, or obediently as taught, or by approaching a story without an open mind, we wrong its very first attribute—its uniqueness, with its sister attribute of freshness. We are getting to be old, jaded readers—instructed, advised readers, victims of summaries and textbooks; and if we write stories as victims of this attitude ourselves, what will happen to us? While we read and while we write, let's forget what we're being forever told and find the fresh world again—of enjoyment and pleasure and the story unspoiled, delighted in or hated for its own sake.

By enjoying, I don't mean to be *easy* on a story. Not all melted, the way William Saroyan at times requests readers to be. I mean only not to bother the story—not interrupt and interpret it on the side as if the conscience were at stake. To see it clear and itself, we must see it objectively.

After all, the constellations, patterns, we are used to seeing in the sky are purely subjective; it is because our combining things, our heroes, existed in the world almost as soon as we did that we were able long ago to see Perseus up there, and not a random scattering of little lights. Let's look at a particular story and see it solitary out in space, not part of some trend. It doesn't matter a bit for the moment who wrote it or when, or what magazine or book it appeared in or got rejected from, or how much or how little money the author got for it or whether he had an agent, or that he received letters in the mail when it was printed, saying, "It is found that your story does not reduce to the elements of a story." We're seeing this story as a little world in space, just as we can isolate one star in the sky by a concentrated vision.

3

THE first thing we notice about our story is that we can't really see the solid outlines of it—it seems bathed in something of its own. It is wrapped in an atmosphere. This is what makes it shine, perhaps, as well as what initially obscures its plain, real shape.

We are bearing in mind that the atmosphere in a story may be its chief glory—and for another thing, that it may be giving us an impression altogether contrary to what lies under it. The brightness may be the result of whizzing in a circle. Some action stories fling off the brightest clouds of obscuring and dazzling light, like ours here. Our penetrating look brings us the suspicion finally that this busy object is quite dark within, for all its clouds of speed, those primary colors of red and yellow and blue. It looks like one of Ernest Hemingway's stories, and it is.

Now a story behaves, it goes through motions—that's part of it. Some stories leave a train of light behind them, meteorlike, so that much later than they strike our eye we may see their meaning like an after-effect. These wildly careening stories are in many ways among the most interesting of all—the kind of story sometimes called apocalyptic. I think of Faulkner's stories as being not meteors but comets; in a way still beyond their extravagance and unexpectedness and disregard of the steadier laws of time and space, Faulkner's stories are cometlike in that they do have a wonderful course of their own: they reappear, in their own time they reiterate their meaning, and by reiteration show a whole further story over and beyond their single significance.

If we have thought of Hemingway's stories, then, as being bare and solid as billiard balls, so scrupulously cleaned of adjectives, of every unneeded word as they are, of being plain throughout as a verb in itself is plain, we may come to think twice about it. The atmosphere that cloaks D. H. Lawrence's stories is of sensation, which is a pure but thick cover, a cloak of self-luminous air, but the atmosphere that surrounds Hemingway's stories is just as thick and to some readers less illuminating. Action can be inscrutable, more than sensation can be. It can be just as voluptuous, too, just as vaporous, and much more desperately concealing.

So the first thing we see about a story is its mystery. And in the best stories, we return at the last to see mystery again. Every good story has mystery—not the puzzle kind, but the mystery of allurement. As we understand the story better, it is likely that the mystery does not necessarily decrease; rather it simply grows more beautiful.

Now, of what is this story composed, the one we're sighting? What is the plot, in other words?

E. M. Forster in his book on the novel makes the acute distinction between plot and narrative thread. A story is a "narrative of events arranged in their time-sequence. A plot is also a narrative of events, the emphasis falling on causality.'' With a plot, instead of keeping on asking, What next? we ask, Why?

Well, in Hemingway's story, which is ''Indian Camp,'' one of his early ones, Nick goes with his father, a doctor, to see a sick Indian woman. She is suffering in labor and the doctor operates on her without an anesthetic. In the bunk above her head, her husband lies with a sore foot. After the operation is over and the child has been successfully born, the husband is found to have slit his throat because he was not able to bear his wife's suffering. Nick asks, ''Is dying hard, Daddy?'' ''No, I think it's pretty easy,'' his father says.

The story is composed of this—the inability to endure suffering. The wish to die rather than face pain. Is this a red and blue world? I see it as dark as night—Hemingway's world is again and again a world of fear. Of physical cruelty, pain, the giving of pain, and for a counter the inability to receive it except in propriety—one way. In Hemingway there is only one way, you know. It is a fear-ridden world, in which the only exorcisement is ritual—the bullfighter's code, the rules of sport, of warfare. This story is over and over again told with a kind of appetite, gusto; and this paradox of essence and effect is one of the hypnotic and incomparable things about Hemingway—his value and his mystery. His imitators lack both value and mystery. Violence in itself is not a story; there is violence and there is the story, or rather the plot, of violence.

How do we get, in Hemingway, that sense of opaqueness? It is not because the stories are stories of action—for action can be radiant, we know—not because they are bare and clean of adjectives and fuss. (Why are feelings and adjectives supposed to be in themselves any more—or any less—illuminating than action and verbs?) To this reader, Hemingway's stories are opaque because they are moralizing stories. And to be moralizing is to be flat-surfaced—to take up your stand behind a shield. The stories aren't really out in the open at all, the outdoors notwithstanding; the arena functions like an ambush, with the author behind taking pot shots at the reader.

Be stoic. We are taught by Hemingway, who is *instructive* by method, that there is a way we had better be. The world is full of fear and danger, says he. We say, All right—it is that. He says, I give you the ceremony. Better not look any closer, but keep to your places. So braveness and fear, instructions and ceremonial to-do, step in front of reality just as surely as sentimentality can. Our belligerent planet Mars has an unknown and unrevealed heart.

But we have to go on from there. For what comes of it? Part of
Hemingway's power comes straight out of this conditioning he imposes
on his stories. In San Francisco there's a painting by Goya, who himself
used light, action, and morality dramatically, of course. The bull ring
and the great tossing wall of spectators are cut in diagonal half by a great
shadow of afternoon. There lies the wonder of the painting—the opaque
paired with the clear, golden sun; half of the action, with dense, clotting
shade. It's like this in Hemingway's plots.

In the same way, one power of Hemingway's famous use of conversation derives from the fact that it's often in translated or broken
sentences—a shadow inserted between the direct speakers. It is an
obscuring and at the same time a magical touch; it illuminates from the
side. It makes us aware of the fact that communication is going on.

As we now picture Hemingway's story, isn't it something like
this—not transparent, not radiant from the front; but from the side, from
without his story, from a moral source, comes its beam of light; and his
story is not radiant, but spotlighted. Don't we feel the kind of excitement
from reading his stories that we more usually feel at a play?

4

As WE all have observed, plot can throw its weight in any of several
ways, varying in their complexity, flexibility, and interest: onto the
narrative, or situation; onto the character; onto the interplay of characters; and onto some higher aspects of character, emotional states, and so
on, which is where the rules leave off, if they've come with us this far,
and the uncharted country begins. Let's look at further stories, still not
seeking to evaluate their authors or the stories among others of their
authors, but taking them up where we find them as they bring out some
aspect or another of plot.

Stephen Crane's "The Bride Comes to Yellow Sky" tells a story of
situation; it is a playful story, using two situations, like counters.

Jack Potter, the town marshal of Yellow Sky, has gone to San Anton'
and gotten married and is bringing his bride home in a Pullman—the
whole errand to be a complete surprise to the town of Yellow Sky. "He
knew full well that his marriage was an important thing to his town. It
could only be exceeded by the burning of the new hotel."

And in Yellow Sky another situation is building up in matching tempo
with the running wheels. A messenger appears in the door of the Weary

Gentleman saloon crying "Scratchy Wilson's drunk and has turned loose with both hands." "Immediately a solemn, chapel-like gloom was upon the place. . . . 'Scratchy Wilson is a wonder with a gun, a perfect wonder, and when he goes on the war-trail, we hunt our holes—naturally.'" Scratchy enters town, pistols in both hands. His "cries of ferocious challenge rang against walls of silence. And his boots had red tops with gilded imprints, of the kind beloved in winter by little sledding boys on the hillsides of New England. . . . He walked with the creeping movement of the midnight cat. As it occurred to him, he roared menacing information. . . . The little fingers of each hand played sometimes in a musician's way. . . . The only sounds were his terrible invitations."

All this is delightful to us not only for itself but for its function of play, of assuring our anticipation; the more ferocious Scratchy is, the more we are charmed. Our sense of the fairness, the proportion of things is gratified when he "comfortably fusiladed the windows of his most intimate friend. The man was playing with this town; it was a toy for him." This plot of situation gives us a kind of kinetic pleasure; just as being on a seesaw is pleasant not only for where we are but for where the other person is.

The train arrives, Jack Potter and bride get off, and Jack's emotion-charged meeting with Yellow Sky is due; and Scratchy Wilson turns out to be its protagonist. They come face to face, and Potter, who says, "I ain't got a gun on me, Scratchy," takes only a minute to make up his mind to be shot on his wedding day.

"If you ain't got a gun, why ain't you got a gun?" Scratchy sneers at the marshal. And Potter says, "I ain't got a gun because I've just come from San Anton' with my wife. I'm married.""Married?" asks Scratchy—he has to ask it several times, uncomprehending. "Married?"

"Seemingly for the first time, he saw the drooping, drowning woman at the other man's side. 'No!' he said. He was like a creature allowed a glimpse of another world. . . . 'Is this the lady?'

"'Yes; this is the lady,' answered Potter.

"'Well,' said Wilson at last, slowly, 'I s'pose it's all off now.'

". . . He was not a student of chivalry; it was merely that in the presence of this foreign condition he was a simple child of the earlier plains. He picked up his starboard revolver, and, placing both weapons in their holsters, he went away. His feet made funnel-shaped tracks in the heavy sand.''

So, in Crane's story, two situations, two forces, gather, meet—or rather are magnetized toward one another, almost—and collide. One is vanquished—the unexpected one—with neatness and absurdity, and the vanquished one exists; all equivalents of comedy.

5

IN Katherine Mansfield's "Miss Brill," there are only one character and only one situation. The narrative is simple, Miss Brill's action consists nearly altogether in sitting down; she does nothing but go and sit in the park, return home and sit on her bed in her little room. Yet considerably more of a story is attempted by this lesser to-do than Crane attempted in "Yellow Sky"; its plot is all implication.

"Miss Brill" is set on a stage of delight. "Although it was so brilliantly fine—the blue sky powdered with gold, and great spots of light like white wine splashed over the *Jardins Publiques*—Miss Brill was glad that she had decided on her fur. . . . [She] put up her hand and touched her fur. Dear little thing!'' We see right off that for Miss Brill delight is a kind of coziness. She sits listening to the band, her Sunday habit, and "Now there came a little flutely bit—very pretty!—a little chain of bright drops. She was sure it would be repeated. It was; she lifted her head and smiled.''

Miss Brill has confidence in her world—anticipation: what will happen next? Ah, but she knows. She's delighted but safe. She sees the others from her little perch, her distance—the gay ones and then those on benches: "Miss Brill had often noticed there was something funny about nearly all of *them*. They were odd, silent, nearly all old, and from the way they stared they looked as though they'd just come from dark little rooms or even—even cupboards!'' For she hasn't identified herself at all.

The drama is slight in this story. There is no collision. Rather the forces meeting in the *Jardins Publiques* have, at the story's end, passed through each other and come out the other side; there has not been a collision, but a change—something much more significant. This is because, though there is one small situation going on, a very large and complex one is implied—the outside world, in fact.

One of the forces in the story is life itself, corresponding to the part of Scratchy Wilson, so to speak. Not violent life—life in the setting of a park on Sunday afternoon in Paris. All it usually does for Miss Brill is promenade stylishly while the band plays, form little tableaux, separate momently into minor, rather darker encounters, and keep in general motion with bright colors and light touches—there are no waving pistols at all, to storm and threaten.

Yet, being life, it does threaten. In what way, at last? Well, how much more deadly to Miss Brill than a flourished pistol is an overheard remark—about *her*. Miss Brill's vision—a vision of love—is brought abruptly face to face with another, ruder vision of love. The boy and girl in love sit down on her bench, but they cannot go on with what they have been saying because of her, though "still soundlessly singing, still with that trembling smile, Miss Brill prepared to listen.

" 'No, not now,' said the girl. 'Not here, I can't.'

" 'But why? Because of that stupid old thing at the end there? . . . Why does she come here at all—who wants her? Why doesn't she keep her silly old mug at home?'

" 'It's her fur which is so funny,' giggled the girl. 'It's exactly like a fried whiting.'

" 'Ah, be off with you!' said the boy in an angry whisper."

So Miss Brill, she who could spare even pity for this world, in her innocence—pity, the spectator's emotion—is defeated. She had allowed herself occasional glimpses of lives not too happy, here in the park, which had moved her to little flutters of sadness. But that too had been coziness—coziness, a remedy visitors seek to take the chill off a strange place with. She hadn't known it wasn't good enough. All through the story she has sat in her "special seat"—another little prop to endurance—and all unknown to her she sat in mortal danger. This is the story. The danger nears, a word is spoken, the blow falls—and Miss Brill retires, ridiculously easy to mow down, as the man with the pistols was easy to stare down in "Yellow Sky," for comedy's sake. But Miss Brill was from the first defenseless and on the losing side, and her defeat is the deeper for it, and one feels sure it is for ever.

6

THE plot of a short story in many instances is quite openly a projection of character. In a highly specialized instance, but a good example, the whole series of ghostly events in *The Turn of the Screw* may obviously be taken as a vision—a set of hallucinations of the governess who tells us the story. The story is a manufactured evidence against the leading character, in effect.

Not always does plot project character, even primarily. William Sansom, a young English writer, might be mentioned as one new writer who pays his highest respect to pure idea. Virginia Woolf too was at least as interested in a beam of light as she was in a tantrum.

In outward semblance, many stories have plots in common—which is of no more account than that many people have blue eyes. Plots are, indeed, what we see with. What's seen is what we're interested in.

On some level all stories are stories of search—which isn't surprising at all. From the intense wild penetration of the hunter in "The Bear" by William Faulkner to the gentle Sunday excursion of Katherine Mansfield's "Miss Brill"; from the cruel errand of Nick's father to the Indian camp in Ernest Hemingway's story to the fantasy of soaring into the realm of the poetic imagination in E. M. Forster's "Celestial Omnibus"; from the fireman seeking the seat of the fire in William Sansom's "Fireman Flower" to the Henry James man in "The Jolly Corner" seeking, with infinite pains and wanderings, the image of himself and what he might have been, through the corridors of a haunted house—in any group of stories we might name as they occur to us, the plot is search. It is the ancient Odyssey and the thing that was ancient when first the Odyssey was sung. Joyce's *Ulysses* is the titan modern work on the specific subject, but when Miss Brill sits in the park, we feel an old key try at an old lock again—she too is looking. Our most ancient dreams help to convince us that her timid Sunday afternoon is the adventure of her life, and measure for us her defeat.

Corresponding to the search involved is always the other side of the coin. On one side of James's coin is search, on the other side is blight. Faulkner is concerned with doom and history, Hemingway with career, ritual, and fate—and so on. Along with search go the rise and fall of life, pride and the dust. And Virginia Woolf sees errand and all alike dissolving in a surpassing mystery.

When plot, whatever it does or however it goes, becomes the outward manifestation of the very germ of the story, then it is purest—then the narrative thread is least objectionable, then it is not in the way. When it is identifiable in every motion and progression of its own with the motion and progression of simple revelation, then it is at its highest use. Plot can be made so beautifully to reveal character, reveal atmosphere and the breathing of it, reveal the secrets of hidden, inner (that is, "real") life, that its very unfolding is a joy. It is a subtle satisfaction—that comes from where? Probably it comes from a deep-seated perception we all carry in us of the beauty of organization—of that less strictly definable thing, of form.

Where does form come from—how do you "get it"? My guess is that form is evolved. It is the residue, the thrown-off shape, of the very act of writing, as I look at it. It is the work, its manifestation in addition to the characters, the plot, the sensory impressions—it is the result of these which comes to more than their mathematical total. It is these plus something more. This something more springs from the whole. It pertains to the essence of the story. From the writer's point of view we might say that form is somehow connected with the process of the story's work—that form *is* the work. From the reader's point of view, we might say that form is connected with recognition; it is what makes us know, in a story, what we are looking at, what unique thing we are for a length of time intensely contemplating. It does seem that the part of the mind which form speaks to and reaches is the memory.

7

IN stories today, form, however acutely and definitely it may be felt, does not necessarily imply a formal structure. It is not accounted for by structure, rather. A story with a "pattern," an exact kind of design, may lack a more compelling over-all quality which we call form. Edgar Allan Poe and other writers whose ultimate aim depended on pattern, on a perfect and dovetailing structure (note the relation to puzzles and to detection and mystery here), might have felt real horror at a story by D. H. Lawrence first of all because of the unmitigated shapelessness of Lawrence's narrative. Lawrence's world of action and conversation is as far from the frozen perfection, the marblelike situations, of Poe as we can imagine; Lawrence's story world is a shambles—a world just let go, like a sketchy housekeeper's un-straightened-up room. More things are important than this dust! Lawrence would say, and he would be as right as the crier of that cry always is.

And what about his characters? Are they real, recognizable, neat men and women? Would you know them if you saw them? Not even, I think, if they began to speak on the street as they speak in the stories, in the very words—they would only appear as deranged people. For the truth seems to be that Lawrence's characters don't really speak their words—not conversationally, not to one another; they are *not* speaking on the street, but are playing like fountains or radiating like the moon or storming like the sea, or their silence is the silence of wicked rocks. It is borne home to us that Lawrence is writing of our human relationships on earth in terms of eternity, and these terms set Lawrence's form.

The author himself appears in authorship in phases like the moon, and sometimes blesses us and sometimes smites us while we stand there under him. But we see that his plots and his characters are alike sacrificed to something; there is something which Lawrence considers as transcending them both. Others besides him have thought that something does. But Lawrence alone, that I have knowledge of now, thinks the transcending thing is found direct through the senses. It is the world of the senses that Lawrence writes in, works in, thinks in, takes as his medium—and if that is strange to us, isn't the loss ours? Through this world he will send his story. It is the plot too; it is his story's reason for being, with sex the channel the senses most deeply, mysteriously, run through, cutting down through layers and centuries and country after country of hypocrisy.

Virginia Woolf presents an interesting variation of this conception; she was an intellectual. Extremely conscious of sex, she was intellectually or philosophically concerned with it. She could make a fantasy of her world, and her people could laugh. But the extreme beauty of her writing is due greatly to one fact, it seems to me: that the imprisonment of life in the word was as much a matter of the senses with her as it was a concern of the intellect. The scent, the gesture, the breath moving from the lips, the sound of the hour striking in the clock, the rippling texture of surface in running water and flowing air—all these things she sought with all her being to apprehend, for they were the palpable shadows and colored reflections of the abstract world of the spirit, the matter that mirrored the reality.

The impressionist dictum at one time that light is the most important actor in the picture can apply to the work of Virginia Woolf; here light does move frequently as a character and on business of its own, from scene to scene, and only itself remains unaffected by cruder and frailer human vision. In one story, "The Searchlight," light is literally the main character.

But it has to be observed that in Mrs. Woolf's stories the beam of light arises not out of the unconscious but out of the conscious being. It is manipulated, like a wand; it touches and discriminates, from here to there, with precise, rather haughty, almost ladylike purpose, to illuminate quite clearly the particular in the abstract world. So near can the sensory come to the philosophic in her stories that the words "breathing," "breath," and the other words which mean this, give us the feeling of a creator ever consciously breathing life into the creation.

While Virginia Woolf uses her senses intellectually, Lawrence uses his intellect sensuously. And while Chekov builds up character, Lawrence breaks down character. These opposites are perpetrated only in one interest, in getting at truth.

D. H. Lawrence is somewhat like the True Princess, who felt beneath forty mattresses that there was a pea under her. Lawrence is as sensitive to falsity as the True Princess was to the pea. And he is just as sure to proclaim the injury.

How can he be so quarrelsome with us while at the same time he is enrapturing us with his extraordinary powers to make us see and feel beauty? But my feeling toward his writing is my feeling toward greatness anywhere. Take it—take it all. It is no laughing matter. It is more pertinent to give in to that beauty of his and better to grit our teeth at his cruelty—for he is cruel—than to laugh at or be annoyed by the shambles he makes of the everyday world.

We all use the everyday world in our stories, and some of us feel inclined or even bound to give it at least a cursory glance and treatment, but Lawrence does not care. He feels no responsibility there at all. He does not care if the mechanics and props of everyday life suffer in his stories from distortion unto absurdity, if his narrative thins and frays away into silliness. Those things aren't what he's concerned with. His plots might remind you of some kind of tropical birds—that are awkward in structure and really impossible-looking when they're on the ground, and then when they take wing and fly, a miracle happens. All that clumsiness and outrageousness is gone; the bird's body becomes astonishingly functional, and iridescent in flight.

8

WILLIAM FAULKNER carries on a plot of development of a kind which I have not yet discussed. The more we read and write. the more clearly we see how many ways there are of *using material*. Some compile meticulously, adding and subtracting and getting a sum which is a story, and which could be graphed if required; sometimes Henry James, who uses this method, seems to be plotting, all exquisitely, graph after graph of different kinds of blights. Other writers distill material, getting clearer

and purer essences as though by some boiling down process—
Lawrence, for example. Faulkner seems to set upon his material and
divine his stories from it.

The furious speed of Faulkner's stories is one of the marks of a
divining writer. His stories seem to race with time, race with the world.
You remember—who could forget?—one sentence of 1600 words in
"The Bear." How this skyscraper could race—like a dinosaur across
the early fields of time—is something to teach us mainly that in the
world of our story-making, wonders never cease. But that sentence runs
along with a strange time-encompassing quality of seeming all to happen
at once; while we are reading we are still hearing the part behind, and the
part before is being anticipated by means of its present part. It makes us
realize how true it is that prose is a structure, in its every part—the
imagination, by instinct or otherwise, is engineered when we write. A
sentence can be in as perfect control as a bridge or a church. Not too
obviously or too exquisitely perhaps, or the reader might start testing as
he goes, which would be fatal to the story.

But the reason Faulkner's unwieldy-looking sentences can race is of
course their high organization—a musical organization. And Faulkner
is highly organized and his evocation does seem to come out of the place
where music comes from. Don't let his turbulence ever blind us; his
structure is there—daring structure. To me, above all other present-day
storytellers he is the one ahead of his time—the most astonishingly
powered and passionate writer we have. "The Bear" is an apocalyptic
story of the end of the wilderness. It ends with the senseless clang on
clang of a man idiotically pounding pieces of his broken gun together
while, in the isolated gum tree over his head, forty or fifty squirrels are
running frantically around. It signifies for one thing the arrival of the
machine age and the squealing treadmill. The story encompasses past
and future, all the past of the land from the Indian times on to this. It has
towering heroic figures, wilderness figures, symbolic figures; and we
get the knowledge in every happening of its happening again, over and
over—and the marvelous whole world of the wilderness, the whole
history of Mississippi.

For in "The Bear" the structure of time is constantly in danger of
being ripped away, torn down by the author—the *whole* time bulges at
the cracks to get in to the present-time of the story. This dilation in time
sense and intractability in space sense, the whole blown-up surface of
the story, has of itself a kind of looming quality, a portentousness. Like

the skin of a balloon, time and space are stretched to hold more, while the story remains in form and function itself.

It is this, most of all, that makes "The Bear" a great deal more than a hunting story. It is a very long story, in five parts, and in Part IV the flimsy partition that keeps the story time apart from whole time flies away entirely. The entire history of the land and a people crowds into a chapter of an expansion, in sentence and paragraph, almost outrageous to the eye alone. Duration of time and extent of space, which always took the accusative case, and were disposed of that way, are let loose now—they are evoked, and tear through the story running backwards and forwards, up and down, into Indian times and the very future, like a pack of beasts from the world's wilderness itself. And this is the beauty of the story. Its self-destruction, self-immolation, is the way it transcends all it might have been had it stayed intact and properly nailed together. There is its wonder.

Sherwood Anderson, it could be said, used this power of expansion in quite another sense in the Winesburg stories—whereby the uneventful and imprisoned life he saw around him became moving and tragic as though another dimension had been added when it passed through his passionate survey—like the same river flowing between deeper walls. In the case of "The Bear," I feel that to Faulkner the escapement of wild time and place must have seemed one *attribute* of the thing he was describing, the lost attribute—just as to Anderson passion was the lost attribute of Winesburg—implicit in it and supplied now, in his stories.

Faulkner in letting time and place out of the box was not being reckless and exhibiting his talents—though what a spectacle they make!—but being true, faithful to his conception of the story at hand. If this alarms many readers, even the very ones most alarmed will have to be the first ones to admit the strict propriety of it.

9

A STORY's major emphasis may fall on the things that make it up—on character, on plot, on its physical or moral world, in sensory or symbolic form. And perhaps the way this emphasis is let fall may determine the value of the story; may determine not how well it is written, but the worth of its being written.

Of course fashion and the habits of understanding stories at given periods in history may play their parts, unconsciously or willfully. But mainly, I venture to think, the way emphasis falls, the value of a story, is the thing nearest dependent upon the individual and personal factor involved, the writer behind the writing.

The fine story writers seem to be in a sense obstructionists. As if they hold back their own best interests. It's a strange illusion. For if we look to the source of the deepest pleasure we receive from a writer, how surprising it seems that this very source is the quondam obstruction. The fact is, in seeking our source of pleasure we have entered another world again. We are speaking of beauty.

And beauty is not a blatant or promiscuous or obvious quality; indeed at her finest she is somehow associated with obstruction—with reticence of a number of kinds. The beauty of ''The Bear'' seems tied up intimately with the reluctance to confine the story to its proper time sequence and space measurements; Faulkner makes fantastic difficulty about time and place both, and the result is beauty. Time after time Lawrence refuses to get his story told, to let his characters talk in any natural way; the story is held up forever, and through so delaying and through such refusal on the author's part, we enter the magical world of pure sense, of evocation—the shortest cut known through the woods.

Could it be that one who carps at difficulties in a writer (''Why didn't he write it like this? Why didn't he write another story?''), at infringements of the rules and lack of performance of duty, fails to take note of beauty? And fails to see straight off that beauty springs from deviation, from desire not to comply but to act inevitably, as long as truth is in sight, whatever that inevitability may mean?

Where does beauty come from, in the short story? Beauty comes from form, from development of idea, from after-effect. It often comes from carefulness, lack of confusion, elimination of waste—and yes, those are the rules. But that can be on occasion a cold kind of beauty, when there are warm kinds. And beware of tidiness. Sometimes spontaneity is the most sparkling kind of beauty—Katherine Mansfield had it. It is a fortuitous circumstance attending the birth of some stories, like a fairy godmother that has—this time—accepted the standing invitation and come smiling in.

Beauty may be missed or forgotten sometimes by the analyzers because it is not a means, not a way of getting the story along, or furthering a thing in the world. For beauty is a result—as form is a result. It *comes*. We are lucky when beauty comes, for often we try, but then when the virtues of our story are counted, beauty is standing behind the door. I think it may be wrong to try for beauty; we should try for other things, and then hope.

Intensity and beauty are qualities that will come out of man's imagination and out of his passion—which use sensitivity for their finding and focusing power. (This can't beg the question quite so hopelessly as assigning the best stories to genius.) It seems to be true that for practical purposes, in writing a story, beauty is in greatest accord with sensitivity.

The two things that cannot be imitated, beauty and sensitivity, are or may be kin to each other. But there is only one of them we can strive for. Sensitivity in ourselves. It is our technique. In the end, our technique is sensitivity, and beauty may be our reward.

A short-story writer can try anything. He has tried anything—but presumably not everything. Variety is, has been, and no doubt will remain endless in possibilities, because the power and stirring of the mind never rests. It is what this power will try that will most pertinently define the short story. Not rules, not aesthetics, not problems and their solution. It is not rules as long as there is imagination; not aesthetics as long as there is passion; not success as long as there is intensity behind the effort that calls forth and communicates, that will try and try again.

And at the other end of the stories is the reader. There is no use really to fear "the reader." The surly old bugaboo who wants his money's worth out of a magazine—yes, he is there (or I suspect it is a she, still wanting her money's worth and having yet to be convinced she's got it); but there is another reader too, perhaps with more at stake.

Inescapably, this reader exists—the same as ourselves; the reader who is also a user of imagination and thought. This reader picks up a story, maybe our new story, and behold, sees it fresh, and meets it with a storehouse of hope and interest.

And, reader and writer, we can wish each other well. Don't we after all want the same thing? A story of beauty and passion and truth?

"The Flash of Fireflies"

Why is it that while the death of the novel is good for post-mortem at least once a year, the short story lives on unmolested? It cannot be because—to borrow their own jargon—literary critics regard it as merely a minor art form. Most of them, if pressed, would express the view that it is a highly specialized and skilful form, closer to poetry, etc. But they would have to be pressed; otherwise they wouldn't bother to discuss it at all. When Chekhov crops up, it is as a playwright, and Katherine Mansfield is a period personality from the Lady Chatterley set. Yet no one suggests that we are practicing a dead art form. And, like a child suffering from healthy neglect, the short story survives.

"To say that no one now much likes novels is to exaggerate very little. The large public which used to find pleasure in prose fictions prefer movies, television, journalism, and books of 'fact,'" Gore Vidal wrote recently (*Encounter,* December 1967). If the cinema and television have taken over so much of the novel's territory, just as photography forced painting into wastelands which may or may not be made to bloom, hasn't the short story been overrun, too? This symposium is shoptalk and it would seem unnecessary for us to go over the old definitions of where and how the short story differs from the novel, but the answer to the question must lie somewhere here. Both novel and story use the same material: human experience. Both have the same aim: to communicate it. Both use the same medium: the written word. There is a general and recurrent dissatisfaction with the novel as a means of netting ultimate reality—another term for the quality of human life—and inevitably there is even a tendency to blame the tools: words have become hopelessly blunted by overuse, dinned to death by admen, and, above all, debased by political creeds that have twisted and changed their meaning. Various ways out have been sought. In England, a return to classicism in technique and a turning to the exoticism of sexual aberration and physical and mental abnormality as an extension of human experience and therefore of subject matter; in Germany and America, a splendid abandon in making a virtue of the vice of the novel's inherent clumsiness by stuffing it not with nineteenth-century horsehair narrative but twentieth-century anecdotal-analytical plastic foam; in France, the "laboratory novel" struggling to get away from the anthropocentric curse of the form and the illusion of depth of the psychological novel, and landing up very much where Virginia Woolf was, years ago, staring at the mark on the wall. Burroughs has invented the reader-participation novel. For the diseased word, George Steiner has even suggested silence.

If the short story is alive while the novel is dead, the reason must lie in approach and method. The short story, as a form and as a *kind of creative vision* must be better equipped to attempt the capture of ultimate reality at a time when (whichever way you choose to see it) we are drawing nearer to the mystery of life or are losing ourselves in a bellowing wilderness of mirrors, as the nature of that reality becomes more fully understood or more bewilderingly concealed by the discoveries of science and the proliferation of communication media outside the printed word.

Certainly the short story always has been more flexible and open to experiment than the novel. Short-story writers always have been subject at the same time to both a stricter technical discipline and a wider freedom than the novelist. Short-story writers have known—and solved by nature of their choice of form—what novelists seem to have discovered in despair only now: the strongest convention of the novel, prolonged coherence of tone, to which even the most experimental of novels must conform unless it is to fall apart, is false to the nature of whatever can be grasped of human reality. How shall I put it? Each of us has a thousand lives and a novel gives a character only one. *For the sake of the form.* The novelist may juggle about with chronology and throw narrative overboard; all the time his characters have the reader by the hand, there is a consistency of relationship throughout the experience that cannot and does not convey the quality of human life, where contact is more like the flash of fireflies, in and out, now here, now there, in darkness. Short-story writers see by the light of the flash; theirs is the art of the only thing one can be sure of—the present moment. Ideally, they have learned to do without explanation of what went before, and what happens beyond this point. How the characters will appear, think, behave, comprehend, tomorrow or at any other time in their lives, is irrelevant. A discrete moment of truth is aimed at—not *the* moment of truth, because the short story doesn't deal in cumulatives.

The problem of how best to take hold of ultimate reality, from the technical and stylistic point of view, is one that the short-story writer is accustomed to solving specifically in relation to an area—event, mental state, mood, appearance—which is heightenedly manifest in a single situation. Take fantasy for an example. Writers are becoming more and more aware of the waviness of the line that separates fantasy from the so-called rational in human perception. It is recognized that fantasy is no more than a shift in angle; to put it another way, the rational is simply another, the most obvious, kind of fantasy. Writers turn to the less obvious fantasy as a wider lens on ultimate reality. But this fantasy is something that changes, merges, emerges, disappears as a pattern does viewed through the bottom of a glass. It is true for the moment when one looks down through the glass; but the same vision does not transform everything one sees, consistently throughout one's whole consciousness. Fantasy in the hands of short-story writers is so much more successful than when in the hands of novelists because it is necessary for it to hold good only for the brief illumination of the situation it dominates. In the series of developing situations of the novel the sustainment of the tone of fantasy becomes a high-pitched ringing in the reader's ears. How many fantasy novels achieve what they set out to do: convey the shift and change, to and fro, beneath, above, and around the world of appearances? The short story recognizes that full comprehension of a particular kind in the reader, like full apprehension of a particular kind in the writer, is something of limited duration. The short story is a fragmented and restless form, a matter of hit or miss, and it is perhaps for this reason that it suits modern consciousness—which seems best expressed as flashes of fearful insight alternating with near-hypnotic states of indifference.

These are technical and stylistic considerations. Marxist criticism sees the survival of an art form in relation to social change. What about the socio-political implications of the short story's survival? George Lukács has said that the novel is a bourgeois art form whose enjoyment presupposes leisure and privacy. It implies the living room, the armchair, the table lamp; just as epic implies the illiterates round the tribal story-teller, and Shakespeare implies the two audiences—that of the people and that of the court—of a feudal age. From this point of view the novel marks the apogee of an exclusive, individualist culture; the nearest it ever got to a popular art form (in the sense of bringing people together in direct participation in an intellectually stimulating experience) was the nineteenth-century custom of reading novels aloud to the family. Here again it would seem that the short story shares the same disadvantages as the novel. It is an art form solitary in communication; yet another sign of the increasing loneliness and isolation of the individual in a competitive society. You cannot enjoy the experience of a short story unless you have certain minimum conditions of privacy in which to read it; and these conditions are those of middle-class life. But of course a short story, by reason of its length and its *completeness,* totally contained in the brief time you give to it, depends less than the novel upon the classic conditions of middle-class life, and perhaps corresponds to the breakup of that life which is taking place. In that case, although the story may outlive the novel, it may become obsolete when the period of disintegration is replaced by new social forms and the art forms that express them. One doesn't have to embrace the dreariness of conventional "social realism" in literature to grant this. That our age is threshing about desperately for a way out of individual human isolation, and that our present art forms are not adequate to it, it is obvious to see in all the tatty dressing-up games, from McLuhan's theories to pop art, in which we seek a substitute for them.

GREGORY FITZ GERALD

The Satiric Short Story: A Definition

IN THE SUMMER 1964 NUMBER OF *Studies in Short Fiction,* EDITOR Frank Hoskins remarked that "a genre as rich and as relatively unexplored as short fiction needs more precise definition." Without, I hope, presumption, I should like to offer the following as an attempt to pin down a corner of this wide canvas called short fiction.

One such corner is satire in the form of the short story. Of course, a basic assumption must be the separate existence of the two genres: "satire" and "short story." The former, in earlier times a mostly formal designation, is now largely a conceptual category, such as "political" in *political novel* or "comic" in *comic poetry;* whereas "short story," though partly a conceptual distinction, is chiefly a formal, a structural designation. Nevertheless, the inevitable overlapping of all literary genre classifications, the logician's *bête noire,* signals the obvious limitations of any too-strict categorizing, too Procrustean an *idée fixe* with respect to their definition.

By *satire* without any attendant qualifying epithet such as *indirect, direct, Menippean,* etc., I do *not* mean any specific formal *structure,* for as Northrop Frye has pointed out, the "word satire now means a tone or quality of art which we may find in *any form:* in a play by Shaw, a novel by Sinclair Lewis or a cartoon by Low.''[1] Obviously, then, "any form" must subsume the short story, which when combined with satire may generate a hybrid form I have designated the "satiric short story."

But the adjective in this compound presents certain problems, because, more likely than its substantive, "satiric" could conceivably suggest the notion that a particular short story possesses only occasional, incidental, and sustained satire. That is, "satiric short story" might reasonably be conceived of as describing short fiction that displays merely desultory touches of adventitious satire. Therefore, let us specifically eliminate this latter possibility by stating unequivocally that the term "satiric short story" as herein employed always presumes that the satire is relatively *sustained* and *unremitting* rather than the opposite; that is, the term designates a *satire* as well as a short story. This distinction, as we shall see later, has some significance.

We all understand that satire "ridicules or holds up to scorn the vices, crimes, and absurdities of men and individuals, of classes and organizations, of societies and civilizations. It does not, however, necessarily make us laugh or even smile; indeed, satire can be quite consciously grim in its effect, as is the case in Orwell's *Nineteen Eighty-Four*."[2] And most authorities concur that "satire inevitably involves what we may call an 'attack' of some sort—if we allow the term 'attack' to subsume more limited, genteel definitions of the satiric office, such as 'exposure' or 'correction' or 'criticism.'"[3] Moreover, no matter what literary form becomes the vehicle of satire, a "satiric fiction," that more than occasionally becomes fantasy in the extremity of its imaginative departure from the literal, is always operative even in apparently "realistic" forms. Edward Rosenheim calls this characteristic "the *fictional* element which is as indispensable to the satirist's art as is the attack itself."[4] Thus the *un*qualified term "satire" now quite generally signifies a conceptual classification of subject matter, not of exterior form, in which the following characteristics appear:

1. [A reductive] attack or censure of man or his follies.
2. An essential meaning which is not consistent with the strictly literal interpretation. . . .
[3.] A domination of the work by the techniques of satire.[5]

Number one, attack, is the *sine qua non* of satire. Number two not only includes irony, reminding us—as Frye says—that satire is "militant irony,"[6] but also includes that fantasying tendency ("the fiction") always found in the satiric vehicle, even though it be essay, oration, dialogue, or some other genre with which (in normal *non*-satiric manifestations) a "fiction" is not ordinarily or indispensably associated. The third point, that "the techniques of satire" always *dominate* the work, provides us with one of the gates with which to bar works containing merely adventitious satiric attack. But what are these techniques of satire?

Any literary device that contributes significantly to reductive attack by ridicule or scorn on any manifestation of vice or folly is a satiric technique. Familiar examples are exaggeration, understatement, caricature, grotesquerie, etc. When such techniques *dominate* any work, it is a satire; when such techniques do *not dominate* a work, or are merely incidental, it is something else: for example, a short story with some satiric touches, *not* a "*satiric* short story." But how, if at all, do such satiric techniques *differ* from other kinds of techniques: of drama, of poetry, or of fiction?

Obviously such techniques (*e.g.,* irony, hyperbole, or even caricature) may also occur in works that cannot accurately be described as satires. This fact suggests that there are at least two varieties of techniques capable of producing either sustained *or* unsustained satiric effects: *1*) the specifically satiric, such as caricature, which not often produce other than satiric effects even in *non*-satiric works;[7] and *2*) those that, like peripety and irony, can produce other effects, such as comedy, pathos, or tragedy, as well as satire, depending on *how* and *to what ends* the writer shapes the techniques.

Since none but a satiric technique (either *1* or *2* above) yields a satiric result, any literary device that produces in its intended audience a mainly *non*-satiric response (for example, of empathy or of sympathy for the object of the attack) will not produce sustained satire.

When one appends to the word *satire* qualifying epithets such as *formal* or *verse*, etc., generating, for instance, "formal verse satire," the resultant compound term usually designates, in addition to its conceptual reference, a specific *structural* form. Among other such qualifiers is the largely structural term *indirect*, which generates the compound "indirect satire." Indirect satire is, of course, widely known as a narrative species with plot and characters. A satiric short story must, therefore, be a *brief* indirect satire. The problem of definition would end here were it not that "indirect satire" traditionally includes much that cannot be accurately designated "short fiction" as we now commonly understand that term; for "*Any narrative or dramatic vehicle* can be adapted to the purposes of indirect satire."[8] While "brief indirect satire" may be a way station en route to our destination, embracing *all* satiric short stories, it is *too* inclusive, not sufficiently precise. Therefore, let us examine another possibility for more discriminating qualification, the term designating that ancient type of satire called "Menippean." Northrop Frye tells us that, named for the cynic Menippus, and occasionally called "Varronian," after one of that ancient's disciples,

> The Menippean satire deals less with people as such than with mental attitudes. Pedants, bigots, cranks, parvenues, virtuosi, enthusiasts, rapacious and incompetent professional men of all kinds, are handled in terms of their occupational approach to life as distinct from their social behavior. The Menippean satire thus . . . [possesses the] ability to handle abstract ideas and theories, and differs from . . . [other types of fiction] in its characterization, which is stylized rather than naturalistic, and presents people as mouthpieces of the ideas they represent.[9]

John M. Aden's definition is even broader—"Menippean satire: either that genre of mixed formal elements as anciently practiced, or the prose satire that has generally succeeded to the name: an indirect mode, with ironic tendencies."[10]

Since in Menippean satire, as Aden defines it, form and concept cohere in a prose narrative, the term obviously excludes the narrative verse satire included by the slightly more comprehensive term "indirect satire" yet does not eliminate prose dramas. But this latter inclusion is more useful to precise definition than not, because dramatic monologues are sometimes classified as short stories and anthologized as such,[11] even though they are very close to the drama and may even be appropriately designated "closet dramas."[12] Thus, without any difficulty and despite an apparent duality of form, satiric dramatic monologues may be logically subsumed under the heading "Menippean."

If now a further, but rather loose and general limitation of *length* be imposed without thereby demanding any more specificity than one does by the term "short" in short story, we have the "brief Menippean satire," a designation that includes all of that fiction that may be classified under the rubric "satiric short story." In fact the classification *Menippean satire* clearly implying a further qualification of brevity, has already been applied to appropriate short stories, for example, to a short story of Eudora Welty's.[13]

"Brief Menippean satire," as defined above, is broad enough to encompass a very wide variety of familiar vehicles for satire, types of brief prose narratives: sketches, fables, fabliaux, fairy tales, yarns, *exempla, märchen,* parables, short short stories, etc. Accordingly, except for the rather indefinite restriction as to length (without insisting on a magazine-editor type of word limit), the "satiric short story" designation as here defined allows as much freedom of inclusion as possible, emphasizing restrictions more relative to its satirical than to its fictional constituents. Logically such freedom embraces a number of specimens that might be excluded by definitions of the *non*-satiric "short story" that debar works having too little (or too much) plot, action, conflict, etc.

As we can readily perceive from the unforeseen effects of something like Defoe's *The Shortest Way with the Dissenters,* the satirist ought to consider carefully his audience. Let us call a major portion of this audience the "intended reader." By the "intended reader" I mean that part of his audience at whom the satirist deliberately aims, whom the satirist regards as having the capacities requisite to the apprehension of his thrusts (and of their instrumental devices). The concept has importance because not every haphazard reader of a satire (who may be to some degree oblivious of its thrusts) is the intended reader. And because "satire is the most consistently and obviously rhetorical of all the major genres. . .,"[14] the satirist will fail to the extent that his intended reader misapprehends him. Naturally enough, then, the satirist's techniques will be conditioned by the nature of this intended reader.

Now having completed the attempt at defining the key constituent terms, I shall try next to assemble them in some hopefully coherent and meaningful order. The "satiric short story" may be defined as a brief Menippean satire (an indirect prose type with characters, plot, conflict, etc.), that sustains throughout a reductive attack upon its object(s); that conveys to its intended reader an import different from its apparent, surface meaning; and that is permeated by satiric techniques.

Some exemplary stories that fit this definition follow: Elizabeth Bowen, "The Good Girl," *The Cat Jumps and Other Stories* (London, 1955); John Collier, "Another American Tragedy," *Fancies and Goodnights* (Garden City, 1954); E. M. Forster, "The Machine Stops," *The Collected Tales of E. M. Forster* (New York, 1947); Ernest Hemingway, "Mr. and Mrs. Elliot," *The Short Stories of Ernest Hemingway* (New York, 1938); Henry James, "Bundle of Letters," *The Complete Tales of Henry James* (Philadelphia, 1962); D. H. Lawrence, "Two Blue Birds," *The Woman Who Rode Away* (New York, 1929); Henry L. Mencken, "The Visionary," *A Book of Burlesques*

(New York, 1920); Somerset Maugham, "Appearance and Reality," *The Complete Short Stories of W. Somerset Maugham,* Vol. II (Garden City, 1953); Flannery O'Conner, "Good Country People," *A Good Man Is Hard to Find* (New York, 1955); Sean O'Faolain, "Childybawn," *The Finest Stories of Sean O'Faolain* (Boston, 1957); and many others.

Indeed, so numerous are the stories that fit the above definition, and so contrasting in nature are they from the *non*-satiric, that it is surprising the satiric short story has received almost no critical attention from the genre specialists.

It is now surely evident that the satiric short story as defined above is a separate sub-genre differing in important respects from non-satiric short stories as well as from other forms of satire. Moreover, the relevance of much of the definition to longer satiric fiction will be immediately evident.

Finally, by approaching the definition of the satiric short story first from the vantage ground of satire, instead of fiction, some—but of course not all—considerable difficulties seem obviated, difficulties that appear to occur inevitably whenever one attempts to find or make a viable definition of the *short story:* conflicting testimony abounds, agreement is all but impossible.[15]

1. "The Nature of Satire," *University of Toronto Quarterly* (October, 1944), p. 75; my italics.

2. Mark Hillegas, "Science Fiction as Satire: A Selected Bibliography," *Satire Newsletter* (Fall, 1963), 20.

3. Edward Rosenheim, Jr.. "Anger as a Fine Art," *College Composition and Communication* (May, 1965), 80. See also his *Swift and the Satirists Art* (Chicago, 1963). p. 18 *et passim;* A. R. Heiserman, *Skelton and Satire* (Chicago, 1961), pp. 297–8; Alvin Kernan, *The Cankered Muse: Satire of the English Renaissance* (New Haven, 1959), p. 7; and others.

4. Rosenheim, *Swift,* pp. 106ff.

5. William E. Haas, "Some Characteristics of Satire," *Satire Newsletter* (Fall, 1965), 2. Because the original six points of the article are, I believe, compressible to these three essential ones, I have here omitted points 3, 4, and 5.

6. *Anatomy of Criticism* (Princeton, 1957), p. 17.

7. Although caricature is a specifically satiric technique, it may, as in Dickens' *Bleak House,* not *dominate* the work, which is therefore not a satire.

8. M. H. Abrams, *A Glossary of Literary Terms* (New York, 1957), p. 86; my italics.

9. Frye, *Anatomy,* p. 309.

10. "Towards a Uniform Satiric Terminology," *Satire Newsletter* (Spring, 1963), p. 31.

11. See, *e.g.,* Ring Lardner's "Haircut," in *Great Modern Short Stories,* Bennett A. Cerf, ed. (New York, 1942), pp. 337–49; and George Milburn's "The Apostate," in *Modern Short Stories,* Robert B. Heilman, ed. (New York, 1950), pp. 315–320.

12. *Encyclopedia of Poetry and Poetics,* Alex Preminger, ed. (Princeton, 1965), p. 530.

13. Jo Allen Bradham, "'A Visit of Charity': Menippean Satire," *Studies in Short Fiction,* I (Summer 1964), 258–63.

14. Alvin B. Kernan, *The Plot of Satire* (New Haven, 1965), p. 25.

15. See, *e.g.,* H. E. Bates, *The Modern Short Story* (Boston, 1941), pp. 15–17; *Story-tellers and Their Art,* Georgianne Trask and Charles Burkhart, eds. (Garden City, 1963), pp. 3–20, *et passim;* and Thomas A. Gullason, "The Short Story: An Underrated Art." *Studies in Short Fiction,* II (Fall, 1964), 13–31.

MORDECAI MARCUS

What is an Initiation Story?

MUCH RECENT criticism, apparently beginning with Brooks and Warren's comments on Hemingway's "The Killers" and Anderson's "I
Want to Know Why" in *Understanding Fiction* (1943), has used the
term "initiation" to describe a theme and a type of story. Ray B. West's
history of *The Short Story in America, 1900–1950* (1952) uses the term
for one of two major types of short story. Several short story textbooks
and textbook manuals employ the term, and other criticism applies it to
novels.

The prevalence of inadequate criticism employing the concept of
initiation suggests that the term requires clarification. I propose to
examine the origins and definitions of this concept, to test it through
application to a variety of stories, and to suggest its usefulness and its
limitations. For the sake of convenience, I will—with the exception of a
few short novels—confine my discussion to short stories.

The name and analytic concept of the initiation story derive basically
from anthropology. The most important rites of most primitive cultures
center around the passage from childhood or adolescence to maturity
and full membership in adult society. Anthropologists call these rites
initiation or puberty ceremonies. These ceremonies involve physical

torture, cutting of various parts of the body, abstention from and ritualistic use of food, isolation, and indoctrination in secret tribal beliefs. According to most anthropologists the purpose of these rites is to test the endurance of the novice, to assure his loyalty to the tribe, and to maintain the power of the adult community. But a few anthropologists believe that they stem from a psychological compulsion to propitiate the adult community or supernatural powers.

Certain "literary anthropologists" propose a concept of initiation apparently based on the idea of propitiating the adult or supernatural world. For example, Joseph Campbell's *The Hero with a Thousand Faces* (1949) describes initiation as a stage in all human life. He derives his description of initiation from the experience of the typical mythical hero as he seeks adjustment and union with the forces of existence, such as the tempting woman and the threatening father. Other writers have analyzed similar initiation rituals in medieval literature.

A brief description of the ways in which fiction can embody ritual will help to show the relationship between these anthropological ideas and the initiation story, and will also be helpful in analyzing certain initiation stories. Ritual is difficult to define and to apprehend because most human behavior follows prescribed patterns unreflectively. Everyday patterns of behavior are recognized as ritualistic only when they are so exaggerated or deliberate as to appear out of the ordinary. Therefore, the formalized behavior of so-called civilized people will appear ritualistic in fiction chiefly under two circumstances: when it involves a response to an unusually trying situation in which a person falls back on socially formalized behavior, or when an individual pattern of behavior results from powerful psychological compulsion. Ritual may appear in fiction in two more guises: through the portrayal of the formalized behavior of primitives or folkpeople and through symbols which suggest mythological parallels in people or action. Certain psychologists and anthropologists, particularly the disciples of Jung, tend to see a basic unity in all these manifestations of ritual, but it is safe to ignore without refuting this questionable doctrine, for it would not seriously alter most of my analysis.

The anthropologist's ideas about initiation would suggest that an initiation story shows adult society deliberately testing and indoctrinating the young, or shows the young compelled in a relatively universal manner to enact certain experiences in order to achieve maturity. But only a very small proportion of works called initiation stories, or meeting the definitions for them, show adults testing or teaching the young. Ritual does occur in some initiation stories, but it is more often of individual than of social origin. Education is always important in an initiation story, but it is usually a direct result of experience rather than of indoctrination. One concludes that the initiation story has only a tangential relationship to the anthropologist's idea of initiation.

The various critical definitions of the initiation story fall into two groups. The first group describes initiation as a passage of the young from ignorance about the external world to some vital knowledge. The second describes initiation as an important self-discovery and a resulting adjustment to life or society. But definitions within these two categories vary considerably.

According to Adrian H. Jaffe and Virgil Scott initiation occurs when "a character, in the course of the story, learns something that he did not know before, and . . . what he learns is already known to, and shared by, the larger group of the world."[1] Several critics, including Brooks and Warren (p. 344), and West (p. 75), explicitly define initiation as a discovery of evil. Brooks and Warren also state that the protagonist seeks to come to terms with his discovery, and West suggests that in learning to live with his knowledge the protagonist begins to achieve self-understanding.

The remarks of Brooks and Warren, and West, about achieving adjustment and self-understanding give their theories continuity with those which make self-understanding central to the initiation story. Curiously balanced between the two classes of definition is Leslie Fiedler's belief that "An initiation is a fall through knowledge to maturity; behind it there persists the myth of the Garden of Eden, the assumption that to know good and evil is to be done with the joy of innocence and to take on the burdens of work and childbearing and death."[2] Less ambiguous concepts of initiation as self-discovery are presented in two discussions of stories by Conrad. Carl Benson believes that *The Shadow Line* presents initiation as "the passage from egocentric youth to human solidarity."[3] Albert J. Guerard finds initiation in *Heart of Darkness* and "The Secret Sharer" to be "progress through temporary reversion and achieved self-knowledge, the theme of man's exploratory descent into the primitive sources of being," but Guerard believes that this knowledge of evil makes us capable of good.[4]

Three of the critics cited insist or imply that initiation stories contain ritual but they offer no distinctions between kinds of ritual. Jaffe and

Scott compare initiation plots to fraternity initiation ceremonies. West suggests that Hemingway is always ritualistic (p. 93), and refers to the "ritual of initiation" in "The Killers" and in Faulkner's "That Evening Sun" (p. 99). (The Faulkner story, I believe, does not present initiation.) Guerard's insistence on psychological compulsion and on the appropriateness of bloodshed in "a true initiation story" suggests that he may consider ritual vital to the form.[5]

A synthesis of these ideas will provide a working definition. An initiation story may be said to show its young protagonist experiencing a significant change of knowledge about the world or himself, or a change of character, or of both, and this change must point or lead him towards an adult world. It may or may not contain some form of ritual, but it should give some evidence that the change is at least likely to have permanent effects.

Initiation stories obviously center on a variety of experiences and the initiations vary in effect. It will be useful, therefore, to divide initiations into types according to their power and effect. First, some initiations lead only to the threshold of maturity and understanding but do not definitely cross it. Such stories emphasize the shocking effect of experience, and their protagonists tend to be distinctly young. Second, some initiations take their protagonists across a threshold of maturity and understanding but leave them enmeshed in a struggle for certainty. These initiations sometimes involve self-discovery. Third, the most decisive initiations carry their protagonists firmly into maturity and understanding, or at least show them decisively embarked toward maturity. These initiations usually center on self-discovery. For convenience, I will call these types tentative, uncompleted, and decisive initiations.

Stories of tentative initiation typically show shocking experiences which leave their protagonists distraught. Since such experiences do not always lead towards maturity, one may demand evidence of permanent effect on the protagonist before ascribing initiation to a story. Stories of very young children offer the greatest problem here. In Chekov's "A Trifle from Life," Katherine Mansfield's "Sun and Moon," and Katherine Anne Porter's "The Circus," young children experience disillusionment in the trustworthiness of an adult, in the permanence of a delightful and picturesque event, and in the joyfulness and sincerity of a circus performance. In each story, a child is violently distressed, while the surrounding adults remain uncomprehending or unsympathetic. Only Miss Porter's story suggests that the disillusioning experience will have long-range effects, and since the suggestion is that they will be damaging, her story raises the possibility that the maturation process in all initiation stories should be further classified according to the proportion of or balance between emotional damage or growth which they show.

Despite one's hesitation to find initiation in these three stories, they are not far removed in theme and structure from many works which critics have called typical initiation stories—for example, several much discussed stories by Hemingway. Among these stories is "Indian Camp," in which Nick Adams watches his father perform a Caesarian operation on an Indian woman and then sees that the woman's husband has killed himself to avoid witnessing her suffering. The story emphasizes Nick's discovery of death, but its conclusion asserts that Nick could not believe he would ever die. If Nick's discovery is to have permanent effects, one must assume that the story's conclusion describes a protective rationalization which cannot last. If this is true, then the story shows an approach to and a temporary withdrawal from mature realization.

Other stories by Hemingway show longer-lasting struggles at thresholds of maturity. "My Old Man" shows its protagonist learning that his father was a cheat despised by various people, and he is left struggling for an adjustment to this bitter knowledge. Hemingway's two stories of adolescent discovery of violence, "The Killers" and "The Battler," are perhaps more problematic than "Indian Camp" and "My Old Man." In "The Killers" Nick Adams is confronted with brutal and somewhat impersonal violence in the actions of the gangsters, and with despairing passivity in the behavior of the prizefighter Andreson. Various details suggest that Nick has never before witnessed such behavior. The end of the story shows Nick struggling for adjustment to his new knowledge, and contrasts his sensitivity to evil and despair with the insensitivity of Sam and George.

This story marks a tentative initiation into maturity, but analysis of its initiation theme has led to irresponsible interpretations. Brooks and Warren propose that Nick experiences "the discovery of evil" (p. 322), but this phrase makes Nick's experience uniquely symbolic of evil in general, which is more weight than the story can carry. Jaffe and Scott, probably building on Brooks and Warren's interpretation, find the story showing "a person who suddenly discovers the basic nature of existence," and claim that it is "about the meaning of life and man's place in the universe'' (pp. 209–210). These interpretations are a far cry from the rather elementary experience of Nick Adams in ''The Killers.''

Quite possibly the idea that an initiation must be profound and universal has misled these critics. Jaffe and Scott's insistence that initiation is always ''into the larger group of the world'' may also mislead them, for Hemingway's heroes are always initiated into a select group. Hemingway's ''The Battler'' records comparable encounters by Nick Adams, but this time he discovers treachery and uncertainty as well as violence. If the experience in ''The Killers'' is to be called *the* initiation into the meaning of existence, one might as well propose the same interpretation for ''The Battler''; but again the idea appears irresponsible. Ray West's idea that ''The Killers'' is an initiation ritual finds little support in the story, for its only ritual element appears to be the operation of the narrow social codes of the gangster and the prizefighter.

Disillusion, uncertainty, and violence also create the tentative initiation of Jody Tiflin in Steinbeck's three-part story ''The Red Pony,'' yet the emphasis in this story is markedly different from that in Hemingway's two stories. Jody's farm life bristles with evidence of the uncertainty of life and the dependence of life on death, but only a series of incidents which involve him deeply begin to bring these truths home to Jody. Steinbeck does not show Jody's final realization, but Jody's feelings after he has seen Billy Buck's struggle to bring the colt to birth suggest that Jody will remember his initiating experiences. ''The Red Pony'' contains occasional suggestions of ritual (chiefly through parallels to primitive rites) in its emphasis on the slaughter of farm animals, and (in the form of individual compulsion) in Jody's constant attention to his pony and to the pregnant mare. In this story Steinbeck's view of the cycle of life is somewhat sacramental. Faulkner's view of nature in ''The Old People'' is distinctly sacramental. In this story, Ike McCaslin is ritualistically initiated into a communion with nature by Sam Fathers, the old Indian-Negro (the rites derive from a primitive culture), after which Ike sees a vision of the buck he has slain. Sam's instructions and Ike's own vision teach him to respect the sacredness of nature. Faulkner's story places less emphasis than does Steinbeck's on the pervasiveness of death, but it does stress the interdependence of life and death. Both of these stories present tentative initiations, for they give only slight evidence that their protagonists are achieving maturity.

Although stories involving some self-discovery usually move beyond tentative and towards uncompleted initiation, self-discovery may be slight enough or sufficiently compounded with other feelings so that it does not lead beyond the tentative. For example, the protagonist of Joyce's "Araby" is disillusioned about the bazaar he longed to visit, and at the same time gains an insight into his own vanity. Perhaps because we see in him little struggle for adjustment, the shame which Joyce's protagonist suffers may seem less of a step towards maturity than the shock which Nick Adams experiences in "The Killers" and "The Battler." Another story which combines some self-discovery with tentative initiation is Dorothy Canfield Fisher's "Sunset at Sixteen," a story about a young girl whose first romantic yearnings and disappointments make her realize that she must experience years of struggle and pain to win through to the final peace of maturity.

The dividing line between tentative and uncompleted initiation is, of course, impossible to establish precisely. Initiation into knowledge of sex and into sexual desire might easily fit all three categories of initiation stories, but in two well known stories such experience illustrates uncompleted initiation. In Anderson's "I Want to Know Why" a boy recognizes moral complexity in the lives of two men whose sexual behavior contrasts with their other actions and reveals a combination of good and evil. Although Anderson's protagonist remains profoundly puzzled, the depth of his concern makes it likely that he will continue to strive for understanding. More complex is the uncompleted initiation in Alberto Moravia's short novel *Agostino,* which portrays a boy of thirteen first learning about the nature of sexual relations, then tortured by his relationship to his young and beautiful widowed mother, and finally unable to gain admittance to a brothel, where he had hoped to destroy his oedipal vision of his mother. Agostino's desperation and seething conflicts perhaps give more assurance that he will struggle towards maturity than does the dilemma of Anderson's protagonist.

Another harsh self-discovery accompanying a discovery about human life occurs in Lionel Trilling's "The Other Margaret." As this highly complex story concludes, a thirteen year old girl is forced to recognize that another person, and presumably all men, are responsible for their moral lives no matter what extenuating circumstances exist. From this insight she immediately moves to recognition of her own responsibility. Although the story ends with the girl weeping uncontrollably, the force with which she makes her discovery, its profoundly personal nature, as well as the girl's intelligence and sensitivity, strongly suggest that her discovery will have permanent effects. The smashing of the clay lamb, which object the protagonist's father identifies with her, is certainly symbolic and may introduce a ritualistic element through association with primitive rites, but ritual, I believe, is not essential to the story.

Self-discovery may be a more gentle correlate of discoveries about human life, as in stories of uncompleted initiation by Jessamyn West and Katherine Mansfield. Miss West's "Sixteen" (the final story in *Cress Delahanty*) portrays a self-centered girl who reluctantly goes home from college to be present at her aged grandfather's death. Details throughout the story suggest that Cress is scornful of the sensibilities of the old, of other people in general, and proud of the rare flowering of her own sensibilities. As her dying grandfather speaks to her of his love for the flower she wears and compares her to his dead wife, Cress realizes that his humanity is like hers, and so she discovers that she has been falsely separating herself from others. The story ends on a note of communion between the dying man and the girl, suggesting that she will change.

A parallel but more complex initiation occurs in Miss Mansfield's "The Garden Party," in which the adolescent protagonist, Laura, is intensely concerned with her relationships to everyone she deals with. Her self-centeredness, unlike Cress Delahanty's, is patronizing, and she is concerned to do what appears right. As the story concludes, Laura discovers the reality and the mystery of death, which discovery seems to ease the burden of living and yet demand that life be understood. Although her problems are not solved, the conclusion suggests that she is in a better position to find life's realities. Laura's almost compulsive concern with the dead man is perhaps psychologically ritualistic, and—as Daniel A. Weiss has observed[6]—her descent to the cottage of the dead man parallels Proserpine's descent to the dead. But these ritual elements are slight.

A somewhat comparable theme is presented in Katherine Anne Porter's "A Grave." This story at first portrays a girl of nine who confronts the mystery of birth and death as she bends over the open body of a pregnant dead rabbit. But it is twenty years later that the meaning of this experience crystallizes for her. Rather than portraying an actual initiation, this story shows a mature person remembering from her years of immaturity a symbol for more recent knowledge. But its revelation that

growth has occurred strongly parallels the initiation theme. Robert Penn
Warren's "Blackberry Winter," which Ray B. West analyzes inten-
sively as an initiation story (pp. 77–80), slightly resembles "A Grave."
Warren presents a series of potentially disillusioning experiences which
a nine year old boy experiences on one day. At the story's end, flashing
ahead twenty-five years to the present, the first-person protagonist
implies that the experiences of that day prefigured all of his subsequent
life. Unlike Miss Porter's story, however, Warren's gives no indication
of how or when the early experience was recognized as a prototype of the
later, and the result is a feeling of melodramatic cheating in the conclusion. West's detailed analysis of the story mistakenly insists that the nine
year old boy understands the meaning of his experience.

Although these stories by Miss Porter and by Warren make a special
use of the initiation theme, they stand at the borderline between stories
of uncompleted and decisive initiation. As one might expect, some
stories of sexual initiation are likely to stand at a similar crossroads, for
initial sexual intercourse is in one sense always decisive but also points
toward character development. Hemingway's somewhat cynical story
"Up in Michigan" portrays the simple disillusionment of a girl who is
half-willingly raped by a man whom she has admired from a distance,
but the story stops rather abruptly after her sexual initiation. Far more
complex is Colette's short novel *Le Blé en Herbe* (translated as *The
Ripening*). In this story, sixteen year old Phillipe spends an idyllic and
yet often bitter summer at the sea-shore in the company of a fifteen year
old girl, Vinca. Both children are pained by the uncertainties of growing
up, but before the summer is over Phillipe has had an extended sexual
initiation with a sensual woman of thirty, and then one brief and
somewhat unsatisfactory intercourse with Vinca. Although Phillipe
develops no sense of sexual guilt from his major experience, its unde-
cided effect on his future, and his great passivity and uncertainty, leave
him still bitter and unhappy. Two symbolic details help communicate
these feelings and add touches of ritual to the story through association
with myth or primitive rite. When Phillipe's lover first invites him into
her house, she presses on him a glass of very cold orangeade, and
Phillipe repeatedly thinks of the bitterness of the drink as he struggles
with his feelings about the woman. When Phillipe returns to the woman's house he tosses a bunch of thistle-flowers into her garden and
accidentally wounds her face. Summoning him into the garden, she

presses a drop of blood onto his hand. The next time Phillipe returns, their sexual affair begins. Both ritualistic details symbolize his partially disillusioning experience.

Moravia's short novel *Luca,* which portrays a more profound and decisive initiation than Colette's, employs a sexual initiation to create its denouement. *Luca* is pervasively ritualistic, often combining psychological compulsion and mythical parallels. The story traces out the struggles of a fifteen year old boy who feels progressively alienated from his mother and father, his school, and his once precious pursuits. He compulsively rejects all contacts because of their hypocrisy and impurity, and proceeds to cut himself off from life. Ritualistically he gives away his most valued possessions, rejects gestures of friendship, and imagines himself passively dead. In a ritualistic game of hide and seek in the dark (an exaggerated version of the cultural ritual of the beckoning but elusive woman), he grows interested in a woman, but she dies before he can keep an appointment with her. Finally, after long illness and delirium, he is initiated into sex by a much older woman, whom he perceives as an earth goddess; and feeling at last in vital contact with all of life, he moves decisively towards mature acceptance.

A fusion of psychological accuracy and familiar archetypes is less certain in Conrad's "The Secret Sharer." Albert J. Guerard finds in this story the archetype of the mythical night journey, which represents a descent into the unconscious.[7] "The Secret Sharer" unquestionably shows psychological ritual: its protagonist must exert himself to an extreme to conceal his double, and he acts in a trance-like manner. Most striking is his compulsion to drive his ship as close to the land as possible, presumably so that he may show Leggatt his gratitude for the experience of self-discovery. How far he has gone beyond the discovery of courage and endurance amidst loneliness remains problematic, but the final sentences of the story reveal that he has achieved a decisive initiation. Numerous psychologists and mythographers have attested to the universality of the myth of the exploratory night journey.

Clearly formalized primitive ritual occurs in two well known stories which portray decisive initiations: Steinbeck's "Flight" and Faulkner's "The Bear." Pepé, the Mexican boy in "Flight," is suddenly projected into manhood when he must bear the consequences of having killed a man over a point of honor. From the story's opening Pepé's behavior shows rituals of his culture: he practices knife throwing, yearns for manhood, dons his father's garments. Perhaps more ritualistic is his flight from the avenging pursuers. The act itself, with foreknowledge that he is probably doomed, is ritualistic, as are his preparations, his course through the mountains, and his final deliberate confrontation of death after his case is hopeless.

The primitivistic ritual in Faulkner's "The Bear" is identical with the ritual in "The Old People," of which story it is a sequel. Sam Fathers marks the forehead of Ike McCaslin with the blood of his first slain deer, thereby bringing Ike into communion with the wilderness and nature. This incident is less detailed in "The Bear" than in "The Old People," but its meanings are much more deeply explored in additional incidents. Other ritualistic details in the story include Ike's abandonment of his watch, gun, and compass before he can get his first glimpse of the bear, Old Ben, and Sam Fathers' patient training of the dog Lion, who is to bring down Old Ben. Both incidents combine psychological compulsion and the sense of a half-intuited myth, the feeling that nature demands a certain rite. More distinctly psychological are the ritualistic intensity with which Ike pores over his grandfather's ledgers in pursuit of evidence of iniquity, and Ike's decision to renounce the land he has inherited from that grandfather and to adopt the Christ-like trade of a carpenter. All of these rituals are part of a decisive initiation: Ike's establishing a correct understanding of what it means to own the land and of how men may redeem their right to own the land. Faulkner's primitive and psychological rituals in this story are always convincing.

Ritualistic elements lend much coherence and power to these stories of decisive initiation, but ritual is not necessary in such a story. F. Scott Fitzgerald's "The Freshest Boy" describes a decisive point in the life of Basil Lee, which turns him away from egoism and snobbery towards self-discovery and social acceptance. Unfortunately, the turning point in the story—Basil's observation of a major frustration in the life of a football hero—is sentimental, as are some of the accompanying details. Fitzgerald's inability to create a vivid event to change his protagonist makes the story unlike most initiation stories, but Basil's final and decisive turn toward maturity is convincing.

The greater prevalence of ritual in stories of decisive rather than tentative or uncompleted initiation is striking, but it is not too difficult to explain. The full initiations which these stories present usually grow out of strong desires for self-discovery rather than from accidents. Use of psychological compulsion and struggle makes it easy for the writer to incorporate primitive or mythological ritual material when it is available. Primitivistic ritual is perhaps too rare in fiction to be generalized about, but it seems chiefly to accompany decisive initiation. Ritual elements are absent from or unimportant in most stories of tentative and uncompleted initiation, and they are not a definite requirement for decisive initiation.

If such stories as several by Hemingway, Anderson, Trilling, and Miss Porter are to remain in the canon of initiation stories—where they have been placed by various critics—a comprehensive definition like the one I have suggested must be adopted. This definition has the virtues of separating stages of initiation and of avoiding insistence on universal and profound meanings. Furthermore, not only should the critic show caution in ascribing ritual to a story, but he should analyze its type and its precise manifestation. These virtues, in turn, may assist careful analysis of meaning and construction. This definition, of course, has the defect of being so broad that almost any story of developing awareness or character can fit it. However, it is possible to exclude stories of simple recognitions about people and perhaps most stories about adults.

The alternative to my broad three-part definition is the close restriction of initiation to what I have called decisive initiation. Such a definition would insist on a clear-cut entrance into the adult world. Ritual would not be a central requirement for the form, but it would be a distinct likelihood. (Some critics, of course, might wish to limit initiation to stories containing ritual.) This definition might reduce the possibility of over-interpretation of stories such as "The Killers" and "Blackberry Winter," but sensibility will always remain more important than critical terms.

We see, then, that a certain anarchy has unnecessarily prevailed in the idea of the initiation story. Its relationships to anthropological ideas, even those of the "literary" anthropologist, are somewhat tenuous, and its use of archetypes and rituals is exaggerated. As is the case with many literary ideas, its central danger lies in its insistence on phenomena where they simply do not exist—in relying on a concept as a matter of faith. If one believes that initiation stories must present ritual, he may find ritual in "Indian Camp" or "The Circus," where they do not exist (except in the manner in which all human behavior is ritualistic). Leslie Fiedler's insistence that initiation is basically a discovery of guilt is an equally mistaken matter of faith. Many of the initiation stories I have discussed lack ritual and guilt.

Clearly defined and applied with sensibility and without fanaticism, the concept of the initiation story may assist thorough understanding of many works of fiction. But without these virtues, it may well serve only as another tool for reductive or misleading interpretation.

1. *Studies in the Short Story* (New York, 1949), p. 155.
2. "From Redemption to Initiation," *New Leader,* 41 (May 26, 1958), 22.
3. "Conrad's Two Stories of Initiation," *PMLA,* LXIX (1954), 49–50.
4. Introduction, *Heart of Darkness* (New York, Signet edition, 1950), p. 14.
5. *Conrad the Novelist* (Cambridge, Mass., 1958), p. 40n.
6. "Crashing the Garden Party," *Modern Fiction Studies,* IV (1958–59), 363–364.
7. *Conrad the Novelist,* p. 26.

EILEEN BALDESHWILER

The Lyric Short Story: The Sketch of A History

WHEN THE HISTORY of the modern short story is written, it will have to take into account two related developments, tracing the course of the larger mass of narratives that, for purposes of clarification we could term "epical," and the smaller group which, to accentuate differences, we might call "lyrical." The larger group of narratives is marked by external action developed "syllogistically" through characters fabricated mainly to forward plot, culminating in a decisive ending that sometimes affords a universal insight, and expressed in the serviceably inconspicuous language of prose realism. The other segment of stories concentrates on internal changes, moods, and feelings, utilizing a variety of structural patterns depending on the shape of the emotion itself, relies for the most part on the open ending, and is expressed in the condensed, evocative, often figured language of the poem. In present day literary theory, the term "lyric" refers of course not so much to structure as to subject and tone, and it is mainly to these aspects of the brief narrative that the adjective is meant to call attention in the phrase "lyrical" story. Obviously, the distinction between prose narrative and verse remains absolute: the "lyrical" story, like any other, includes the essentials of storytelling—persons with some degree of verisimilitude engaged in a unified action in time—and the medium remains prose. Looking at the "lyrical" narrative historically, one sees that some writers, a minority, devoted themselves exclusively to this form, while others were able to utilize the "epical" mode as well. Still, there exists a definite line of development within the "lyrical" vein, explicitly so titled as early as 1921 by Conrad Aiken, in a review of *Bliss and Other Stories.* The purpose of the present essay is to sketch the outline of this history by indicating briefly the writers that we need to examine and by suggesting something of their special contributions.

It seems clear that it is in the loosely structured, yet unified, sketches of Turgenev's *A Sportsman's Notebook,* with their subtle discrimination of shades of emotion, their famous "shimmering" tone and lovingly detached attention to the physical details of natural objects and scenes that the lyrical story first emerges as a distinctive form. Episodic in construction, few of the pieces revolve around a conventional plot; rather, more often than not, the author gently leads us through an interlude of time depicted by means of minute, impressionistic touches—not without occasional motifs or semi-symbolic figures—in such a way that the senses are alerted and the feelings softened and made reflective. At first glance, one thinks of Turgenev as working on a canvas crowded with characters, yet the more insistent impression is of a few distinct personages, each of whom is complete within his own aura, his own emotional tone and setting. Through the tactful managing of aesthetic distance and the use of a narrator-observer perfectly attuned to the nuances of nature and human feeling, Turgenev carefully controls and subtly shades tone. Although he works within the limits of naturalism, Turgenev exhibits a supreme power of cloaking all in a dream-like incandescence, of casting the gently melancholy light of his own vision uniformly over natural objects and human events.

Despite his respect and admiration for Turgenev, Chekhov, the next practitioner of the lyric story, works in a different vein, devoting almost his entire attention to reporting small, emotionally laden situations from the point of view of two or three characters. Forsaking the trappings of conventional plot as did Turgenev, Chekhov concentrates his attention on severely limited occasions, diffusing over them a humorous or melancholy light and reporting them with the absolute fidelity of naturalistic art. At times, however, these self-imposed limitations are transcended and Chekhov's story achieves a larger, freer, more musical dimension. Representative of the pieces that rise to the level of truly poetic utterance are "The Schoolmistress," 'Easter Eve," "The Bishop," "Gusev," and "The Lady with the Dog," although these are foreshadowed by such earlier sketches as "The Student" and "The Pipe."

The "musicality" of Chekhov's major stories is exactly described by D. S. Mirsky's comment that while the author's prose is not "melodious," the architectonics of his stories is akin to that of a musical composition. "At once fluid and precise," the narratives are built on "very complicated curves . . . calculated with the utmost precision." The structure of a Chekhov story, then, is "a series of points marking out with precision the lines discerned by him in the tangled web of consciousness." According to Mirsky, Chekhov

> excels in the art of tracing the first stages of an emotional process, in indicating those first symptoms of a deviation when to the general eye, and to the conscious eye of the subject in question, the nascent curve still seems to coincide with a straight line. An infinitesimal touch, which at first hardly arrests the reader's attention, gives a hint at the direction the story is going to take. It is then repeated as a leit-motif, and at each repetition the true equation of the curve becomes more important, and it ends by shooting away in a direction very different from that of the original straight line.

Thus in "The Lady with the Dog" the straight line is the hero's attitude towards his vacation affair with the young wife, an intrigue that he regards as passing and even trivial, while the "curve" is created in the growth of his overwhelming and all-pervasive love for her. (Mirsky adds that in many of Chekhov's stories these lines are complicated by "a rich and mellow atmosphere" arising from the abundance of emotionally significant detail. The effect, then, is poetical, even lyrical, and, as in lyric, it is not plot development that arouses interest. On the contrary, the reader experiences "infection" by the poet's mood. To Mirsky, Chekhov's stories are, in short, "lyrical monoliths": the episodes are themselves deeply conditioned by the whole and without significance apart from it.)

There is a sense in which all of Chekhov's work is symbolical, but in some stories symbols perform central structural functions. The symbols of "The Lady with the Dog" are perhaps least well defined, but certain large metaphors—mostly related to place—are important vehicles of extended meaning. Thus the sea, the hotel room, the provincial concert hall, the house behind the barbed fence, the Yalta resort, all signify states of mind (freedom, imprisonment, vulgarity, longing) and suggest meaning beyond mere physical fact. In "The Schoolmistress," symbols

The Lyric Short Story: The Sketch of a History

205

are more precise and more limited in effect. Objects like the teacher's faded photograph of her mother, which has a direct relation to the girl's hallucinatory vision of the woman in the railway carriage, both unify the story and underline the tragic theme of contrast between what is and what might have been as they recapitulate the past and insert it violently into the present. The difficult, painful journey by cart to the town is itself conventionally symbolic of the entrance into one's tragic destiny, here elaborated by the romantic encounter at the crossroads, the accident at the pond, and the "descent into hell" at the village tavern.

It is traditional "natural" symbols that dominate "Easter Eve," one of the most appealing of all Chekhov's narratives. Here, the symbolism of the Christian Resurrection surrounds Ieronim's account of the death of his fellow monk and the earthly end of a perfect love of charity. Ferrying his passengers across the river to the monastery for the Paschal service, Ieronim questions the meaning of suffering, loneliness, and pain even as he and his companion view with ecstasy the scene of the great Easter fire on the far side of the stream. Thus it is as much through the plethora of suggestion surrounding such traditional symbols as a river passage, the Resurrection, light and darkness, as by means of action or characterization that Chekhov dramatizes profound human emotions. In "Gusev," possibly an atypical Chekhov work, the subject is the death at sea of a simple Russian soldier returning to his village after a campaign in the East. The story gains its flavor by certain devices used to characterize the soldier, for example, a foil in the person of the "intellectual" Pavel, and to suggest the quality of his inner life, particularly the delirious dreams of Gusev's return to the snowbound village, with its terrifying motif of the bull's head without eyes, and the account of the meaningless fight with Chinese men, counterpointed by the exquisite scene of the boatmen with the canaries. As the dying Pavel bitterly chattered, "Gusev was looking at the little window and was not listening. A boat was swaying on the transparent, soft, turquoise water all bathed in hot, dazzling sunshine. In it there were naked Chinamen holding up cages with canaries and calling out: 'It sings, It sings!'" The rapid alternation of scenes in the sick bay with dream sequences and idyllic interludes such as the scenes glimpsed through the porthole, with accompanying shifts of tone, becomes a major structural device and creates an extremely vivid, surrealistic effect.

When Chekhov, like Turgenev, raises tone to the level of a major device, we see an important step away from the conventional tale of reported action (the "epical" story) toward a condition approaching that of the lyric poem. Besides freeing the short story from the limitations of conventional plot, Turgenev and Chekhov consciously exploited language itself to express more sharply states of feeling and subtle changes in emotion. With these authors, the locus of narrative art has moved from external action to internal states of mind, and the plot line will hereafter consist, in this mode, of tracing complex emotions to a closing cadence utterly unlike the reasoned resolution of the conventional cause-and-effect narrative. It is here that we observe the birth of the "open" story. Besides the use of the emotional curve, other new patterns of story organization are beginning to emerge, such as the alternation of scenes and moods for a "surrealistic" effect, the circling around a central dilemma or set of feelings, the record of a moment of intense feeling or perception which contains its own significant form.

The English disciples of Turgenev and Chekhov, especially A. E. Coppard and Katherine Mansfield, exploited some of these innovations in their own way. In Coppard, outward action is again strictly subordinated to inner feelings, for all is directed to portraying the intense moment (as in "Dusky Ruth") or in tracing its secret sources ("The Field of Mustard") or showing the growth of personhood through deep emotional involvement ("Fishmonger's Fiddle"), or the profound though fitful emergence of individual identity ("The Hurly Burly"). Coppard, moreover, can use language with some of the "piety," delicacy, and precision of the English metaphysicals, as Ford Madox Ford has pointed out. In addition, an important source of his poetic effects is his carefully controlled use of setting. The closing section of "The Field of Mustard" affords a fair sampling of the blend of these factors in Coppard's narratives as we see strong infusion of feeling, delicate use of verbal devices including rhythm, continuity of mood among character, setting and theme, and metaphoric use of natural detail. As the unhappy women huddle together along the path of their way home from an afternoon's faggot-gathering in the autumn wood and when each has revealed her former love for the romantic rake Rufus Blackthorn, Rose expresses her envy for Dinah, who has at least the joy of her children.

> "Ain't you got a fire of your own indoors?" grumbled Dinah.
> "Yes."
> "Well, why don't you set by it then!" Dinah's faggot caught the briars of a hedge that overhung, and she tilted round with a mild oath. A covey of partridges feeding beyond scurried away with ruckling cries. One foolish bird dashed into the telegraph wires and dropped dead.

"They're good children, Dinah, yours are. And they make you a valentine, and give you a ribbon on your birthday, I expect?"

"They're naught but a racket from cockcrow till the old man snores—and then its worse."

"Oh, but the creatures, Dinah!"

"You—you got your quiet trim house, and only your man to look after, a kind man, and you'll set with him in the evenings and play your dominoes or your draughts, and he'll look at you—the nice man—over the board, and stroke your hand now and again."

The wind hustled the two women close together, and as they stumbled under their burdens Dinah Lock stretched out a hand and touched the other woman's arm. "I like you, Rose, I wish you was a man."

Rose did not reply. Again they were quiet, voiceless, and thus in fading light they came to their homes. But how windy, dispossessed, and ravaged roved the darkening world! Clouds were borne frantically across the heavens, as if in a rout of battle, and the lovely earth seemed to sigh in grief at some calamity all unknown to men.

Less sure in the development of her own voice, Katherine Mansfield, like Coppard, sometimes achieves the exact balance between realistic detail and delicate suggestiveness that the lyric story demands. Occasionally, as in "The Escape," Miss Mansfield is extremely successful in her use of the epiphany to reflect and resolve emotional complexities. One or two of the earliest pieces show the author's experiments in the pastel mood-piece, for example, "Spring Pictures" and "The Wind Blows." A more sustained lyricism occurs in the mature, two-part story composed of "The Prelude" and "At the Bay." A number of readers have approached "The Prelude" as a novelistic excursus, while others see it as a naturalistic portrayal of a moment of family life and again others take it as representing the culminating appearance of the child Kezia, the autobiographical cipher for the Miss Mansfield herself. If, however, one places Linda Burnell at the center of the narrative—where she quite properly belongs—the story immediately appears as a delicate tracing of the ebb and flow of the woman's emotional life at a crucial period in her development. This life, though presented within a densely realistic context, is most effectively revealed through several powerful symbols: the dream sequences, birds, and especially the aloe tree. Growing on a grassy mound in the drive before the Burnells' house in the country, the tree occupies a focal point as well in the revelation of Linda's consciousness. The gnarled, ancient, seldom-blooming aloe, with its sharp-edged leaves and its roots clutching the earth like claws, is an effective "objective correlative" for the woman with her tangled emotional life of love and hatred, sensitivity and cruelty, fertility and sterility.

In a scene near the close of the story, the tree provides an effective culminating image for the feelings and themes the narrative has developed. As solitary as the ancient tree, Linda Burnell is obsessed by desires of fright and escape. As she and her mother leave the cribbage-playing couple in the drawing room for a moonlight walk in the cool park, this episode takes place:

> "I have been looking at the aloe," said Mrs. Fairfield. "I believe it is going to flower this year. Look at the top there. Are those buds, or is it only an effect of light?"
>
> As they stood on the steps, the high grassy bank on which the aloe rested rose up like a wave, and the aloe seemed to ride upon it like a ship with the oars lifted. Bright moonlight hung upon the lifted oars like water, and on the green wave glittered the dew.
>
> "Do you feel it, too," said Linda . . . "Don't you feel that it is coming towards us?"
>
> She dreamed that she was caught up out of the cold water into the ship with the lifted oars and the budding mast. Now the oars fell striking quickly, quickly. They rowed far away over the top of the garden trees, the paddocks and the dark bush beyond. Ah, she heard herself cry: "Faster! Faster!" to those who were rowing.

Thus, in an interior monologue built around mingled images of imprisonment and flight, love and hatred, Katherine Mansfield reveals the deeply complex emotional life of the protagonist, while surrounding it with a profusion of sensuous detail and minor episodes. Elizabeth Bowen has suggested that when Miss Mansfield's "other side—the high-strung susceptibility, the almost hallucinatory floatingness" unites with her "factual firmness," a unique blend of narrative qualities results. It is this occasionally successful and even eloquent combination that is Miss Mansfield's "signature" among story writers in the lyric vein.

To call D. H. Lawrence a poetic writer is, in the mouths of many, to do no more than call attention to the overpowering sensuality and passion of some of his most characteristic work or to glance at the vein of natural mysticism that occasionally gleams there. Yet when in his shorter pieces Lawrence permits structure itself to be guided by the shape of feeling he can—despite the limitations of his language—

achieve a directly lyrical effect. Although overburdened with thematic considerations, a story like "The Blind Man" illustrates in part this achievement. Other pieces, like "The Christening," provide clearer examples of Lawrence's capacity to portray a group in the throes of intense and contradictory feelings while deriving the narrative's structure from the very ebb and flow of emotion.

Virginia Woolf, likewise, moves the locus of narrative from autonomous external action to interior life. Aside from their interest as illustrative of a rather well thought out epistemology and its accompanying morality, Mrs. Woolf's delicately wrought *Monday or Tuesday* pieces exemplify the use of all the arts of language at the service of narrative whose sole concern is to represent the curve of feeling. The title sketch itself, with its exquisite, forever elusive motif of the heron in flight and its suggestion of the ultimate linking of inner and outer space, shows essentially poetic gifts at work. "A Summing Up" and "The String Quartet," delicately sensuous revelations of the self to itself, each with its climactic epiphany, offer excellent illustrations of Mrs. Woolf's handling of lyric narrative, although the much-anthologized "Kew Gardens" also reveals her essential talents. In "Kew Gardens" Mrs. Woolf depicts, with precise sensory detail and in a strictly sustained tone of what might be called reflective torpor, the passing of a July afternoon when the garden is at the height of its beauty. Groups of people drift along, fragmentary conversations occur, hinting larger tragedies and comedies, a snail inches its way along a leaf. The rhythm is languorous, the pace slow but pervaded by a current of excitement, and the whole pulsates with teeming life, an effect achieved of the piling up of sound, smell, and color images. The opening and closing sections are classic—

> From the oval-shaped flower-bed there rose perhaps a hundred stalks spreading into heart-shaped or tongue-shaped leaves half-way up and unfurling at the tip red or blue or yellow petals marked with spots of colour raised upon the surface; and from the red, blue, or yellow gloom of the throat emerged a straight bar, rough with gold dust and slightly clubbed at the end. The petals were voluminous enough to be stirred by the summer breeze, and when they moved, the red, blue and yellow lights passed one over the other, staining an inch of the brown earth beneath with a spot of the most intricate colour. The light fell either upon the smooth, grey back of a pebble, or, the shell of a snail with its brown, circular veins, or falling into a raindrop, it expanded with such intensity of red, blue and yellow the thin walls of water

that one expected them to burst and disappear. . . . Then the breeze stirred
rather more briskly overhead and the colour was flashed into air above, into
the eyes of the men and women who walk in Kew Gardens in July.

.   .   .   .

Thus one couple after another with much the same irregular and aimless
movement passed the flower-bed and were enveloped in layer after layer of
green blue vapour, in which at first their bodies had substance and a dash of
colour, but later both substance and colour dissolved in the green-blue atmosphere. How hot it was! So hot that even the thrush chose to hop, like a
mechanical bird, in the shadow of the flowers, with long pauses between one
movement and the next; instead of rambling vaguely the white butterflies
danced one above another, making with their white shifting flakes the outline of a shattered column above the tallest flowers . . . Yellow and black,
pink and snow white, shapes of all these colours, men, women, and children
. . . wavered and sought shade beneath the trees. . . . but their voices
went wavering from them as if they were flames lolling from the thick waxen
bodies of candles. . . Wordless voices, breaking the silence suddenly. . . .
But there was no silence; all the time the motor omnibuses were turning their
wheels and changing their gear; like a vast nest of Chinese boxes all of
wrought steel turning ceaselessly one within another the city murmured;
on top of which the voices cried aloud and the petals of myriads of flowers
flashed their colours into the air.

Virtually abandoning external action, choosing as a subject shifts of
emotion more subtle and more private than those depicted by Turgenev
or Lawrence, tracing with the diction and rhythms of the poet the "fall of
the atoms on the mind," Mrs. Woolf definitively abandoned the conventional short story to choose new subjects, new themes, new structures,
and new language. Like that of Turgenev, her work marks an almost
total break between old and new. Later writers in the lyric vein, especially the Americans, may—with the exception of Sherwood
Anderson—be viewed as elaborators rather than discoverers in this
mode.

Everyone knows the egregious failures of *Winesburg, Ohio*, but not
everyone sufficiently credits its successes. For cutting the story free
once for all from the tale, the moral fable, the romantic reverie, the
journalistic *jeu*, Anderson places us all in his debt, but he follows the
best practitioners of the lyric story in his fusing of the skills of the
naturalistic writer with those of the poet. I have written elsewhere of his
circular, hovering, "Chinese box" structure, of the fragmentation of
chronological sequence, the repetitive, incantatory rhythmic effects, the
ritualized dialogue, the use of natural symbols, the insistence that all

other narrative elements must be subordinated to the shape and growth of the emerging emotion. ''Sophistication'' and ''Hands,'' from the *Winesburg* volume, provide respectively a less and a more disciplined example of his characteristic achievement, although ''Death in the Woods'' represents his art at its highest point.

A very different voice is that of Conrad Aiken, the only one of the lyrical short story writers who is also an accomplished poet and thus a kind of test case. While stories like ''The Dark City'' and—in a different way—''Strange Moonlight'' demonstrate Aiken's mastery of sensuous detail, his ability to create structure from interwoven motifs (see the moonlight-gold-goldfinch-medal-peachtree cluster) and his variation of delicately shifting tones and straightforward chronological structure for the sake of a culminating emotion, still his fondness for the allegorical, the hallucinatory, and the lush inhibit Aiken's success with the pure lyrical narrative.

Far more relentless in curbing a tendency to romanticism is Katherine Anne Porter. The success of stories like ''The Circus'' rests on Miss Porter's ability to achieve maximum effect with a minimum of materials through a careful control of mood, impeccable selection of detail, and the sparest possible external action, which is in turn always responsible to the movement of inner feeling. ''The Grave'' is both a more profound and a more unified instance of short story art as it moves freely backward and forward in time, quietly utilizing natural symbolism and an excellent example of the epiphanic ending. Miss Porter works through indirection and omission, shunning the fulsome, the over-elaborated and the strained. At best, her work achieves the severity of structure and purity of language that mark for instance the great sonnets of our language, although her precedents are entirely within the narrative tradition. Her ability to seize a nexus of complex feeling and to capture its nuances in precise but evocative language is rivalled only by that of her contemporary and admirer, Eudora Welty.

Doubtless there are lyrical elements in Miss Welty's ''Death of a Traveling Salesman,'' ''A Worn Path,'' ''Livvie,'' and ''Powerhouse,'' stories marked by a broad range of suggestion, careful management of tone, the use of metaphor as a major structural device, and the abandonment of conventional plot sequence for the sake of the presentation of a developing emotion or pattern of feeling. The same traits appear in purer form in ''A Curtain of Green'' and ''A Memory,'' the latter reminiscent in its different way of Anderson's treatment of adolescent emotion recollected in adult tranquillity. Although Miss Welty is a master of the suggestively concrete detail, she moves further away from naturalism than either Anderson or Katherine Anne Porter. Perhaps what is different in her is a greater detachment, a higher degree of negative capability, than either of the other writers possesses. Her tone is alert, yet retrospective, and she is probing springs of feeling that lie at the exact border between the silent, unconscious life of memory and desire and the daylight dream of order. Imagery and symbol (the Edenic complex in ''A Curtain of Green,'' the picture-frame metaphor in ''A Memory'') are totally responsive to and consumed by passion; they not only assist expression, they are themselves ''expressive.'' In many ways, Miss Welty's language is as delicate as Virginia Woolf's though it has nothing in it of the precious or the diffuse. One of her characteristic interests is the reconciliation of opposites, and the structural pattern of her stories sometimes arises from a dialectical movement from pole to pole of feeling or attitude.

Finally, in a discussion of the American lyrical short story, one would want to mention the work of a young writer of varied talents, John Updike. At a far reach from the expansive Olinger stories is the kind of achievement hinted at in ''Sunday Teasing'' (*The Same Door*) and brought much closer to fruition in the title story of *The Music School*, as well as in ''Harv is Plowing Now'' and ''Leaves,'' from the same volume. In the latter story the reader is struck equally by the variety and disparity of the materials and by the faultlessness of their integration, a union created far below—or above—the level of story-line, theme, or motif. ''Leaves'' may best be described as a sophisticated quest story in the modern manner; at the same time it is an intense probing of the perennial question of moral guilt and of man's movement in and out of purely natural processes, and it is overlain with a profound sense of beauty, reflected or ''expressed'' in its own art. The manner is ostensibly descriptive and essayistic; details of action are presented in hints and indirections and kept carefully subordinated to an estimate of their effect and meaning. The issue of How to be gradually modulates to the question of What to say, thus the reflexive references to the writing of the story: ''And what are these pages but leaves? Why do I produce them but to thrust, by some subjective photosynthesis, my guilt into Nature, where there is no guilt''? Updike's method of construction is to present isolated blocks of description that are yet joined by a continuity of persistent inquiry in the narrative voice. In ''Leaves,'' the author also creates a unifying motif in the grape leaves, with their analogue in Whitman's "Leaves of Grass," to which Mr. Updike refers in the unexpectedly dramatic close of the story.

Here, then, is a sketch of the form an extended account of the development of the lyric story might take, tracing, as it will have to do, a strong line from the inception of this mode with Turgenev, through Chekhov and his English disciples, to Sherwood Anderson and such contemporaries as Eudora Welty and John Updike. Certainly, other writers will need to be taken into consideration, and the work of the authors examined here must be more fully and more carefully assessed. But even to look at the history of the short story from the point of view suggested will tend to make clear that there is, alongside the flow of the realistic, conventional, "epical" narrative that constitutes the mainstream, a parallel development of a mode which can be perfectly distinguished by its characteristic subjects, structures, tone, and language. No complete account of the growth of the serious story can afford to neglect this phase of literary history.

RICHARD KOSTELANETZ

Notes on the American Short Story Today

All media are active metaphors in their power to translate experience into new forms. —Marshall McLuhan

The Americans have handled the short story form so wonderfully that one can say that it is a national art form. —Frank O'Connor

The medium is a metaphor in its ability to offer an image of experience which, though not an exact replica, in some way recreates experience; and in contrast to the novel, whose length makes it capable of presenting a broad picture of reality, the short story devotes its attention to a small area of human existence. If, however, this microcosm is sufficiently resonant, the short story will become a complex symbol for larger worlds. On its surface it may portray a single situation, but in its depths it can comment upon universal issues. For this reason, as a medium the short story is more metaphoric than the novel, which in turn is more metaphoric than reportage. In the great modern short stories, the techniques of representation stem not from realism, which emulates reportage, but from symbolism, which descends from poetry.

The nature of realism as a literary mode is discussed in the following passage from Erich Auerbach's *Mimesis,* perhaps as profound a study of the various forms of reality in literature as has ever been written. Here Auerbach describes the style of representation in Homer's *Odyssey:*

> All this is scrupulously externalized and narrated in leisurely fashion. The two women express their feelings in copious direct discourse. Feelings though they are, with only a slight admixture of the most general considerations upon human destiny, the syntactical connection between part and part is perfectly clear, no contour is blurred. . . . Clearly outlined, brightly and uniformly illuminated, men and things stand out in a realm where everything is visible; and not less clear—wholly expressed, orderly even in their ardor—are the feelings and thoughts of the persons involved.

Evidently, what distinguishes nearly all the best works of modern literature is the rejection of this kind of realism as a literary mode; and since short works of fiction are—by their nature—uncomfortable with lengthy, detailed portraits, the contemporary short story, in all Western literatures, accentuates this non-realistic tendency. But in America, as nowhere else, short-story writers from the times of Washington Irving, Hawthorne, Poe, and Melville to the present have always discarded realism for elliptical and symbolic representational styles. To this day, the best American short stories have presented (1) experiences which are not typical but so extreme that they strain the reader's "willing suspension of disbelief," and (2) actions which are not explained by the author but are presented without editorial comment for the reader's interpretation. The author depicts in depth rather than in breadth, and the world described is not varied and definable but narrow, disordered and ambiguous. What American short-story writers have always offered is a vision of life that must transcend reportage with metaphor if it is to succeed as literature.

Of course, many novelists today are still in the realist tradition, but even the best of them write works that are less interesting, less provocative—indeed, of lesser stature. Yet some of the realistic fiction writers, like Mary McCarthy in America and like Dan Jacobson in England, support their work with essays in which they try to discount the particular achievements of great nonrealistic modern writers. These critics assert, in short, that we measure a novelist by how many full-bodied characters he can create, by how wise and authoritative his narrative voice is, and by how accurately he evokes the reality of what he describes. In fact, we can use these criteria to judge Tolstoy, Dickens and George Eliot; but, when we use them to judge Faulkner, Proust, Gide, and Joyce, they become irrelevant and reactionary since they do not subsume the modern writers' special intentions and achievements. Just as the political reactionary wants to abolish the income tax and return to the free-economy days of yore, so the reactionary novelist-critic wants to discredit the innovations in the form, perception, and content of modern writing. Although this double-barreled defensive maneuver has some conversational notoriety, it has but little influence upon the most important fiction writers today.

A rejection of realism and its concomitant values is a prerequisite for realizing a second ambition of contemporary fiction writers—to stake out for fiction its own unique territory. If a color film can transport us to life in an exotic land more intimately and completely than prose, the novel would be foolish to compete; if a poem can present a concise image, fiction writers should not try to equal poetic economy with the less precise tools of prose. If sociologists and sociological journalists can define shifting patterns of social feeling, and if the essayist can change social behavior and literary taste, the novelist may well pass up both these tasks. Indeed, when a novel provides the most accurate portrait of bad working conditions in the Chicago meat-packing houses—as Upton Sinclair's *The Jungle* did—then the novel's impact represents, not the achievement of fiction, but the failure of sociology to do better. Modern novelists have realized that the essence of fiction is prose style—no other medium can imitate it; and without a special, heightened language, no work of fiction is truly interesting as literature. At the center of the fiction writer's purposes, then, is the creation of a unique style which enables him to penetrate the experience fiction best describes—not the quantifiable, verifiable elements of society and man (really the realm of reportage) but the hidden qualitative phenomena that only a man of vision, the novelist, can perceive.

The revolution against literary realism corresponds to a shift in the structure of the short story. The traditional mode was linear development: things happened realistically, in credible and usually chronological succession, until the story created a pattern of expectation that was concluded by the story's logical end (or sometimes undercut by an equally credible, but less predictable, reversal). Whereas the old short story (whose doddering contemporary heirs are the mystery and the pulp-slick) emphasized the ending (which packed as much surprise and moral punch as possible), the modern short story emphasizes the middle. Unlike their predecessors, contemporary writers of short stories devote their energies largely to the techniques of telling—the use of figurative language, metaphor, the evocation of sharply symbolic (rather than comprehensive) details, well-turned phrases, strategic placement of the climax, manipulation of the point of view, and similar devices—in order to create a fiction not of surface and clarity but of depth and complexity. In modern short works of fiction, plot, tone and (often) theme are established fairly quickly, and the story becomes an elaboration of the opening elements: it is intensified rather than developed. Moreover, in modern short works of fiction, the narrator is rarely a reliable observer—indeed, his unreliability itself often becomes the fiction's central issue. Although Frank O'Connor's assertion that, "in the great modern short stories, there is no character with whom the reader can identify himself" is not true for every first-rate short story (exceptions include works by Samuel Beckett, Faulkner, and Sherwood Anderson), his perception is certainly more often true of short stories than of long works of fiction. In modern short stories, the reader observes the scene instead of participating in it.

Ideally, in modern short stories, each new paragraph should offer a succession of surprises or intensifying symbols; and since the writers concentrate intensely upon shaping every moment of the stories, the resulting fiction is closer in form to poetry than it is to traditional fiction. This is also why the best new short stories can be more *rereadable* than the old ones. Whereas foreknowledge that the wife sold her hair to buy the fob and the husband sold his watch to buy the comb may keep us from enjoying O. Henry's "The Gift of the Magi" a second time, the sheer beauty of style, the esthetic economy, the symbolic perfection, the balanced conflict of moral issues, and the depth and scope of human truths in great modern short stories—such as Joyce's "The Dead," Isaac Babel's "The Sin of Jesus," Kafka's "The Penal Colony," and Hemingway's "A Clean, Well-Lighted Place"—make them worth reading again and again.

II

The modern short story of Chekhov, Joyce, and Hemingway departed from the traditional form. The past few years have presented signs of a new, similarly international development both within and against the modernist canon. These new formal changes are rather quiet and subtle, but they are distinctive enough to suggest another reshaping of the structure of the short story. In Joyce's pervasively influential theory of the short story we remember, the fiction turned upon an epiphany, a moment of revelation in which, in Harry Levin's words, "amid the most encumbered circumstances it suddenly happens that the veil is lifted, the burthen of the mystery laid bare, and the ultimate secret of things made manifest." The epiphany, then, became a technique for jelling the narrative and locking the story's import into place. The classic example is the "Pok" of opening the champagne bottle in Joyce's "Ivy Day in the Committee Room," the gush of air bestowing meaning on the entire story. What made this method revolutionary was the shifting of the focal point of the story from its end—as in (say) Boccaccio, Voltaire, and Balzac—to a spot within the body of the text, usually near (but not at) the end.

In the new short story, on the other hand, the epiphany is abolished, and the writer's theme or perception is diffused throughout the work, which becomes, in effect, a succession of revelatory moments. Donald Barthelme's "To London and Rome" (1963), for instance, is a series of very brief scenes in each of which an excess of money permits the narrator to commit some ridiculous act. One event is not enough to convey the theme, and no one scene is necessarily more important than another; but, through repetition and cumulative impact, the story establishes its point. A similar strategy shapes such a thoroughly ironic work as Jorge Luis Borges' "Pierre Menard, Author of Don Quixote" (1939), essentially a parody of a critical article about a writer whose "admirable ambition was to produce [out of his own mind] pages which would coincide—word for word and line for line—with" *Don Quixote*; here Borges' attitude towards the absurdity of some literary values and styles is diffused in every paragraph of the story. Neither Barthelme nor Borges announces his themes, though in Barthelme the theme is more clearly implied than in Borges. This recent shift in the structure of the modern short story pulls the genre further away from its roots in narrative (which, in our time, is more successfully appropriated by history and reportage) and pushes it closer to the nonlinear spatial forms of modern poetry.

Although the origins of this new short story lie in the past—in Maupassant (particularly "La Horla," *not* "The Necklace"), in Chekhov ("A Boring Story"), in Alfred Jarry ("The Supermale"), in some of the fiction of Franz Kafka and Isaac Babel, and in most of Jean-Paul Sartre's early stories—the change itself is largely the accomplishment of post-war writers: in England, of Samuel Beckett,

Dylan Thomas, Ted Hughes, and B. S. Johnson; in Sweden, of Stig Dagerman; in Russia, of Abram Tertz; in France, of Alain Robbe-Grillet and Pierre Gascard; in Italy, of Tommaso Landolfi and Vera Cacciatore; in Spanish America, of Jorge Luis Borges and Adolfo Bioy Casares; in Germany, of Klaus Roehler, Günter Eich, and Jakov Lind; in Ghana, of Peter Kwame Buahin; and in America, of Donald Barthelme, William Burroughs, Kenneth Koch, Jack Ludwig, James Purdy, Hubert Selby, Jr., Thomas Pynchon, and Curtis Zahn (but not, at least not yet, of Bernard Malamud or Isaac Bashevis Singer).

III

The esthetic development of the modern short story, then, may be divided into three distinct historical stages; and what has happened in American literature, our example for the moment, has parallels in English and continental fiction. In the pre-1920 short stories of (say) Henry James, Armbrose Bierce or Edith Wharton, the pace of the story is—as A. M. Wright has noted—leisurely; most of the important events and thoughts, as well as themes, are fairly explicitly presented; the characters are more exceptional than average; the story's meaning emerges from its surface action; the presentation of events is strictly chronological; the representational mode is a realism seemingly calculated to produce a shock of familiar recognition; the narrator is (except in James) always omniscient; the tone and plot are fairly optimistic, if not moralistic; and the end of the story coincides with the logical termination of the action.

In the short stories of the 1920's—those of Hemingway, Faulkner, and Katherine Anne Porter—the action is greatly pruned until the story appears rather plotless. Yet every detail serves an artistic function; nothing seems unconsidered or accidental. The short stories in the Twenties exhibit greater emotional complexity and ambiguity, as well as a more discriminating sense of emphasis and an increased brevity of representation (in short, a modified, more selective, realism). Their authors let the crucial thoughts and themes remain implicit and elusive, often presenting them in symbolic form; chronology is distorted, usually through flashbacks; the overall attitude is unsentimental, if not aggressively pessimistic; and the characters emerge as fairly undistinguished, typical people who seem, nonetheless, hardly attached either to each other or to traditional social institutions. Instead of concentrating on plot development, the authors resort to rhetorical strategies of parallelism and repetition; the narrator often speaks in the first person and may be a major participant in the action rather than just an observer of it; and the story's end comes as an anticlimax after the earlier epiphany.

The American short stories of the 1940's—particularly those of Lionel Trilling, Shirley Jackson, Mary McCarthy, Delmore Schwartz, J. D. Salinger, and J. F. Powers—are descended directly from the short stories of the 1920's. But, whereas the writers in the Twenties were obsessed by meaninglessness (epitomized by Hemingway's "A Clean, Well-Lighted Place"), the writers in the Forties represented something of a reaction: not only did they favor a more nearly chronological plot with an ending that clamped the fiction into a thematic vise, but they also displayed an overarching concern with moral ambiguity. The 1950's, in retrospect, seem to have been an eclectic decade, productive of little truly original work in the short story, but of many masterly, almost studied, realizations of essentially earlier styles. The chief common tendency in writers as varied as Bernard Malamud, Saul Bellow, Carson McCullers, Flannery O'Connor, and George P. Elliott is towards the development, usually through plot, of an effective symbolic character or situation; and the major theme of short stories during this decade is moral failure—either the inability of a certain moral code to cope with the realities of existence, or (conversely) the individual's inability to find a viable morality.

In the 1960's, the modernist impetus revives, and some of the works during this decade illustrate the third stage in the esthetic development of the modern short story. In these works, the narrative is more discontinuous and the chronology even more distorted (perhaps as a reflection of the formal revolution implicit in quantum theory and in electronic media). Rather than push his characters through a plot, the author fills in the picture, often changing his (and the reader's) attitude towards the scene. The story sometimes gives the impression that it could go on forever—its ending seems less an integral conclusion than a reflection of the author's artistic decision to stop. Particularly in rendering human consciousness (and in using first-person narrators), the writers are more elliptical; they execute transitions in time, scene and (Tillie Olsen, in particular) point of view more sharply, sometimes even without conspicuous notice. Their characters are more radically marginal, if not irrefutably isolated; and most of their stories have extremely limited, if not nonexistent, moral dimensions. Though hardly sentimental, the stories are less ruthlessly pessimistic than their predecessors; and unlike the narrators in the stories of the Forties, the narrators in those of the Sixties rarely make any discoveries (indeed, their inability to understand is often the reader's discovery). The prose style of the stories, while not traditionally literary, is characterized by the use of heightened language that only print can produce, and many of the writers experiment with more original and economical ways to exploit the medium of the printed book. Finally, the stories suggest that a crucial shift in the use of symbolism has occurred: although certain objects, characters, and events have symbolic dimensions, in most of the stories the central theme is not evoked primarily through symbols. (In rare cases, however, the story as a whole becomes a symbol: for example, the milieu portrayed in Thomas Pynchon's ''Entropy'' is symbolic of the scientific concept named in the title.) Not one of these writers can claim to represent things accurately (the rejection of literary realism is complete), but they do evoke actions and mental processes directly, even though the significance of these events generally remains implicit. The meanings of the stories are comparatively clear and definite, although the unconventional techniques may put off the unwary or lazy reader. Thus, not only do the writers of these new short stories endeavor to find a special technique that enhances the experience (for example, Irvin Faust's great mad character Jake Bluffstein needs an over-the-shoulder, third-person narrator—just as Beckett's narrator requires a twisting, dulling prose style); but, more radically, they emphasize the technical elements so strongly that the story can even become a nonnarrative succession of fragmented impressions whose connecting strands fall into place when (and not until) the story is finished or reread. In addition, the main interest is often centered less upon the plot or theme than upon the processes of composition, which are sometimes so conspicuously exposed that they cannot help dominating the story. The short stories of the 1960's represent, then, an extension of the modern revolution, on modernism's terms; and in America at least, the most recent stories take off from, rather than react against, the most fruitful decade for short works of fiction—the 1920's.

IV

In recent American fiction, many of the best works—both long and short—express one of two complementary themes: the absurdity of society and the madness of the self. The European absurd novel (of, say, Sartre and Albert Camus) reveals through description of rather normal activities a disjunction between values and behavior, intention and effect, belief and reality, which proves so broad and irrefutable that it renders the world meaningless. In contrast, the American absurd novel is—like European absurd theatre—an exuberant, nonrealistic portrait of thoroughly ridiculous events which, *in toto,* suggest that the world is ultimately senseless. In the novel form, the absurd writer can take on history itself (as Thomas Pynchon, John Barth and Joseph Heller do) and show in a sprawling, diffuse narrative that history—both in its single events and on the whole—is absurd. Given the limitations of the short story, the absurdist writer is able to treat only a single experience. In Samuel Beckett's brilliant but undeservedly unknown short stories, the action immediately attains metaphysical overtones; but American short-story writers confine their absurd vision to more modest, mundane activities. To Donald Barthelme, in many of his stories, the capacity to spend large amounts of money renders life absurd. To Kenneth Koch, in "The Postcard Collection" (which perhaps echoes Jorge Luis Borges), the absurd activity is the vain attempt to define in declarative sentences the ambiguous experience of art; to Bernard Malamud, in "Naked Nude," it is the artist's irrational and indestructible devotion to his own work; and to Jack Ludwig, in "Thoreau in California," it is all situations that reveal the nonsensical discrepancy between social demands and images on the one hand and individual desires and identities on the other.

In treating the madness of the self—a theme better suited to the short story's capacities—the writer in recent American fiction describes psychological derangement *from the inside.* That is, he dissects the workings of the mad mind itself, instead of carefully noting external symptoms. This internal portraiture distinguishes (say) the first part of Dostoyevsky's *Notes from Underground* from the rather objective representation of a madman's odd behavior in Herman Melville's "Bartleby." Nowadays, the external portraiture seems better suited to the medium that deals best with surface symptoms, the movies; while fiction and poetry (Sylvia Plath, *et al.*) seem better suited to conveying the *feel* of madness. In recent short stories the portraits of mental imbalance range from Michael Rumaker's institutionalized young man, who comes to accept a toy as a human being, to Irvin Faust's Jake Bluffstein, who imagines himself becoming the Messiah of the Jews.

Saul Bellow's Herzog, in the story "Sono and Moso" (later revised and included in the novel), suffers from severe, inexplicable depression, whereas H. W. Blattner's "Sound of a Drunken Drummer" echoes Malcolm Lowry's *Under the Volcano* (1947) in depicting the alcoholic's disjointed consciousness.

Of course, not all of the best recent short stories can be said to express one or the other of these two themes. Influenced by the modern tradition of experiment in multiple points of view, many young writers, invariably products of classes in creative writing, have produced accomplished, rather academic, semblances; Tillie Olsen, however, has employed this technique—in "Tell Me a Riddle"—with such emotional depth, structural fluency, deftness and beauty of language that the story as a whole transcends its ancestry. She has successfully adapted what was originally a novelistic technique to the short-story form, defining the scene and its people from several, differing perspectives; and she never ceases to weave beautiful figures as in the description of the dying grandmother: "Light she grew, like a bird, and like a bird, sound bubbled in her throat while the body fluttered in agony." In value, "Tell Me a Riddle" is surely among the great works of American fiction of recent years.

James Purdy's interests and achievement are more difficult to define. On the one hand, his best novel so far, *Malcolm* (1960), is a minor masterpiece in the absurd tradition—taut, resonant, and almost European in its strong control of every element. In his stories, on the other hand, he has perfected the modern technique of keeping everything implicit and of creating a pregnant moment—a situation, a dialogue, or even a line—that suggests many things. In context, the rather simple line that concludes Purdy's "Goodnight, Sweetheart"—"'God,' Miss Miranda whispered. 'Dear God'"—achieves its power by suggesting a multitude of prayers. Mastery of compression, together with sensitivity, characterizes Purdy's best work, especially his two early stories, "Don't Call Me By My Right Name" and "63: Dream Palace," both of which were written in the Fifties.

Unlike nearly all contemporary writers, Thomas Pynchon builds his fiction upon sophisticated scientific ideas. The structure of his novel *V.* (1963) reflects the concept of reality expressed in quantum theory, and his story "Entropy" (mentioned above) subsumes two possible senses of the scientific term used as the title. Simply and roughly, the term "entropy" signifies, in thermodynamics, "a measure of disorder within a closed system'' or, in information theory, ''a measure of disorder within language.'' In the first sense of ''entropy,'' Pynchon's story depicts the imminence of the heat-death: if the earth's temperature should stay constant at 37° F., then human life would become, on its surface, randomly disordered and would come to exhibit, at its base, stasis. In the second sense of ''entropy,'' the story depicts— explicitly—the failure of Saul (ironically, an information theorist) and his wife to communicate with each other, and —implicitly—the failure of everyone to communicate at the Washington party. In the story's scene, then, entropy in these two senses has reached maximal levels.

V

The overarching theme of the best contemporary short stories is less the imminent apocalypse our political history would suggest than the meaninglessness that would seem the inevitable outcome of our intellectual development. Just as absent as an omniscient narrator (even the third-person narrator is close or over the shoulder) is the definite moral stance; and where one can discern a moral statement in these stories, its authority seems pragmatic and tenuous. Mrs. Blattner suggests only one criterion for judging the alcoholism and high-class prostitution of her character—it drove her to her death; but can we condemn Fiedelman's abductors if they forced him to paint what he believes to be a great picture? With Donald Barthelme's and Kenneth Koch's narrators, moral judgments would seem to emerge from a critique of the styles—they make fools of themselves; therefore, they are not worth emulating. This overarching nihilism debases the satirical impulse, surely implicit in (say) Barthelme and Koch, which as it refuses to offer contrasts turns satire into irony; and irony too is intrinsic in what we have come to call ''black humor''—comedy which suggests that there is a gaping pit in life. This world-view, too, probably accounts for the open form of these stories—the only event that seems capable of terminating an action is the death of a major character; otherwise, as we noted, the story seems capable of going on forever. Open form, as many critics have noted, is characteristic of an age that feels it does not have a strong hold on experience.

The period from 1960 to 1965 has witnessed, I believe, an ascendancy of the short story. Not only has the experimental impulse revived to produce some successful works, particularly in the broken continuity

and the heightened economy of Barthelme and Olsen; but a number of new short-story writers have emerged: most of the writers discussed in this essay, as well Bruce Jay Friedman, William Burroughs, Uli Beigel, Curtis Zahn, Myron Taube, John Yount, Hubert Selby, Jr., Ivan Gold, Susan Sontag, and Philip Roth. None of them has written many stories (in sharp contrast to such repetitious writers as John O'Hara and John Updike), possibly because they regard the writing of a short story as a difficult art that requires nearly as much planning as a novel and nearly as much precise execution as a poem. This great attention is necessary, especially if the short story as a form is to salvage its own identity. The Sixties, so far, have been a good decade for short works of fiction.

A SELECTED, ANNOTATED BIBLIOGRAPHY
OF THE SHORT STORY

I. ESSAY COLLECTIONS AND FICTION BIBLIOGRAPHIES

Aldridge, J. W., ed. *Critiques and Essays on Modern Fiction, 1920– 1951*. New York: The Ronald Press, 1952.

The essays collected here are primarily on the novel. See, however, the extensive general bibliography on fiction compiled by R. W. Stallman, pp. 553–610.

Calderwood, James L., and Harold E. Toliver, eds. *Perspectives on Fiction*. New York: Oxford University Press, 1968.

Although the collection contains some general essays on the nature of fiction and narrative forms, the focus is on the novel.

Chekhov, Anton. *Letters on the Short Story, the Drama, and Other Literary Topics*. Ed. Louis S. Friedland. New York: Dover Publications, 1966.

This translation by Constance Garnett, originally published in 1924, contains comments by Chekhov on his own stories as well as on the stories of others.

Current-García, Eugene, and Walton Patrick, eds. *What is the Short Story?* Rev. ed. New York: Scott, Foresman and Co., 1974.

Although this is primarily a short story anthology, it contains a generous selection of mostly American criticism on the short story arranged in chronological order. Articles listed below which are included in this collection are so noted. The book also contains a four-page general bibliography on the short story.

Gullason, Thomas A., and Leonard Casper, eds. *The World of Short Fiction: An International Collection.* 2nd ed. New York: Harper & Row, 1971. Contains a six-page general bibliography on short fiction.

Kumar, Shiv, and Keith McKean, eds. *Critical Approaches to Fiction.* New York: McGraw-Hill, 1968.

Only four of the selected essays are on the short story: the Bader, Stroud, and Marcus articles which are collected in the present volume, and Chapter One of Ray B. West's *The Short Story in America.*

Rideout, Walter B., and James K. Robinson, eds. *A College Book of Modern Fiction.* Evanston, Illinois: Row, Peterson and Co., 1961.

This short story anthology includes twelve essays on fiction, only four of which are on the short story specifically: the Welty, Stroud, and Friedman articles which are collected in the present volume, and the "Convention" chapter of Sean O'Faolain's *The Short Story.*

Smith, Frank R. "Periodical Articles on the American Short Story: A Selected, Annotated Bibliography." *Bulletin of Bibliography,* 23 (January-April 1960), 9–12; (May-August 1960), 46–48; (September-December 1960), 69–72; (January-April 1961), 95–96.

This checklist of articles published between 1920 and 1950 is coded to indicate relative value of the items. Finding very few articles that give serious critical attention to the short story, Smith suggests his work might almost be considered a "negative" bibliography.

Stevick, Philip, ed. *The Theory of the Novel.* New York: The Free Press, 1967.

The essays selected are all on the novel. See, however, the twenty-two page bibliography on fiction, pp. 407–28.

Summers, Hollis, ed. *Discussions of the Short Story.* Boston: D. C. Heath & Co., 1963.

The nine general essays on the short story are the Poe, Matthews, Jarrell, and Bader selections included in the present volume; Ray B. West's Chapter One, Sean O'Faolain's chapter on "Convention," a chapter each from Percy Lubbock's *Craft of Fiction* and Kenneth Payson Kempton's *The Short Story,* and Bret Harte's "The Rise of

the Short Story.'' Also includes seven additional essays on specific
short story writers.

Thurston, Jarvis, ed. *Reading Modern Short Stories.* Glenview, Illinois: Scott, Foresman and Co., 1955.

This short story anthology contains a four-page general bibliography
on fiction.

Thurston, Jarvis, O. B. Emerson, Carl Hartman, and Elizabeth Wright,
eds. *Short Fiction Criticism: A Checklist of Interpretation Since 1925
of Stories and Novelettes (American, British, Continental), 1800–
1958.* Denver: Alan Swallow, 1960.

This checklist of interpretations of individual stories was brought up
to date by Elizabeth Wright in the Summer 1969 issue of *Studies in
Short Fiction,* and has been supplemented by Ms. Wright, George
Hendrick, and Warren Walker in each Summer issue since then.

Trask, Georgianne, and Charles Burkhart, eds. *Storytellers and Their
Art.* New York: Doubleday Anchor, 1963.

A valuable collection of comments on the short story form by practitioners from Chekhov to Capote. See especially Part I: ''Definitions
of the Short Story'' and ''Short Story vs. Novel,'' pp. 3–30.

Walker, Warren S., comp. *Twentieth-Century Short Story Explication:
Interpretations, 1900–1966, of Short Fiction Since 1800.* 2nd ed.
Hamden, Connecticut: The Shoe String Press, Inc., 1967.

Checklist of interpretations of individual stories.

II. BOOK-LENGTH STUDIES AND HISTORIES

Beachcroft, T. O. *The Modest Art: A Survey of the Short Story in
English.* London: Oxford University Press, 1968.

An historical survey of the major figures of the English short story
from Chaucer to Doris Lessing. The result of the basic difference
between antique stories (listening) and modern stories (reading) is
that the modern short story writer attempts to portray rather than
expound. He removes his own personality from the story and presents
the flash of insight through poetic methods.

Canby, Henry S. *The Short Story in English.* New York: Holt, Rinehart
and Winston, Inc., 1909, reprinted 1932.

The romantic movement gave birth to the modern short story; Poe is
the first important figure in the changing fashions of story-telling
since Chaucer. The rest of the nineteenth century and the first of the

twentieth has applied Poe's theory of single effect to new subjects, primarily the contrasts of civilizations in flux.

Canby, Henry S., and Alfred Dashiell. *A Study of the Short Story.* Rev. ed. New York: Henry Holt and Co., Inc., 1935.

A short story anthology with a long introduction based on *The Short Story in English.* A survey of the development of short fiction from the varieties of medieval forms (all best represented in *Canterbury Tales*) through the American local color story of the turn of the century. The comments on how the short story combines the elements of the exemplum, the essay, the novella, the gothic romance, and the romantic sketch, are still helpful.

Esenwein, J. Berg. *Writing the Short-Story: A Practical Handbook on the Rise, Structure, Writing and Sale of the Modern Short-Story.* New York: Hinds, Noble and Eldredge, 1909.

One of the best known of the early "how-to" books. Discusses what a short story is not: not a condensed novel, an episode, a synopsis, a biography, a sketch, or a tale. Lists seven basic characteristics that add up to the following definition: "A Short-Story is a brief, imaginative narrative, unfolding a single predominating incident and a single chief character, it contains a plot, the details of which are so compressed, and the whole treatment so organized, as to produce a single impression."

Grabo, Carl H. *The Art of the Short Story.* New York: Charles Scribner's Sons, 1913.

A craft book for aspiring writers. Discusses the underlying principles of all narrative writing such as point of view, plot, character, dialogue, the unities, and description. The only difference between the short story and the novel is that the short story is more exacting in the selective process and more unified in action, place and time. The short story aims at a single effect. Writers of longer narratives aim at a variety of effects which "more nearly mirror the complexities of emotional life."

Kempton, Kenneth Payson. *The Short Story.* Cambridge: Harvard University Press, 1947.

A book on the technique of the short story for aspiring writers. Basic principle is that "a good story entails an unwritten contract between its writer, the editor, and its reader, and that good story writing must reconcile these often conflicting points of view. . . ." Quite detailed and full of illustrations, but still just a craft book.

Newman, Frances. *The Short Story's Mutations: From Petronius to Paul Morand*. New York: B. W. Huebsch, Inc., 1924.

Although most of this book is story anthology, the inter-chapters chart the story's evolution from the "Matron of Ephesus" to Morand's "The Nordic Night"—an evolution of subtly changing techniques growing out of shifting philosophic attitudes. The broad movement is from the ironic mode to the impressionistic.

O'Brien, Edward J. *The Advance of the American Short Story*. Rev. ed. New York: Dodd, Mead and Co., 1931.

A survey of the development of the American short story from Irving to Sherwood Anderson. The focus is on contributions to the form by various authors: Irving's development of the story from the 18th century essay, Hawthorne's discovery of the subjective method for psychological fiction, Poe's formalizing, Harte's caricaturing, James' development of the "central intelligence," and Anderson's freeing the story from O. Henry formalism.

————. *The Dance of the Machines: The American Short Story and the Industrial Age*. New York: The Macaulay Co., 1929.

Chapter four of this rambling polemic against machine-like standardization in the industrial age describes thirty characteristics which the short story ("the most typical American form") shares with the machine: e.g., it is patterned, impersonal, standardized, speeded-up, and cheap.

O'Faolain, Sean. *The Short Story*. New York: The Devin-Adair Co., 1951.

A book on the technique of the short story which says that technique is the "least part of the business." O'Faolain illustrates his thesis that personality is the most important element by describing the personal struggles of Daudet, Chekhov, and de Maupassant. However, he does his duty to the assigned subject of the book by also discussing the technical problems of convention, subject, construction, and language.

Pain, Barry. *The Short Story*. London: Martin Secker, 1916.

One of a series of pamphlets on various genres. The primary distinction between the short story and the novel is that the short story, because of its dependence on suggestive devices, demands more of the reader's participation. "The novelist gives more to the reader and asks less of him. The short-story writer gives less and asks more."

Pattee, Fred Lewis. *The Development of the American Short Story.* New
York: Harper and Row, 1923.
The most detailed and historically full survey of the American short
story from Irving to O. Henry. Charts the changes in taste of the
short-story reading public and indicates the major contributions to the
form of such "classic" practitioners as Irving, Hawthorne, Poe, and
Harte. Surveys the effect of the "Annuals," the "Ladies' Books,"
local color, Matthew's *Philosophy of the Short Story,* and the writing
handbooks.

Peden, William. *The American Short Story: Front Line in the National
Defense of Literature.* Boston: Houghton Mifflin Co., 1964.
Discussion of major trends in the American short story since 1940.
The center of the book consists of a chapter on those writers who focus
on everyday life in contemporary society (Cheever, O'Hara, Peter
Taylor, Updike, Powers, and Salinger) and a chapter on those who are
preoccupied with the grotesque, abnormal, and bizarre (McCullers,
O'Connor, Purdy, Capote, and Tennessee Williams). An additional
chapter surveys other short story subjects such as the war, minorities,
regions, and science fiction.

Ross, Danforth. *The American Short Story.* Minneapolis: University of
Minnesota Press, 1961.
No. 14 of the Pamphlets on American Writers Series. A sketchy
survey which measures American stories since Poe against Aristotelian criteria of action, unity, tension, and irony. Ends with the Beat
Generation writers who rebel against the Poe-Aristotle tradition by
using shock tactics.

Ward, Alfred C. *Aspects of the Modern Short Story: English and
American.* London: University of London Press, Ltd., 1924.
Brief dicussions of representative stories of twenty-three different
writers. In the introduction, Ward lists five rather simplistic characteristics of the parable form by which to judge the short story.
However, he does note that the short story is ideally suited to the
impressionistic effect and the territory of the unconscious.

West, Ray B., Jr. *The Short Story in America: 1900–1950.* Chicago:
Henry Regnery, Co., 1952.
Probably the most familiar and most often recommended history of
the American short story. I assume it attempts to take up where Fred
Lewis Pattee's book leaves off, but it lacks the completeness or the

continuity necessary for an adequate history. Chapter I, "The American Short Story at Mid-Century," is a short survey in itself of the development of the short story since Irving, Hawthorne and Poe. Chapter IV is devoted completely to Hemingway and Faulkner.

Williams, William Carlos. *A Beginning on the Short Story: Notes.* Yonkers, New York: The Alicat Bookshop Press, 1950.

In these "Notes" from a writers workshop session, Williams makes several interesting, if fragmentary and impressionistic, remarks about the form: the short story, as contrasted with the novel, is a brush stroke instead of a picture. Stressing virtuosity instead of story structure, it is "one single flight of the imagination, complete: up and down." It is best suited to depicting the life of "briefness," "brokenness and heterogeneity."

Wright, Austin. *The American Short Story in the Twenties.* Chicago: University of Chicago Press, 1961.

Using a canon of 220 stories, one set selected from the twenties and the other from the immediately preceding period, Wright examines differing themes and techniques to test the usual judgments of what the "modern short story" is. The examination is belabored for some four hundred pages and only ends in proving that the short story of the twenties is different from the short story of the naturalists.

III. SPECIAL SERIES

A. *Kenyon Review International Symposium on the Short Story.*

Contributions from short story writers from all over the world on the nature of the form, its current economic status, its history, and its significance. Plans were announced in 1970 for the publication of a single volume of the symposium, but the project was postponed indefinitely without explanation.

Part I, 30, Issue 4, 1968, 443–90. Christian Stead (England), Herbert Gold (United States), Erin Kŏs (Yugoslavia), Nadine Gordimer (South Africa), Benedict Kiely (Ireland), Hugh Hood (Canada), Henrietta Drake-Brockman (Australia), Carlo Cassola (Italy).

Part II, 31, Issue I, 1969, 58–94. William Saroyan (United States), Jun Eto (Japan), Maurice Shadbolt (New Zealand), Chanakya Sen (India), John Wain (England), Hans Bender (West Germany), and "An Agent's View" by James Oliver Brown.

Part III, 31, Issue 4, 1969, 450–502. Ana Maria Maute (Spain), Torbork Nedreaas (Norway), George Garrett (United States), Elizabeth Taylor (England), Ezekiel Mphahlele (South Africa), Elizabeth Harrower (Australia), Mario Picchi (Italy), Junzo Shono (Japan), Khushwant Singh (India).
Part IV, 32, Issue I, 1970, 78–108. Jack Cope (South Africa), James T. Farrell (United States), Edward Hyams (England), Luigi Barzini (Italy), David Ballantyne (New Zealand), H. E. Bates (England).

B. *Studies in Short Fiction History of the English Short Story.*

Duncan, Edgar Hill. "Short Fiction in Medieval English: A Survey," *Studies in Short Fiction,* 9 (Winter 1972), 1–28.

A survey of short pieces in the Old English period, primarily in verse, which have in common the characteristic of "artfully telling a story in a relatively brief compass" and which focus on "singleness of character, of action, and/or of impression." The fall of the angels and the fall of man in the *Genesis B,* the flight of the Israelites and crossing of the Red Sea in the *Exodus,* the St. Guthlac poems, and *The Dream of the Rood* are analyzed.

————. "Short Fiction in Medieval English: II. The Middle English Period." *Studies in Short Fiction,* 11 (Summer 1974), 227–41.

A brief sampling of short fiction elements in the "shorter romance" form, the exemplary narrative, the beast tale, and the fabliau introduced to Middle English by the French. Also noted are paraphrases of biblical stories, saints' lives, and the dream visions of *Pearl* and Chaucer's "The Book of Duchess" and the "Prologue to the Legend of Good Women."

Schlauch, Margaret. "English Short Fiction in the 15th and 16th Centuries." *Studies in Short Fiction,* 3 (Summer 1966), 393–434.

A survey of types of short fiction from the romantic *lai* to the *exemplum,* and from the bawdy *fabliau* to the *novella.* Her conclusions are that modern short story writers are heirs both in subject matter (e.g., internal psychological conflict) and technique (e.g., importance of dialogue) to a long tradition that antedates the 17th century, a tradition that is still worth studying.

Mish, Charles C. "English Short Fiction in the Seventeenth Century." *Studies in Short Fiction,* 6 (Spring 1969), 223–330.

He divides the period into two parts: 1600–1660, in which short fiction declined into sterile imitation and preciousness, and 1660–1700, in which it was revitalized by the French influence of such as Mme. de Lafayette's *Princess de Cleves*. The French direction toward interiorization, psychological analysis and verisimilitude in action and setting, combined with the English style of the self-conscious narrator, moves fiction toward the novel of the eighteenth century.

Boyce, Benjamin. "English Short Fiction in the Eighteenth Century: A Preliminary View." *Studies in Short Fiction.* 5 (Winter 1968), 95–112.

Discusses the types of short fiction found in the periodicals and inserted in novels: character sketch, oriental tale, stories of passion. Usually the purpose was didactic and the mode was either "hovering pathos" or "hovering irony." The most distinctive characteristic is the formal, even elegant, language.

Harris, Wendell V. "English Short Fiction in the Nineteenth Century." *Studies in Short Fiction,* 6 (Fall 1968), 1–93.

After distinguishing between "short fiction" appearing before 1880 and "short story" after 1880, Harris surveys examples from both periods. The turning point, as one might expect, is the definition posed by Brander Matthews which first appeared in *The Saturday Review* in 1884.

IV. ARTICLES AND PARTS OF BOOKS

"The Art of the Short Story: Principles and Practices in the United States." *Times Literary Supplement,* September 17, 1954, pp. xl, xlii. Also included in *American Writing Today: Its Independence and Vigor.* Ed. Allan Angoff. New York: New York University Press, 1957, pp. 176–91. A survey of the development of the American short story. Suggests that the form thrived in prose-conscious nineteenth-century America because it fulfilled a poetic need. American stories are usually better than British ones because the wide divergence of places in America makes the artist aware of the multifariousness of life; he is compelled to subdue, order, and yet preserve that experience in the short story.

Backus, Joseph M. "'He Came Into Her Line of Vision Walking Backward': Nonsequential Sequence-Signals in Short Story Openings." *Language Learning,* 15 (1965), 67–83.

A sequence signal is a word indicating that the sentence in which it appears follows another sentence on which it depends for its meaning. The short story makes frequent use of such signals out of sequence. For example in the first sentence of Mary King's "The Honey House" ("He came into her line of vision walking backward. . . ."), the personal pronouns are referentless and thus out of sequence. The effect of the device is to pique the reader's curiosity, to plunge him *in media res,* and to reflect the slow process of identification by which he confronts the new experience.

Baker, Falcon O. "Short Stories for the Millions." *Saturday Review,* 19 Dec. 1953, pp. 7–9, 48–49. (Also in *What is the Short Story?*)

As a result of Brooks and Warren's *Understanding Fiction* and the New Criticism's focus on form, the short story writer has begun to ignore entertainment value and the ordinary reader. Critics and editors have so disparaged the formula story that they have created another formula—"the literary formula of the unresolved impasse."

Baker, Howard. "The Contemporary Short Story." *Southern Review,* 3 (Winter 1938), 576–96.

A long review article of *Best American Stories of 1937* and fifteen other collections. Everything "worth saying about the short story bears in one way or another on the point that writing must be built up from a substructure of ideas." Urges that the short story be made deliberately much more intellectual than it usually is, or is recognized as being.

Beck, Warren. "Art and Formula in the Short Story." *College English,* 5 (November 1943), 55–62.

Discussion of the difference between the popular short story and the literary short story. There is no sharp technical distinction; the literary story is the assertion of a different outlook—a protest against deceptive sentimentalizing of reality.

———. "Conception and Technique." *College English,* 11 (March 1950), 308–17.

Asserts the primacy of conception in fiction and the relative dependence of technique.

Beebe, Maurice. "A Survey of Short Story Textbooks." *College English,* 18 (January 1957), 237–43.

A review of forty short-story textbook anthologies in print at the time; the best one is still Brooks and Warren's *Understanding Fiction,* the model for all critical readers since 1943.

Bierce, Ambrose. "The Short Story." *The Collected Works of Ambrose Bierce*. 1911; rpt. New York: Gordian Press, Inc., 1966. X, 234–48.
Criticizes Howells and the realistic school: "to them nothing is probable outside the narrow domain of the commonplace man's most commonplace experience. . . . the truest eye is that which discerns the shadow and the portent, the dead hands reaching, the light that is the heart of darkness."

Bleifuss, William. "The Short Story in Text and Intact." *College English*, 23 (February 1962), 402–08.
A supplement to Beebe's review, covering twenty-seven short story texts published from 1957 to 1961.

Boynton, Percy H. "American Authors of Today: The Short Story." *English Journal*, 12 (May 1923), 325–33.
The interest in technique has died down in short stories in the periodicals. The search now is for new subject matter, most of which is found in the realm of the supernatural or in far away exotic places.

Brickell, Herschel. "The Contemporary Short Story." *The University of Kansas City Review*, 15 (Summer 1949), 267–70.
Makes several generalizations about the decline of quality magazines willing to publish fiction, about the trend of the short story to be more subjective, psychological, and poetic, and about the lack of writers who find the short story a natural and inevitable form. Many writers of promise who began with the short story have now turned to the novel.

————. "What Happened to the Short Story?" *Atlantic Monthly*, 188 (September 1951), 74–76. (Also in *What is the Short Story?*) We have reached a very high plateau in the development of the American short story. Modern writers have succeeded in breaking the story away from its formal frame by drawing it nearer to poetry "in the precise and beautiful use of language" and by making it a "slice of the mind and the spirit rather than the body."

Canby, Henry S. "Free Fiction." *Atlantic Monthly*, 116 (July 1915), 60–68 (Also in *What is the Short Story?*)
Criticism of the "well-made," "formula" story of the day, because it is based more on convention than life, especially when contrasted with the "reality" of Chekhov's stories. The multitudinous situations, impressions, and incidents in modern life are perhaps incapable of presentation in a novel because of their very impermanence, but they are "admirably adapted to the short story because of their vividness and their deep if narrow significance."

————. "On the Short Story." *Dial,* 31 (October 16, 1901), 271–73. (Also in *What is the Short Story?*)

The novel-writer aims at a natural method of transcription; the short story writer adopts the artificial method of selecting only what bears on his narrow purpose—the conveying of vivid impressions of one phase of a situation or character. The short story which "forsakes its natural field to delve deep into the mystery of things or the confusion of psychological character-subtleties is usually a flat failure."

Clarke, John H. "Transition in the American Negro Short Story." *Phylon,* 21 (Winter 1960), 360–66. A shorter version of this article appears as the introduction to *American Negro Short Stories.* Ed. John Henrik Clarke. New York: Hill and Wang, 1966. A brief historical survey of the American Negro short story from Dunbar and Chesnutt at the turn of the century, through the Harlem literary renascence of the twenties, to the emergence of Richard Wright, who marked the end of the double standard for Negro writers.

Colum, Mary M. "The American Short Story." *Dial,* 62 (April 19, 1917), 345–47.

Review of O'Brien's *Best Stories of 1916* and Harry T. Baker's writing manual, *The Contemporary Short Story.* Criticism of the commercial standardization of the form. The short story is not so close to the novel, but rather somewhere between the drama and the essay form. The real writers of the day—Frost, Masters, Lowell— present short stories in the guise of free verse or polyphonic prose.

Cory, Herbert Ellsworth. "The Senility of the Short Story." *Dial,* 62 (May 3, 1917), 379–81. (Also in *What is the Short Story?*)

The short story has become obsessed with a unity which is abnormally artificial and intense. Seldom attaining high seriousness, it is a literature of feverish excitement, "the blood kinsman of the quick-lunch, the vaudeville, and the joy-ride."

Current-García, Eugene and Walter R. Patrick. "Introduction." *American Short Stories.* Rev. ed., 1964, pp. xi-liv.

An historical survey of the American short story through four periods: romanticism, realism, naturalism, and the modern period of both traditionalists (those who have carried on the Poe-De Maupassant-James tradition) and experimentalists (those who have focused more on the fragmented inner world of the mind).

————, eds. *Short Stories of the Western World.* Glenview, Illinois: Scott, Foresman and Co., 1969.

This anthology includes lengthy and detailed introductory comments on four different historical periods in the development of the short story.

Dawson, W. J. "The Modern Short Story." *North American Review,* 190 (December 1909), 799–810.
Applying the critical test that a short story must be complete in itself and consist of a single incident, Dawson can dismiss stories by Dickens and Hardy and praise those by Kipling, Stevenson, Poe and Hawthorne. "The finest writing in a short story is that which takes us quickest to the very heart of the matter in hand."

Dollerup, Cay. "The Concepts of 'Tension,' 'Intensity,' and 'Suspense' in Short-Story Theory." *Orbis Litterarum,* 25 (1970), 314–37.
Heavily documented survey of critical theory in German, Danish, and English on the concepts of intensity or tension in the short story and how these terms have been applied to linguistic rhythm, contrast, character, structure, and reader suspense in the form.

Dyer, Walter A. "A Short Story Orgy." *Bookman,* 51 (April 1920), 217–23.
Mostly thumbnail sketches of some twenty-seven short story collections published during the year, but prefaced by some general considerations on the lack of any common denominator that may be applied to the form.

Eastman, Richard M. "The Open Parable: Demonstration and Definition." *College English,* 22 (October 1960), 15–18. Also appears in *Approaches to the Short Story.* Ed. Neil D. Isaacs and Louis H. Leiter. San Francisco: Chandler.
Using his own original story as an example, Eastman describes the parable form perfected by Kafka and Beckett. It differs from the traditional parable because its "designed instability" leaves its ethical analogy open to the interpretation of the reader.

Elliott, George P. "A Defense of Fiction." *Hudson Review,* 16 (1963), 9–48. Reprinted as an introduction to *Types of Prose Fiction.* Ed. George P. Elliott. New York: Random House, 1964, pp. 3–30.
Discussion of four basic impulses that mingle with the story-telling impulse: "to dream, to tell what happened, to explain the nature of things, and to make a likeness."

————. "Exploring the Province of the Short Story." *Harpers,* 230 (April 1965), 111–16.

A review of seven collections including Cheever's *Brigadier and the Golf Widow,* Singer's *Short Friday,* and O'Hara's *The Horse Knows the Way.* "The worst pitfall a writer dealing in extremes must watch out for is depersonalizing his characters. At the brink, people are apt to behave much alike, less according to their personal natures than according to human nature generally."

Engstrom, Alfred G. "The Formal Short Story in France and its Development Before 1850." *Studies in Philology,* 42 (July 1945), 627–39.

After making distinctions between the *Nouvelle* and the *Conte* (a complex line of action vs. a compressed one), Engstrom points out the lack of any significant examples of *Conte* until Mérimée's *Mateo Falcone* (1829), the first formal short story in French literature. The only other significant contributors to the form before 1850 are Balzac and Gautier.

Farrell, James T. "Nonsense and the Short Story," *The League of Frightened Philistines and Other Papers.* New York: Vanguard Press, Inc., 1945 (written in 1937), pp. 72–81.

Ridicules the crop of short-story writing handbooks that sprang from Brander Matthews' *Philosophy of the Short-Story.* Their focus on form has made technical facility a value and has falsified the material of life. The typical American short story either affirms the ideological aims of capitalism or patronizes those of lower economic origin.

————. "The Short Story," *The League of Frightened Philistines and Other Papers.* New York: Vanguard Press, 1945 (written in 1935), pp. 136–48.

Decries the inadequacy of many revolutionary social critics practicing the short story form. Too often the revolutionary point of view appears more glued on than integral to the story.

Fitz Gerald, Gregory. "Introduction." *Modern Satiric Stories: The Impropriety Principle.* Glenview, Illinois: Scott, Foresman and Co., 1971, pp. 2–47.

Expansion of Fitz Gerald's article which is reprinted in the present volume. The three part definition of the satiric short story is considerably bolstered by examples divided into types: allegories, science fiction, fantastic and realistic satires, monologues, and parodies.

Also includes bibliographies of short story, satire, and science fiction criticism.

Fuller, Henry B. "New Forms of Short Fiction." *Dial,* 62 (March 8, 1917), 167–69. Survey of the types of magazine and newspaper fiction of the period and how popular taste and the demands of weekly publication conditioned them.

Gardner, John and Lennis Dunlap, eds. *The Forms of Fiction.* New York: Random House, 1962.

This text anthology includes descriptions of the various forms of short fiction: sketch, fable, yarn, tale, short story, and short novel.

Geismar, Maxwell. "The American Short Story Today." *Studies on the Left,* 4 (Spring 1964), 21–27.

Criticizes the Salinger-Roth-Malamud-Updike coterie for their stress on craftsmanship of the well-made story and their ignoring of the social realities of the time. Even though there is much excitement in contemporary life, the "American artist has been shrinking further and further into the labyrinthian recesses of the tormented and isolated psyche, of the individual soul."

Gerould, Katherine Fullerton. "The American Short Story." *Yale Review,* NS 13 (July 1924), 642–63.

Urges that the short story be read as critically as the novel. Poses the following requirements for the form: it must be well-made; it must give us situation, suspense, and climax; and it must focus on a significant event which is either truly momentous for the character or typical of the lives of many people.

Gold, Herbert. "The Novel and the Story—the Long and Short of It." *Fiction of the Fifties.* Ed. Herbert Gold. Garden City, New York: Doubleday & Co., Inc., 1959, pp. 12–15.

The short story since Joyce has concerned itself with "scene and incident, striking hot, like the lyrical poem." The novel since Dostoyevsky and Tolstoy has made "the whole man face the whole world."

Gullason, Thomas A. "Revelation and Evolution: A Neglected Dimension of the Short Story." *Studies in Short Fiction,* 10 (Fall 1973), 347–56.

Challenges Mark Schorer's distinction between the short story as an "art of moral revelation" and the novel as an "art of moral evolution." Analyzes Lawrence's "The Horse Dealer's Daughter" and

Steinbeck's "The Chrysanthemums" to show the short story embodies both revelation and evolution.

Harte, Bret. "The Rise of the Short Story." *Cornhill Magazine,* 7 (July 1899), 1–8. (Also in *Discussions of the Short Story* and *What is the Short Story?*)

More properly, Harte's subject is the "rise" of the local color story in America, which he says is the true American story—as opposed to the earlier stories by Irving which had English models.

Hartley, L. P. "In Defense of the Short Story." *The Novelist's Responsibility.* London: Hamish Hamilton, 1967, pp. 157–59.

A brief consideration of why short stories are not popular when collected in a single book; mainly it is reader laziness, for each story requires such close concentration.

Hicks, Granville. "The Art of the Short Story." *Saturday Review,* 41 (December 20, 1958), 16.

A review of *Best American Short Stories of 1958* and *Stanford Short Stories–1958.* An emotional experience for the reader, rather than plot or character, is the focus for the modern short story.

Howe, Irving. "Tone in the Short Story." *Sewanee Review,* 57 (Winter 1949), 141–52.

Review of *Best American Short Stories of 1948, Prize Stories of 1948,* and collections of stories by Delmore Schwartz, Isaac Babel, and others. Because the short story lacks prolonged characterization and the independent momentum of the novel, it depends more on those technical devices or inflections of style we call tone. "A novel written in one dominant tone becomes intolerable; a story too often deviating from it risks chaos."

Howells, William Dean. "Some Anomalies of the Short Story." *North American Review,* 173 (September 1901), 422–32.

The basic anomaly is that while readers seem to enjoy stories in the magazines, they do not read them when collected in a volume. Each story requires so much of the reader's energy that several together exhaust him. One of the basic defects of the short story in comparison to the novel is that it creates no memorable characters.

Hull, Helen R. "The Literary Drug Traffic." *Dial,* 67 (Sept. 6, 1919), 190–92.

The majority of short stories in the mass magazines are a mild literary dope, read by people who wish a substitute for their childhood day-dreaming and phantasying. "If there were a desire for stories with vitality or humor or beauty or vision or comment, there might be more such stories."

Joselyn, Sister Mary, O.S.B. "Edward Joseph O'Brien and the American Short Story." *Studies in Short Fiction,* 3 (Fall 1965), 1–15.

Attempts a synthesis of O'Brien's philosophic and aesthetic attitudes which may have determined his choices of "best stories." Discusses also O'Brien's contribution to the history, theory, and growth of the American short story.

Kostelanetz, Richard. "The Short Story in Search of Status." *Twentieth Century,* 174 (Autumn 1965), 65–69.

Substantially the same article which appears in this collection under the title, "Notes on the American Short Story Today."

Langbaum, Robert. "Best Short Stories." *Commentary,* 24 (August 1957), 171–73.

Review of *Best American Short Stories of 1956.* Many of the stories deal either with minority groups ("For the minority culture offers definable mores which, in the more serious stories, can then be used to accentuate the lack of mores in the majority culture.") or with the majority culture through odd points of view, most commonly that of childhood.

Marler, Robert F. "From Tale to Short Story: The Emergence of a New Genre in the 1850's." *American Literature,* 46 (May 1974), 153–69.

Using Northrop Frye's distinction between the tale (embodies "stylized figures which expand into psychological archetypes") and the short story (deals with characters who wear their "*personae* or social masks"). Marler surveys the critical condemnation of the tale form and the increasing emphasis on realism in the 1850's. The broad shift is from Poe's overt romance to Melville's mimetic portrayals, especially in "Bartleby, the Scrivener."

Matson, Esther. "The Short Story." *Outlook,* 121 (March 5, 1919), 406–09.

A consideration of why the short story had such an enormous appeal at the time. Instead of playing on our intellectual or spiritual natures, the short story plays on emotion, and at this time "our nerves are painfully close to the surface." The danger of the short story is that the writer "must often be tempted to harp upon the emotions that depress and devitalize instead of invigorate."

Maugham, W. Somerset. "The Short Story." *Points of View: Five Essays*. Garden City, New York: Doubleday & Co., Inc., 1958, pp. 163–212.

This long and "desultory essay," as Maugham himself calls it, combines his earlier "Introduction" to *Tellers of Tales: 100 Short Stories from the United States, England, France, Russia and Germany*. New York: Doubleday, Doran & Co., Inc., 1939, pp. xiii–xxxix; and "The Short Story." *Essays by Divers Hands: Being the Transactions of the Royal Society of Literature of the United Kingdom,* XXV, n.s. Ed. Sir Edward Marsh. London: Geoffrey Cumberlege, Oxford University Press, 1950, pp. 120–34. As might be expected, Maugham's preference is for the "well-made story exemplified by De Maupassant's "The Necklace." However, most of the essay deals with Chekhov and Mansfield biographical material.

May, Charles E. "The Short Story in the College Classroom: A Survey of Textbooks Published in the Sixties." *College English,* 33 (Jan. 1972), 488–512.

An omnibus review of 110 short-story textbooks published in America between 1961 and 1970. The texts are classified according to methods of organization (elements of fiction, thematic categories, modes of fiction, major authors, etc.) and evaluated according to the apparatus (critical commentary, study questions, teacher manuals, bibliographies) featured in each.

Millet, F. B. "The Short Story." *Contemporary American Authors: A Critical Survey*. New York: Harcourt, Brace and Co., 1940, pp. 85–97. An adequate survey of the American short story from the nineties to the forties. The emphasis is on influences on the form: rise of the large circulation slicks, Chekhov, O'Brien, and the aesthetic forces of both objective and subjective naturalism.

Mirrielees, Edith R. "The American Short Story." *Atlantic Monthly,* 167 (June 1941), 714–22.

A complaint about the decline of consistently maintained talent in short story writing since 1920. The promising writer who begins in the little magazines aims toward the wider popularity of the slicks; his quality declines accordingly.

———. "Short Stories, 1950." *College English,* 12 (May 1951), 425–32.

A survey of the American short story during the first fifty years of the twentieth century, focusing especially on the typical subject matter of short stories in the late forties. Notes the increase of stories about childhood, stories of the supernatural, and stories sparked by racial and economic oppressions. Also notes a shift away from individual character interest to general significance of the situation or predicament.

Moffett, James. "Telling Stories: Methods of Abstraction in Fiction." *ETC.* 21 (December 1964), 425–50.

Charts a sequence covering "entire range" of ways in which stories can be told, from the most subjective and personal (interior monologue and dramatic monologue) to the most objective and impersonal (anonymous narration); includes examples of each type. The progression is the basis for *Points of View: An Anthology of Short Stories.* Ed. James Moffett and Kenneth R. McElheny. New York: New American Library, 1966.

Munson, Gorham. "The Recapture of the Storyable." *The University Review,* 10 (Autumn 1943), 37–44.

A brief survey of the short story's escape from the O. Henry formula. The best short-story writers are concerned only with three questions: "have I discovered a storyable incident? how shall I cast my actors? who would best tell it?" To define "storyable" he turns to James' description of the writer's subject as a "tiny nugget" with a "hard latent value."

Newman, Frances. "The American Short Story in the First Twenty-Five Years of the Twentieth Century," *Bookman,* 63 (April 1926), 186–93.

There is little difference between a popular magazine story published in the first five years of the century and one published in the same type of magazine in the five years past. Those writers who are aware of Chekhov and Freud and who try to see below the surfaces of their characters publish in the little magazines.

Oates, Joyce Carol. "The Short Story." *Southern Humanities Review,* 5 (Summer 1971), 213–14.

The short story is a "dream verbalized," a manifestation of desire. Its most interesting aspect is its "mystery."

O'Conner, Flannery. "Writing Short Stories." *Mystery and Manners.* Ed. Sally and Robert Fitzgerald. New York: Farrar, Straus & Giroux, 1969, pp. 87–106.

In this lecture at a Southern Writers Conference, O'Connor discusses the two qualities necessary for the short story: "sense of manners," which one gets from the texture of his immediate surroundings; and "sense of mystery," which is always the mystery of personality— "showing how some specific folks *will* do, *will* do in spite of everything."

O'Connor, Frank. "Prospectus for an Anthology." *Nation,* 183 (November 3, 1956), 395–96.

His preference is for American, Russian, and Irish stories because they reveal a keen sense of human loneliness. "Sometimes I question myself and wonder whether I am attracted by certain great stories because they express an underlying mood of my own, or whether I am attracted to them because they are written close to the source of story telling itself."

O'Faolain, Sean. "The Secret of the Short Story." *United Nations World,* 3 (March 1949), 37–38.

The secret lies in the French word *constater,* "meaning to establish the state or truth of a thing, to sum it up." Exploring why some countries are more accomplished in the short story form than others, O'Faolain concludes that "the more firmly organized a country is the less room there is for the short-story, for the intimate close-up, the odd slant, or the unique comment."

Overstreet, Bonaro. "Little Story, What Now?" *Saturday Review of Literature,* 24 (November 22, 1941), 3–5, 25–26. (Also in *What is the Short Story?*)

A reply to protests that the current story is unpleasant and abnormal and that it has no plot. Having lost the faiths of the nineteenth century which underpinned a confident life of action (that one could tell the difference between right and wrong and that a reliable correspondence exists between inner character and outward behavior), the modern story-teller is concerned with psychological materials, not with events in the objective world.

Patrick, Walton R. "Poetic Style in the Contemporary Short Story." *College Composition and Communication,* 18 (May 1957), 77–84.

The poetic style appears more consistently in the short story than in the novel because metaphorical dilations are essential to the writer who "strives to pack the utmost meaning into his restricted space."

Pattee, Fred Lewis. "The Present Stage of the Short Story." *English Journal,* 12 (September 1923), 439–49.

A reaction to the teaching of the short story in the schools as a new genre which has made steady progress in America from the crude toward the perfect. All that Poe said had already been said by Aristotle: the form flourished because English novels were not protected by copyright. Short stories give us only fleeting sensations while novels give us a philosophy of life.

Peden, William. "The American Short Story During the Twenties," *Studies in Short Fiction,* 10 (Fall 1973), 367–71.

Highly abbreviated account of the causes of the explosion of short stories during the Twenties: e.g., the new freedom from plotted stories, new emphasis on "now-ness," the boom of little magazines, and the influence of cinematic techniques.

———. "The American Short Story Since 1940." *Story,* 142 (Sept.-Oct. 1963), 117–25.

Brief survey of the significant writers. Reprinted as Chapter 3 in his book, *The American Short Story.*

———. "Introduction." *Short Fiction: Shape and Substance.* New York: Houghton Mifflin Co., 1971, pp. 1–51.

After quoting several previous attempts at definition, Peden offers his own "modest" definition: "A short story is a piece of prose fiction short enough to be read at one sitting and in which a character or a group of characters gets from here to there."

———. "Publishers, Publishing and the Recent American Short Story." *Studies in Short Fiction,* 1 (Fall 1964), 33–44.

Substantially the same article appears as Chapter Two of Peden's *The American Short Story.* Criticism of the mass circulation slicks' failure to encourage the growth of the short story. Survey of the type of fiction published in the slicks and how it is determined by the big advertisers. Survey of the little magazines and quarterlies which do support quality stories, but live a financially precarious existence.

Perkins, Frederick B. "Preface." *Devil-Puzzlers and Other Studies.* New York: G. P. Putnam's Sons, 1877. (Also in *What is the Short Story?*)

The short story compares with other prose types as the lyric does with the epic or narrative poem. A really fine story such as one by Poe, Hawthorne, Hoffman, or Tieck is "the production of a faculty lofty, unique and rare."

Perry, Bliss. "The Short Story." *A Study of Prose Fiction.* Boston and New York: Houghton Mifflin Co., 1902, pp. 300–34.

The short story differs from the novel by presenting unique and original characters, by focussing on fragments of reality, and by making use of the poetic devices of impressionism and symbolism.

"The Persistent Mystery of the Modern Short Story." *Current Opinion,* 67 (August 1919), 119–20.

A very brief survey of some attempts to define and keep abreast of "a literary form which puzzles the critics and often perplexes the reader."

Pochman, Henry A. "Germanic Materials and Motifs in the Short Story." *German Culture in America: Philosophic and Literary Influences: 1600–1900.* Madison: University of Wisconsin Press, 1957, pp. 367–408.

Documents Irving's indebtedness to various German sources for much of his work, the influence of Tieck, Hoffmann, and Chamisso on Hawthorne and Poe, and Poe's debt to Schlegel for his theory of the short story.

Pritchett, V. S. "Short Stories." *Harper's Bazaar,* 87 (July 1953), 31, 113, (Also in *What is the Short Story?*)

The short story is a hybrid, owing much to the quickness and objectivity of the cinema, much to the poet and the newspaper reporter, and everything to the "restlessness, the alert nerve, the scientific eye and the short breath of contemporary life." Makes an interesting point about the collapse of standards, conventions and values which has so bewildered the impersonal novelist but has been the making of the story writer—"who can catch any piece of life as it flies and make his personal performance out of it."

Pugh, Edwin. "The Decay of the Short Story." *Living Age,* 259 (November 14, 1908), 387–95. Originally appeared in *The Fortnightly Review.*

The English short story has fallen into decay for the same reasons that the American short story has—the rise of the popular magazines which demand stories in the Poe mode, stories with "snap," "vim," "crispness," "breeziness."

Rosenfield, Isaac. "Great American Desert." *New Republic* 109 (October 1943), 461.

Review of *Best American Short Stories of 1943.* Too many stories are written from the study of technique, not from the "obsession of the personal." The form has settled down to a "middle age conservatism of thwarting the imagination."

———. "A Year of the Short Story." *New Republic,* 111 (October 23, 1944), 540–42.

Review of *Best American Short Stories of 1944.* "None of the stories is in any sense an experiment with language or form; and yet, by adapting form to theme . . . they show what the proper uses of freedom are in raising expression from a living death.''

Saroyan, William. ''What is a Story?'' *Saturday Review of Literature,* 11 (January 5, 1935), 409. (Also in *What is the Short Story?*)

The important distinction to be made is not between short story and novel, but between created things and imitated things. The created thing is ''living substance, mutability, substance growing.''

Seldes, Gilbert. ''The Best Butter.'' *Dial,* 72 (April 1922), 427–30.

Review of *Best American Short Stories of 1921* and *Prize Stories of 1921.* The American short story is ''by all odds the weakest, most trivial, most stupid, most insignificant art work produced in this country and perhaps in any country.'' The subjects are trivial and vulgar; the technique shows no experimentation.

Shaw, Harry. ''Some Clinical Notes.'' *Saturday Review of Literature,* 24 (November 22, 1941), 3, 23–25. (Also in *What is the Short Story?*)

The lack of worthwhile short stories at the time is the result of a shift in reader preference to the magazine article. While story technique has remained static, article writing has developed new appealing methods to interest the reader.

''Short Stories: Past, Present and Future.'' *Publisher's Weekly,* 198 (December 14, 1970), 12–15.

Report of Doubleday's day-long symposium (November 20, 1970) to honor publication of *Fifty Years of the American Short Story,* ed. William Abrahams. One of the panelists, Wallace Stegner, pointed out, ''There has hardly been any systematic criticism in this country of the short story . . . we badly need a good critical history of it.''

Smertenko, Johan J. ''The American Short Story.'' *Bookman,* 56 (January 1923), 584–87.

The rise of mass circulation magazines dependent on advertising has caused the deterioration of the short story. A number of magazines should be endowed to publish the best stories of both the masters and the promising unknown writers.

Smith, Horatio E. ''The Development of Brief Narrative in Modern French Literature: A Statement of the Problem.'' *PMLA,* 32 (1917), 583–97.

Surveys the confusion between the *conte* and *nouvelle* and calls for a critical investigation of the practice and theory of the French forms similar to those published on the American short story and the German *Nouvelle*.

Stanford, Derek. "A Larger Latitude: Three Themes in the Nineties Short Story." *Contemporary Revew,* 210 (February 1967), 96–104. The themes are: the life of sex, illustrated by the work of Ella D'Arcy and George Egerton; the life of art, as seen in Arthur Symon's *Spiritual Adventures;* bohemian and *declassée* existence, reflected in stories by Henry Harland and George Gissing.

Strong, L. A. G. "The Art of the Short Story." *Essays by Divers Hands: Being the Transactions of the Royal Society of Literature of the United Kingdom,* XXIII, n.s. Ed. Hon. Harold Nicholson. London: Geoffrey Cumberlege, Oxford University Press, 1947, pp. 37–51. Survey of the rise of the English short story in the nineties and how it split into the two streams of serious and commercial short stories. The only rule for the short story is that it give the reader a sense of a completed experience.

———. "Concerning Short Stories." *Bookman,* 75 (November 1932), 709–12. (Also in *What is the Short Story?*) Urges that critics and editors stop arguing about what a short story is and agree that the only thing that matters is that it be a piece of short prose fiction which has an aim worthy of an artist and succeed in that aim.

———. "The Short Story: Notes at Random." *Lovat Dickson's Magazine,* 2 (March 1934), 281–91. Urges the return to narrative to invigorate the "somewhat anaemic body of the contemporary English short story." The new freedom in the short story, primarily due to the influence of Chekhov, has led too many writers snobbishly to scorn plot and situation.

Suckow, Ruth. "The Short Story." *Saturday Review of Literature,* 4 (November 19, 1927), 317–18. An extreme reaction to the formulizing of the genre. No one can define the short story; any such attempt is a "fundamental stupidity." An esthetic method for dealing with diversity and multiplicity, the short story has always been a natural expression for American life, a life so multitudinous "that its meaning could be caught only in fragments, perceived only by will-o'-the-wisp gleams, preserved only in tiny pieces of perfection."

Sullivan, Walter, "Revelation in the Short Story: A Note on Methodology." *Vanderbilt Studies in Humanities,* vol. 1. Ed. Richmond C. Beatty, John Philip Hyatt, and Monroe K. Spears. Nashville: Vanderbilt University Press, 1951, 106–12.

The fundamental methodological concept of the short story is a change of view from innocence to knowledge. The change can be either "logical" (coming at the end of the story), or "anticipated" (coming near the beginning); it can be either "intra-concatinate" (occurring within the main character) or "extra-concatinate" (occurring within a peripheral character). Thus defined the short story did not begin until the final year of the nineteenth century; *The Dubliners* marks the completion of its development.

Tannen, Yoli. "Is a Puzzlement." *Masses and Mainstream,* 10 (January 1957), 14–18.

A review of *The Best American Stories of 1956.* The serious stories are in the little magazines which no one reads; the rest are the non-distinctive ones appearing in the big magazines. The problem of the "literary" writer seems to be his unwillingness to deal with the typical "white middle-class Protestant"; he prefers instead to focus on the comparatively simple delineation of the racial minority.

Villa, José Garcia. "The Contemporary Short Story." *Prairie Schooner,* (Fall 1936), 231–33.

The short story is taking on the characteristics of the sketch or the essay. The slice of life theory often neglects the integrative function of a short story and ignores its basically dramatic nature. "The mere episode—functionless, directionless, and pointless—is not a story."

West, Ray B. "The American Short Story." *The Writer in the Room.* Detroit: Michigan State University Press, 1968, pp. 185–204. Originally appeared as his "Introduction" to *American Short Stories.* New York: Thomas Y. Crowell Co., 1959.

Contrasts the short story's "microscopic" focus on inner motives with the novel's "telescopic" view of man from the outside. The novel is concerned with man's attempt to control nature through social institutions; the short story presents the individual's confrontation with nature as an indifferent force.

————. "The Modern Short Story and the Highest Forms of Art." *English Journal,* 46 (December 1957), 531–39.

The rise of the short story in the nineteenth century is a result of the shift in narrative view from the "telescopic" (viewing nature and society from the outside) to the "microscopic" (viewing the unseen world of inner motives and impulses).

Wharton, Edith. "Telling a Short Story." *The Writing of Fiction.* New York: Charles Scribner's Sons, 1925, pp. 33–58.

The chief technical difference between the novel and the short story is that the novel focuses on character while the short story focuses on situation; "and it follows that the effect produced by the short story depends almost entirely on its form, or presentation."